KNOWING, SEEING, BEING

Knowing, Seeing, Being

Jonathan Edwards, Emily Dickinson, Marianne Moore, and the American Typological Tradition

Jennifer L. Leader

University of Massachusetts Press
Amherst and Boston

Copyright © 2016 by University of Massachusetts Press
All rights reserved
Owing to space limitations, page 247 constitutes an extension of this copyright page.
Printed in the United States of America

ISBN 978-1-62534-180-8 (paper); 179-2 (hardcover)

Designed by Jack Harrison
Set in Adobe Caslon Pro
Printed and bound by The Maple-Vail Book Manufacturing Group

Library of Congress Cataloging-in-Publication Data
Names: Leader, Jennifer L., 1967–
Title: Knowing, seeing, being : Jonathan Edwards, Emily Dickinson,
Marianne Moore, and the American typological tradition / Jennifer L. Leader.
Description: Amherst : University of Massachusetts Press, c2016. |
Includes bibliographical references and index.
Identifiers: LCCN 2015040305| ISBN 9781625341808 (pbk. : alk. paper) |
ISBN 9781625341792 (hardcover : alk. paper)
Subjects: LCSH: Edwards, Jonathan, 1703-1758—Criticism and interpretation. |
Edwards, Jonathan, 1703-1758—Influence. |
Dickinson, Emily, 1830-1886—Criticism and interpretation. |
Moore, Marianne, 1887-1972—Criticism and interpretation. |
Typology (Theology) in literature. | Nature in literature. | Belief, Problem of (Literature) |
Hermeneutics—History. | Christianity and literature—United States—History.
Classification: LCC PS742 .L43 2016 | DDC 810.9—dc23
LC record available at http://lccn.loc.gov/2015040305

British Library Cataloguing in Publication Data
A catalogue record for this book is available from the British Library.

And it came to pass, as he sat at meat with them, he took bread, and blessed it, and brake, and gave to them.

And their eyes were opened, and they knew him; and he vanished out of their sight.

And they said one to another, Did not our heart burn within us, while he talked with us by the way, and while he opened to us the scriptures?

Luke 24:30–32

Contents

Acknowledgments

It was my great good fortune to have entered the scholarly profession in a moment of various kinds of renaissances in Edwards, Dickinson, and Moore studies and to have inherited the fruits of others' contemporaneous researching and editing labors. I am also deeply grateful for the personal guidance and encouragement of many people during the years I spent thinking about, writing, and rewriting this book.

I especially thank Elizabeth Fuller at the Rosenbach Free Library of Philadelphia, Betty Clements at the Claremont School of Theology Library, Mary Lynn of Skidmore College, and the librarians at the Brooklyn Historical Society and the Dickinson College Library for their aid in accessing and understanding archival and resource materials. Thank you also to Lyndsay Taylor, Jonathan Lew, Adam Miller, and Brian Ebersole for their help with access to scholarly materials, as well as to the English Department at Duquesne University for its support in the early stages of this work.

I've had the great privilege and joy to meet many thoughtful and generous scholars whose work and advice have spurred me on. To mention just a few of these, my especial thanks go to Linda Leavell, who allowed me to read a galley version of her wonderful Moore biography before it came to print and who has unstintingly answered the many Moore questions I've thrown her way. I want to express my sincerest thanks to Jane Eberwein, certainly for her personal words of guidance and affirmation of this project, but also for the enormous depth and breadth of her original scholarship, work that has become a lasting foundation for the next generation of scholars working with Dickinson and her religious influences. Likewise, my heartfelt thanks go to Rowena Revis Jones, herself the author of several important studies on Dickinson and religion, who generously read an entire draft of this book and provided invaluable feedback and suggestions.

I want to express my deepest appreciation to Cristanne Miller, without whom this book simply would not be. Cris, whose groundbreaking feminist scholarship, generosity of spirit, and thoughtful guidance held the door open for me in more ways than I can list here, helped me at every stage in this complicated process (twice!). Profound thanks to her for her enormous patience and tolerance of my humor, for affirming the value of examining this strange trio in my original proposal years ago and then challenging me to be bolder in my conclusions than I wanted to be, and for her rare good gift for a kind of editing that teaches and that, through the years, has given my own best voice back to me.

Finally, gratitude beyond words goes to my father, Ron Leader, whose faithful daily labors provided the broad childhood place from which I could read and think and be; to my mother, Jean Leader, herself a historian and genealogist whose keen intellect I have sorely missed in the writing of this book; and to my husband, Jonathan Avrigean, whose loving presence has provided the ground upon which this book could grow.

KNOWING, SEEING, BEING

Introduction

A History of the Work of Typology

An alternative genealogy of American letters might very well begin with the tale of cultural connections among three authors and the history of two books. The authors are the unlikely trio of Jonathan Edwards (1703–1758), Emily Dickinson (1830–1886), and Marianne Moore (1887–1972), and the books, the Protestant Scriptures and Edwards's *History of the Work of Redemption.* The latter text was the eighteenth-century theologian's attempt to bring the King James Bible to bear on Christian experience in the New World. Edwards wanted to show how God's providential and unifying typological handiwork was at play not only in the historical time frame described in Scripture, but also in recorded history outside the Old and New Testaments and even in the natural realm of the Connecticut Valley itself. In so doing, Edwards employed the time-honored pattern of presenting corporeal, historical types as foreshadowing spiritual, ahistorical antitypes—not for the purpose of diminishing the present world but rather to affirm its lasting importance by folding human existence into God's larger and eternal story of glory and redemption. Thus, for instance, as Edwards explains in *A History,* when God shows the childless Abraham the sky full of stars in Genesis 15 and tells him "so shall thy seed be," a "blessing [of] all the families of the earth was now made known" (*WJE* 9:161). The promise given to Abraham connected him not only to future generations he would never meet but also to an eternal plan set in motion before his creation, a now-and-not-yet relationship indicated in the signifying stars. For, as Edwards observes in one of his source notebooks, previous to the making of the world, stars "were designed by the Creator to be a type of the saints [the future Church], the spiritual seed of Abraham; and the seeming multitude of them, which is much greater than the real multitudes of visible stars, was designed as a type of the multitude of the saints" (*WJE* 11:60n3). *A History of the Work of Redemption* was based on a series of sermons Edwards delivered in 1739 and part of a larger project he never completed or published. After its first publication by his son in 1774, the text (broadly interpreted) was one among many cultural and religious impetuses providing justification for the new republic's divine mandate for independence from England by virtue of the nation's part in a larger redemptive plan.

By the middle of the nineteenth century, more than sixty thousand copies of an 1838 edition of the *History* had been distributed by the American Tract Society; the book's broader influence as historiography was recognized by George Bancroft in his 1840 *History of the United States.* In fact, according to the religious historian John Wilson,

> it may not be too much to suggest that Edwards's history was as influential as any other single book in fixing the cultural parameters of nineteenth-century American Protestant culture. It securely anchored American experience in a cosmic setting, locating it by means of reference to sacred Scripture and investing it with preeminent significance for concluding the drama of Christian redemption. It legitimated the social experiment that was the new American culture. (82)

Emily Dickinson, deeply cognizant not only of the Bible but also of the various streams of typological thought within the broader culture of her day, would have been exposed to the *History* during her time at Mount Holyoke Female Seminary, if nowhere else; the text was one of the seminary founder Mary Lyon's favorite works (and Edwards was one of her favorite authors), and she read from it nightly to her students. Dickinson experimented with many variations on the typological themes and dynamics she inherited. Redirecting her emphasis from the sacred to the secular and from the vast church of the redeemed to particular loved ones, she mourns the "Absence of an Eye" in one poem, for example, by establishing a new, if faint, typological connection between the beloved dead and "the Routes of Stars" overhead whose "superior Eyes / Include Us – as they go –" (F771 B).

After a period of dormancy, Edwards's philosophical and theological legacies were unearthed again in the twentieth century—this time in a general sense by the neoorthodox movement and, more specifically, by H. R. Niebuhr in his influential 1937 work *The Kingdom of God in Amer-*

ica. In his analysis of American sociohistorical movements, Niebuhr accorded a seminal role in the formation of American culture to the redemptive and eschatological impulses exemplified by Edwards in his *History*. Marianne Moore, always an independent and eclectic thinker, came to a cultural awareness of this notion of American experience lived in the light of eternal ramifications through multiple channels. Like Edwards and Dickinson, Moore grew up in a Protestant denomination aligned with the Reformed theological tradition, a heritage influenced by Augustine and traced forward from the Reformers through the Puritans and beyond; in adulthood her study of the Bible continued in Presbyterian settings as well. Later in life Moore was also an admirer and acquaintance of another leading thinker in the neoorthodox movement, H. R. Niebuhr's brother Reinhold, one of the preeminent theologians of his day and among the last to exert broad popular influence on American culture. Jointly the Niebuhr brothers' call for Christianity's active engagement with culture and for a return to an acknowledgment of the ethical pertinence of Scripture harkens back to a particularly Edwardsean strain of American Calvinism: a tradition that emphasizes God's extreme alterity, His immanent involvement in earthly affairs, and the need for divine revelation to perceive the connection between the two. Writing in an age when denominations were splitting over arguments concerning the Bible's authority, Moore's brilliant modernist poetics embrace and transform the doubts of the twentieth century to suggest "how by darkness a star is perfected" ("By Disposition of Angels"). In this Christmas poem, for instance, Moore repeatedly questions the old typological connections that somehow bind the star and angels to the Nativity of Christ and to the individual observer. Yet even when "uproot[ed]" by reason from symbolic associations, the speaker finds that the relationship between the observer, the natural object, and the eternity of the departed "saints" (to use Jonathan Edwards's word) persists; she concludes, "steadier than steady, star dazzling me, live and elate, / no need to say, how like some we have known; too like her, / too like him, and a-quiver forever" (*CP* 142).

In truth, the story of recurring literary motifs and cultural encounters among these three writers could have been told in a myriad of ways: although inhabiting three different centuries, Edwards, Dickinson, and Moore share deep affinities for the King James Bible, for the natural sciences (in settings in which science and faith were not considered conflicting categories), and for a particularly American brand of Reformed hermeneutics (at a time when theologians still shaped the way people read and thought about the way language works). In this book I assert that arranging these figures along the lines of this shared heritage reveals a deep structure of American metaphysical thought that has heretofore been largely unexamined. While it is a truism that the Bible has had a tremendous influence on American letters, one of the many erasures of the Perry Miller school of thought is of epistemological categories that might delineate and juxtapose currents of religious philosophy beyond the Transcendental, both within and across the boundaries of writers' works. In fact, early training in the Protestant Scriptures did more than shape (or discourage) religious belief; it also shaped, via specific theological traditions, underlying assumptions about the authority, transparency, and trustworthiness of all language to contain or mediate reality. This book makes a beginning toward filling in that gap by locating and articulating ways Edwards, Dickinson, and Moore received and transformed both models of language and depictions of the natural world from within their own Reformed typological heritage.

I do not argue for directly causal relationships (though both Dickinson and Moore were highly aware of some aspects of Edwards's work in their formative years). Rather, I posit that all three partake of this common biblical and cultural tradition as they grapple with the manner in which the immanent and transcendent worlds might be in a consequential relation to each other—and, as time progressed, with the non-essentialist language to describe that dialectic. The palimpsest of the Reformed tradition accounts for remarkable similarities in the ways these writers approach matters of aesthetics, subjectivity, ontology, phenomenology, and ethics. Analyzing their typological practices reveals profound and recurring sets of questions they jointly pose concerning the "Book of Nature" and its relation to characteristics of spiritual knowledge, to the roles of perception, desire, and beauty, and to the construction of individual subjectivity. Thus, in Edwards's, Dickinson's, and Moore's work, spiritual knowing, or apprehension, is often configured as a process of dynamic revelation from outside the self, and apperception becomes a kind of ethical relationship. These writers ask: How is seeing informed by revelation? How does language connect the seen (physical) and unseen (spiritual) realms? And how does perception put the self into relation with what is seen? Furthermore, each author uses the natural world to illustrate how being can be a state of progressive becoming as they variously consider: What is selfhood, and how does the self occupy the uncomfortable gap between the now and not yet, mortality and eternity?

Concomitantly, in *Knowing, Seeing, Being,* I show Edwards, Dickinson, and Moore as philosophical participants, in their own fashions, in eighteenth-, nineteenth-, and twentieth-century exegetical debates, and hence as vitally engaged with their own moments in the history of American biblical hermeneutics. As avid readers and scrutinizers of their own religious communities, they were highly aware of ongoing controversies during their lifetimes concerning the primacy of figurative, dynamic, or metaphorical interpretive language versus that of literal, rational, propositional, or "common sense" modes. Their proclivities for tracing a narrow middle path between these two historically shifting positions often put them at crosscurrents not only with mainstream Reformed thinking of their day but also with philosophical premises that arose from deism, Scottish Common Sense philosophy (later the Princeton Scholasticism), Unitarianism, Transcendentalism, and scientific materialism.

While the substance of this book begins with the eighteenth century, it is important to note that the practice of typological interpretation began not with Edwards or even the Puritans, of course, but with the earliest Christians. In its most basic sense, typology is a method of biblical exegesis in which a person, event, or practice in the Old Testament—a type—is read as a "foreshadowing" or prefiguration of the New Testament Christ, the antitype. The tradition is based on several key New Testament passages in the Gospels, the Pauline Epistles, and the Book of Hebrews that indicate Christ as the fulfillment not only of Old Testament prophecies but also of the very fabric of Jewish history and identity, its key figures, and Levitical laws. In this manner, the Old Testament was read through the New, and the Christian religion gained a sense of narrative fit as a part of the ongoing story of God's revelation to humankind. As this hermeneutical tradition continued its development throughout the Reformation and beyond, types came to be drawn from the New Testament as well as the Old, and in addition to the incarnation of Christ, the second coming of Christ and fulfillment of His kingdom might also stand as antitypes.

The chief characteristic that distinguishes typology from allegory, symbolism, or Platonic correspondence is that type and antitype are both considered to be *real;* that is, although the antitype serves as the teleological end and fulfillment of the type, both are ontologically distinct entities and both exist as historical personages or events within the framework of linear time. This distinction, however, is complicated by the fact that type and antitype are also always read *sub specie aeternitatis,* that is, in the light of eternity. As Eric Auerbach observes in his classic study "Figura," while "promise and fulfillment are real historical events," they also are

> the tentative form of something eternal and timeless; they point not only to the concrete future, but also to something that always has been and always will be; they point to something which is in need of interpretation, which will indeed be fulfilled in the concrete future, but which is at all times present, fulfilled in God's providence, which knows no difference of time. This eternal thing is already figured in them, and thus they are both tentative fragmentary reality, and veiled eternal reality. This becomes eminently clear in the sacrament of the sacrifice, the Last Supper, the *pascha nostrum,* which is *figura Christi.* (53, 59–60)

The type and antitype, then, are part of two time schemes: the temporal, chronological unfolding of events and the eternally present now.

Throughout the history of the Christian Church, the amount of interpretive leeway allowed for typological explication has fluctuated between two greatly contested positions: that which privileged the mystical, figurative, and broadly allegorical senses of the text and a more narrow stance that limits typology to its strictly literal and historical references found in the Old Testament. Ultimately, by the fifth century, the figurative School of Alexandria had prevailed; the basic method of hermeneutics throughout the Middle Ages was based on the Augustinian and Aquinan fourfold senses of interpretation: historical, allegorical, tropological, and anagogical (eschatological). It was against this tradition of "mere" allegory and its manifold possibilities for the idiosyncratic interpretation of hidden mystical truths that the Protestant Reformers raised the cry of *sola scriptura.* Key leaders such as William Tyndale and Martin Luther vigorously opposed the fourfold method of interpretation and posited in its place a more constrained system of types and antitypes which had been largely subsumed under the broader medieval allegorical rubric. It was this more restricted understanding of typology that Calvin in his *Institutes* instructs biblical scholars to use as "the key" to relating the Old Testament to the New. Consequently, with the return to close examination of Greek and Hebrew biblical texts as opposed to emphasis on church tradition, typology gained a new ascendance as an authorized method of reinforcing the primary importance of what the Protestant Reformers believed to be the Bible's historical and literal unity. As Barbara Kiefer Lewalski observes, "The characteristic Protestant approach takes the Bible not as a multi-level allegory, but as a complex literary work whose full literal meaning is revealed only by careful attention to its poetic texture and to its pervasive symbolic mode—typology" (117).

In the two generations immediately preceding Edwards, Calvin's emphasis on typology played a role in the development of federal and covenant theology and was a major influence on Puritan exegetes such as William Ames (1576–1632), whose book *Medulla Theologiae* "became the textbook of American Calvinism until well into the eighteenth-century" (Brumm 29). Typological handbooks systematizing individual type-antitype pairings between the Testaments became increasingly popular among Puritan divines. One of the most widely read of these works, *The Figures or Types of the Old Testament, by which Christ and the Heavenly Things of the Gospel were Preached and Shadowed to the People of God of Old* (1673), was written by Increase Mather's brother Samuel and exerted great influence on Edwards's own typological writings. Based on a series of sermons Mather gave in Dublin from 1666 to 1668 to correct what he perceived to be the Anglicans' excessively allegorical methods of interpretation, the book offers an extremely narrow definition of typology that would become the standard orthodox position: "A Type is some outward or sensible thing ordained of God under the Old Testament, to represent and hold forth something of Christ in the New." Thus, Mather continues, "men must not *indulge their own Fancies* as the Popish Writers use to do, with their Allegorical Senses, as they call them; except we have some Scripture ground for it. It is not safe to make any thing a Type meerly upon our own fansies and imaginations" (52, 55).

At the same time the Reformers and their heirs were reclaiming typology, there was also broad precedent in Protestant thought for finding signs in the natural world of God's design and character. Such musings derived their impetus from multiple passages in Scripture such as Psalm 19, which begins, "The heavens declare the glory of God; and the firmament sheweth his handywork." In his *Institutes*, Calvin appreciates the natural beauty of the world and instructs the regenerate not to "decline to take a pious delight in the clear and manifest works of God" in "this most beautiful theater"; they should "contemplate the immense treasures of wisdom and goodness exhibited in the creatures, as in so many mirrors [of God]" (1.14.20–21). Indeed, seventeenth-century Reformed ministers were deeply conversant with the Calvinist theology of nature, and Puritan divines in the generations before Edwards were expected to be able to give a rational account for God's systematic design of the universe in consonance with His character. Concomitantly, scientific advances were not a threat to the authority of the Bible but rather a useful help in the development of natural theology.

As the scion of these theological traditions, Jonathan Edwards famously extrapolated typological methodologies from the reading of biblical texts to the reading of the natural landscape of the Connecticut Valley. Using a metaphysical lens that he had an especial affinity for, Augustine's dictum "Believe that you may understand," Edwards formalized the way religious knowledge illuminated Christians through the Book of Nature in a manner similar to the way it was believed that written Scripture did. Doing so was both an attempt to intellectualize his own mystical experiences with nature and also part of his larger philosophical assertion that spiritual, or "affective," knowledge was a valid epistemological category in the age of British empiricism. In Edwards's system of natural typology, images in the natural world become divine language; by reading them, one enacts the way God "transforms the heart into divine image and changes the life to the divine pattern" of being (*WJE* 14:92). For Edwards, the heaven-bestowed apperception of divine beauty—the "divine and supernatural light," as he called it in a sermon of the same name—also illuminates all that is "real and true," and from this intimacy of sight comes transformation of the self and its desires that results in a radical and fundamental change toward a God-ward orientation of being. This tripartite knowing/seeing/being-in-relation is the cornerstone of Edwards's theological metaphysics, as well as the philosophical focus of this book.

The chapters that follow are grouped into three sections, each of which concentrates on a single author. I begin each section with a biographical essay in which I delineate in succession the way Edwards, Dickinson, and Moore were engaged at the personal, familial, and intellectual levels with their Reformed tradition. In these chapters I examine some of the streams through which the writers would have come by the Reformed typological tradition, as well as some of their own approaches to the Bible. These contextual biographies lay the foundation for the following chapter or chapters in each section, in which I explicate some of their explorations of typological relationships in their work, as well as consider interactions between their writing and that of their literary and theological contemporaries.

Part I, "Jonathan Edwards," serves as a reintroduction to the theologian and his literary metaphysics for readers who may be unfamiliar with the findings of a recent renaissance in Edwards studies. The twenty-first-century completion of the Yale *Works* of Edwards, as well as a spate of historical and bibliographical research on the divine, call for a reestimation of any remaining notions of Edwards as intellectually isolated or backward-thinking; instead, Edwards worked at the philosophical cutting edge of his day, and he developed his theories not only in light of classic Reformed writings but also as part of a transatlantic post-Reformed, Dissenting, and English Enlightenment conversation in which he vigorously participated. In chapter 2 I assert that Jonathan Edwards's natural typology ought to be considered a literary device in its own right and that his radical and comprehensive conception of being as a kind of being-in-relation-to-the-Other poses an alternative American model to the Neoplatonic "Correspondences" in Emerson's *Nature*. This chapter, "Beauty and the Eye of the Beholder: Being and Desire in Jonathan Edwards's Natural Typology," unfolds Edwards's natural typology vis-à-vis this relational ontology. In Edwards's universe there is no essential object or self that exists on its own, apart from an eternally signifying matrix of divine, discursive exchange (what Stephen H. Daniel has deemed a state of "being-in-relation"). Edwards locates his typological model for knowing, seeing, and being in the relationship among the members of the Trinity. His eighteenth-century defense of the Trinity as both an appellation and a broader concept becomes an important placeholder for the evocative role of the figural in biblical exegesis in following generations.

Part II, "Emily Dickinson," situates the poet in an Amherst that was neither terrorized by imprecatory hellfire sermons nor assailed by threats to the faith from Darwin and the sciences, as was once imagined. Instead, Dickinson grew up in an environment congenial to both critical thought and hermeneutical investigation, dual emphases that helped foster the centrality of her own religious imagination. Dickinson freely modifies elements of this Reformed typological heritage to suit her own poetic purposes, and her uses of the natural world in an attempt to bridge the gap between the physical and the spiritual are by turns comforting, satiric, and uncanny. In chapter 4, "Reading with 'Compound Vision': Emily Dickinson and the Nineteenth-Century 'Paper Wars,'" I investigate two of Dickinson's primary typological stances as they relate to concepts of revelation and perception. Her interest in these matters was not idiosyncratic; it was contemporaneous with very heated arguments about the role of personal experience and of figural language in biblical exegesis that were occurring at seminaries and among such Reformed leaders as Horace Bushnell, Charles Wadsworth, and Edwards Amasa Park. These poems also contain Dickinson's most overt replies to the training in natural theology she received from the all-pervasive Amherst figure Edward Hitchcock. In chapter 5, "'Myself—the Term between': Dickinson's Typology of Split Subjectivity," I examine poems in which the type-antitype relationship causes the experience of an agonizing ontological division for Dickinson's speakers. This split is similar to the division between flesh and spirit described in the Pauline letters, one that Horace Bushnell called the "double sense" and Ralph Waldo Emerson the "double consciousness." When Dickinson's poems are viewed in this light, a subgenre emerges; the subject in these poems, even against its will, becomes a subject-in-process, signifying beyond itself, falling forward toward an infinitely receding spiritual antitype, which in turn summons the subject's split between flesh and spirit. From this perspective, Dickinson's famed "nature is a Haunted House" epistolary dialogue with T. W. Higginson becomes a subtle rejoinder to the sunnier Unitarian's belief in the human ability to read the Book of Nature (L 459A).

In Part III, "Marianne Moore," I explicate the poet's reception and reappropriation of typological hermeneutics via her early and later religious influences and affinities. Moore's formative years occurred during the early twentieth-century fundamentalist/modernist controversies concerning the historical accuracy and inspiration of biblical texts. She was not sheltered from these controversies but early on was exposed to multiple principles of exegesis that, in turn, lent themselves to the literal and figural registers of her poetry. Neither emblematic, symbolic, nor Neoplatonic, Moore's natural animals and plants, I argue, can profitably be understood as types that embody ontological difference, that enact a dynamic semiotic relation with their ideational antitypes, and that inhabit an ethical epistemological category of "in-betweenness" and "integration." In chapter 7, "'Part Terrestrial, and Part Celestial': 'The Real' and 'The Actual' in Moore's Revisionist Typology," I document for the first time Moore's deep intellectual and poetic engagement with an early twentieth-century group of moderate Bible scholars who came to be known as the "believing critics." I trace these hermeneutical principles forward into her animal poems of the thirties and forties and argue that in poems such as "The Jerboa" and "The Plumet Basilisk," the denizens of the natural world open a space in which there need not be a distinction between the literal and the figural, the sacred and the secular, or the "Real" and the "Actual," as she phrases it at one point in terms she borrows from the theologian P. T. Forsyth. In chapter 8 I juxtapose typological aspects of the avant-garde poetry Moore wrote before her work with *The Dial* (1907–1925) with characteristics of her more popularly focused post–World War II poetry. I argue in this chapter,

"'Integration Too Tough for Infraction': Being, Ethics, and Aesthetics in Early and Late Moore," that despite changes in style, Moore's oeuvre during her long career retains a philosophical, meta-poetic unity. Furthermore, there is a tripartite focus on the ethical, the aesthetic, and the semiotic in Moore's later work that is illustrated by her relationship with the theologian Reinhold Niebuhr. Proceeding by contiguity, contingency, and what Roland Hagenbüchle has termed in Emily Dickinson's poetry "metonymically constructed metaphor," Moore ultimately refuses to construct an essentialist, egotistic subject position that may be ontologically separated from the web of signifying discourse—the type-antitype relationship itself ("Precision" 41).

Finally, in each section I make use of the work of the philosophers Emmanuel Levinas and Jean-Luc Marion, who provide a suggestive postmodern vocabulary that helps unpack these writers' correspondences. Levinas's conceptions of the complete alterity of the Other offer an epistemological and phenomenological framework through which natural and supernatural phenomena might be considered in ethical and non-subsuming relation to each other. Marion, in his extension of Levinas and in his own exploration of consequential relations between the viewer and the viewed, provides a useful reconception of the notions of "idol" and "icon." Marion's philosophy finally attempts to liberate the notion of God from a limiting being/nonbeing duality; instead, in a gloss on Heidegger, he posits that a "Gød without Being" subverts all binaries, ultimately giving being itself as a gift of agape. Their thought sheds light on the way Edwards, Dickinson, and Moore all participate in ongoing epistemological, aesthetic, and ontological frameworks that might best be described as a typological philosophical tradition in American letters.

I
JONATHAN EDWARDS

1
Jonathan Edwards
A Reconsideration

"Perhaps there is not one leaf of a tree, nor spire of grass, but what has effects all over the universe, and will have to the end of eternity," Jonathan Edwards wrote as a young graduate student at Yale, more than a century before Walt Whitman penned *Leaves of Grass* (*WJE* 6:204). The Jonathan Edwards who authored a vast set of mystical private notebooks and who inhabited a joyous, God-filled universe of plenitude and desire, of divine intimacy and human physicality, seems worlds away from the Edwards of anthologized fame who is so often introduced to students in their survey courses. "Sinners in the Hands of an Angry God" was indeed the best selling of Edwards's American publications during his lifetime; yet, as Norman Fiering points out, "less than two percent" of all of Edwards's sermons "pertain to the afterlife of the damned," while 15 percent of the sermons that had been published by 1980 were "of the imprecatory type"—"a fact," he continues, "that tells us more about Edwards's various editors than about the author" (*Moral Thought* 204). But to be fair, there are many Jonathan Edwardses. The enormous scope of this eighteenth-century divine's erudition, public and personal writings, and historical influence makes him a crucial and controversial figure to students of American history, philosophy, theology, and literature alike. Laid claim to so stridently by so many (and for so long: the process of dividing up Edwards's intellectual legacy began shortly after his death in 1758), Edwards's identity as cultural icon and architect of the American mind is still up for grabs: the internecine debates initiated at the beginning of the twentieth century continue unabated as to whether Edwards the thinker was primarily indebted to the Enlightenment or to Calvinism and the

Bible; whether he was a synthesizer or an inventor; whether he was the last Puritan or the first modernist, a postmodernist or a medievalist.[1]

One of the most enduring of these Edwardses is the one famously envisioned by Perry Miller. This Edwards clandestinely throws off the chains of the old Calvinist mindset in order to transmute its tradition of typology into a genesis of natural romanticism. Miller traces this line from the early Puritans to Edwards, then from Edwards to Emerson, to Thoreau, to Frost and other modernists.[2] (F. O. Matthiessen's 1941 *American Renaissance: Art and Expression in the Age of Emerson and Whitman*—a text that is now as famous for its near exclusion of Emily Dickinson and Harriet Beecher Stowe as it is for its delineation of the continuities between Emerson, Hawthorne, Melville, Whitman, and Thoreau—helped codify this lineage for several generations of literary scholars.) Yet another formidable Edwards emerged in the 1970s as the masterly rhetorician who sets the stage for American exceptionalism in Sacvan Bercovitch's *Puritan Origins of the American Self* and *The American Jeremiad*.[3] As David Laurence notes, however, in these twentieth-century models,

> American literature forms a continuous series in which Puritanism and Edwards have importance by dint of their precedence in the genetic chain; yet American writing only becomes Literature with the nineteenth century flowers atop the long, prickly, and rarely blossoming stalk that stretches back through the colonial past. Within the limits of this teleological ordering, Edwards must be situated outside the literary. He must belong more to the prehistory than to the history of American literature. (231)

With the notable exception of Elisa New's insightful work *The Line's Eye: Poetic Experience, American Sight*—and more recent books by Carole Lynn Stewart (*Strange Jeremiahs: Civil Religion and the Literary Imaginations of Jonathan Edwards, Herman Melville, and W. E. B. Du Bois*) and Andrea Knutson (*American Spaces of Conversion: The Conductive Imaginaries of Edwards, Emerson, and James*)—contemporary literary scholars have fallen strangely silent concerning the possibility of more substantively incorporating Edwards's achievements as a writer and thinker into the American literary canon.

Meanwhile, scholars of American history, philosophy, and religion entered the new millennium with two new Edwards biographies and a spate of fine books that make significant advances toward establishing once and for all the originality of Edwards's Biblicism, philosophy, and metaphysics, his rich engagement with both secular and religious transatlantic thought, and his lasting contributions to theological communities on both sides of the Atlantic—a renaissance that happily coincided with the marking of Edwards's three-hundredth birthday. Furthermore, in 2008 Yale University Press published the last of its physical volumes of *The Works of Jonathan Edwards*—volume 26, the *Catalogues of Books*.[4] Remarkably, this is the first published resource since 1931 to attempt to delineate the reading lists Edwards kept. As the volume's editor Peter J. Thuesen notes, the *Catalogues of Books*—bibliographic listings and analyses of all that we know of what Edwards read, lent, had access to, or wished to acquire—now "enable us to track Edwards's reading at every stage of his career, affording us the most comprehensive view yet of his own intellectual evolution" (Editor's Introduction 3).[5] Given these resources, literary and cultural reevaluations of Edwards may now take place alongside a much grander backdrop of his intellectual, spiritual, and metaphysical vision than earlier generations were privileged to have.

Such a literary reestimation must necessarily dismantle some of the long-cherished assumptions Perry Miller set forth in his 1940 essay "From Edwards to Emerson." Most notably, Edwards's language-based methodology for the creation of types is both more complex and less transgressive than has been supposed from Miller's earlier readings of the natural types as precursors to the symbolic Correspondences of American Transcendentalism. Disentangling Edwards from an anachronistic placement at the head of a certain kind of American renaissance serves at least two purposes. First, by setting Edwards aright in his historical, religious, and philosophical contexts, we may more clearly determine where his individual brilliance as a writer lies. Second, by identifying where Edwards receives and transmits his own traditions, we can become more consciously aware of other, more endemic continuities of theme and philosophical approach in American letters which have heretofore been camouflaged. In short, reincorporating Edwards into an American literary genealogy requires that we name and then locate corresponding elements in the writings of later generations who were influenced either by Edwards directly or by Reformed cultural and hermeneutical mechanisms (or responses to those mechanisms) that Edwards helped to forward.

The Jonathan Edwards that this book attempts to portray is an author of considerable literary skill and self-awareness whose typological writings continually re-present the poetics of the human heart and its compelling desire for, yet fear of, intimacy.[6] His sermons and treatises explore the experiences of finding meaning, comfort, fulfillment, and even ecstasy in relation to the divine Other at the same time that they underline the dizzying loss of control and fear of exposure that such an intimacy would bring. Edwards's use of language attempts to mirror what the experience of such a relationship with the divine Other might be like: life would not be a straitjacketed existence of moral, intellectual, and aesthetic similitude but, in his own words, "lively," open, expansive, dynamic. In order to convey such a life, Edwards reinvented an already inherently relational typology and forged it from an amalgam of biblical hermeneutics he inherited from his family's Reformed tradition, the contemporary science and philosophy he avidly studied, and his own deeply felt experiences in nature.

Jonathan Edwards was born in 1703, in East Windsor, Connecticut, the fifth child and only boy in a family of ten sisters.[7] His father, Timothy Edwards, was a clergyman who led a number of successful revivals, and his mother, Esther Stoddard Edwards, was the daughter of an even more famous revivalist, the Reverend Solomon Stoddard of Northampton, Massachusetts. Consequently, Edwards grew up with the privileges of education and opportunity afforded to an only son whose extended family formed much of the Connecticut River Valley's religious, military, commercial, and ruling elite.[8] A brilliant and precocious student, he attended Yale College for his undergraduate and M.A. degrees between 1716 and 1722. After holding two pastorates for a short time and serving briefly as a tutor at Yale, at the age of twenty-three Edwards was called to assist his famous grandfather Stoddard in Northampton. When Stoddard died in 1729, Edwards assumed his pulpit, serving there for twenty years until he was dismissed by the congregation in 1750 over a conflict concerning admission to the communion sacraments. Edwards spent the next eight years as a pastor and missionary to the Mahican Indians in the frontier village of Stockbridge, Massachusetts, a position in which, freed from his former duties calling for extensive preparation of sermons, he wrote four of his major treatises. When Edwards's son-in-law the Reverend Aaron Burr Sr., president of the College of New Jersey (now Princeton), died in 1757, the board of trustees chose Edwards to be his successor. Edwards reluctantly agreed, probably wishing to devote more time to his studies than the position would allow. He died only a few months after he was installed in Princeton, however, from smallpox contracted from an inoculation—the victim, perhaps, of his own progressive thinking. (Edward Jenner would not develop his universally effective vaccine for nearly forty more years.)

While Edwards's spiritual development was certainly guided by the highly intellectual and devout environment provided by his parents, Timothy and Esther, his early belief in a God that could be both sovereign and loving was neither unquestioning nor without private struggles. Edwards recalls in his "Personal Narrative" that as a young man, he was "full of objections against the doctrine of God's sovereignty, in choosing whom he would to eternal life, and rejecting whom he please; leaving them eternally to perish, and be everlastingly tormented in hell. It used to appear like a horrible doctrine to me" (*WJE* 16:791–92).[9] In his seventeenth year, Edwards underwent a spiritual crisis, the results of which he was never able to explain in terms of a logical progression of thought; instead he relates that inexplicably "there came into my soul, and was as it were diffused through it, a sense of the glory of the divine being: a new sense, quite different from anything ever experienced before" (*WJE* 16:792). Of this change the newly minted nineteen-year-old Yale graduate would write in an idea notebook, "We drink in strange notions of holiness from our childhood, as if it were a melancholy, morose, sour and unpleasant thing; but there is nothing in it but what is sweet and ravishingly lovely. 'Tis the highest beauty and amiableness, vastly above all other beauties" (*WJE* 13:163).

While the King James Bible was always central to his interpretation of conversion, the natural world quickly became intrinsic to his vision of the relationship between the human and the divine as well. From his youth Edwards had felt the presence of God in the outdoors. Once he was given a "new sense" of "the divine being," as he relates in his "Personal Narrative," he found that "the appearance of everything was altered. . . . God's excellency, his wisdom, his purity and love, seemed to appear in everything; in the sun, moon and stars; in the clouds, and blue sky; in the grass, flowers, trees; in the water, and all nature; which used greatly to fix my mind" (*WJE* 16:793–94). God's holiness, no longer something "melancholy, morose, [and] sour," rather brought "inexpressible purity, brightness, peacefulness and ravishment to the soul." He depicts this relationship between the human and divine as

> a little white flower, as we see in the spring of the year; low and humble on the ground, opening its bosom, to receive the pleasant beams of the sun's glory; rejoicing as it were, in a calm rapture; diffusing around a sweet fragrancy; standing peacefully and lovingly, in the midst of other flowers round about; all in like manner opening their bosoms, to drink in the light of the sun. (796)

The image of a commonplace "little white flower" oriented toward the sun/Son becomes in Edwards's narration an emotionally charged image by which to link a material reality with an immaterial one. As if it were a Venn diagram in which the circles of physical and spiritual experience are briefly overlaid, Edwards's emotional apperception of the flower "opening its bosom, to receive the pleasant beams of the sun's glory" becomes for him an affective experience (involving both the mind and the emotions) of his own soul in mutual relationship with God. With this new spiritual discernment, nature—as experienced through the senses and meditative engagement—becomes a language of God, instructive of His personal attributes and qualities. In his twenty-fifth year, Edwards began his "Images of Divine Things" notebook to record the way that elements of the natural world (types) both pointed toward and were reified by divine personages and principles (antitypes). He made entries in his natural typology notebook until the last months of his life.

When Edwards the seasoned clergyman became a leader of the New England revivals, he expounded upon this concept of the "new sense" as part of his larger defenses of the revival movements. In works such as *The Distinguishing Marks of a Work of the Spirit of God* (1741) and *A Treatise Concerning Religious Affections* (1746) (texts whose influences would reach long into the nineteenth century), Edwards attempts to evaluate and clarify the signs and consequences of these revivals in order to show how the phenomenon indicated that God was truly working among His people, and that parishioners were not acting out of short-lived and excessive emotionalism, or "enthusiasm," as the critics termed it. He writes in *Religious Affections* that the new sense is "entirely above nature, altogether of a different kind from anything that men find within themselves by nature, or only in the exercise of natural principles"; instead, "through the saving influences of the Spirit of God, there is a new inward perception or sensation of their minds" that is "as entirely diverse from anything that is perceived in them, by natural men, as the sweet taste of honey is diverse from the ideas men get of honey by only looking on it, and feeling of it" (*WJE* 2:205, 206). The new spiritual sense, which Edwards also terms "grace in the hearts of the saints," is the way "God does . . . communicate himself, and make the creature partaker of the divine nature (the Spirit of God communicating itself in its own proper nature)" (203).[10]

While the biographical facts of Edwards's life and the scope of his major teachings are not much in dispute, there has been a great deal of literary-historical infighting concerning the numerous sources behind

Edwards's terminology and ideas in his descriptions of the new spiritual sense. As M. X. Lesser summarizes in his introduction to Edwards's *Sermons and Discourses, 1734–1738,* the new spiritual sense

> is a way of knowing akin to John Locke's empirical model in *An Essay Concerning Human Understanding,* a "new simple idea" unmediated by thought or logic; or to the transforming light of Isaac Newton's *Optiks* made metaphor, the reconciliation of God and man in the physics of the natural world; or the *sensus suavitatis* of John Calvin's *Institutes of the Christian Religion,* a sense of sweetness in the promise of divine assurance, a taste of salvation. It is perhaps all these and a little beyond, the confluence of Edwards' philosophical, scientific, and theological thought, the new language of old belief. (*WJE* 19:10)

This fundamental eclecticism of Edwards's thought, though certainly exceptional in its ingenuity and breadth, was also part and parcel of the amalgam of Reformed and Enlightenment assumptions that constituted the intellectual milieu in which he was raised.

Indeed, reassessments of the relationship between Edwards's conception of a divinely bestowed "new sense" and traditional Reformed thought have failed to bear out Perry Miller's influential claims that Edwards's epistemologies were chiefly a product of Enlightenment skepticism and a forerunner of American symbolist Transcendentalism. Miller's main contention was that Edwards's "rhetoric of sensation," or sense language of "a new simple idea," was directly linked to the divine's very early reading of Locke's *Essay Concerning Human Understanding.* In his 1948 introduction to the first and last complete edition of *Images of Divine Things* to be published until the 1993 Yale *Works* edition, Miller asserts that Edwards, inspired by his newfound Lockean sensationalism, was persuaded to make "a still more radical break with the past: an exaltation of nature to a level of authority coequal with revelation"; this was "an indirect confession that for him, as for all men after him, nature had become as compelling a way of God's speaking, if God speaks at all, as Scripture" (28, 29). Edwards was now "quoting Scripture to confirm the meaning of natural phenomena, not adducing natural images to confirm the meaning of Scripture" (36). Thus, Miller concludes, Edwards, "in his most secret moments," was the unwitting forerunner of Emerson (39). Rescued by Miller for his modernist project, an Edwards sanitized of his embarrassingly religious belief system could be admired for the fact that "he was, on the deepest level of his being, moving with the times" (38).[11]

Although this last observation by Miller is certainly correct, the "times" Edwards was moving with were post-Reformation and British latitudinarian, when scientific, philosophical, and religious thought were more often than not viewed as complementary rather than antagonistic. Thorough investigations into Edwards's background reading and philosophical sources—and, most convincingly, vigorous reexaminations of the entire body of Edwards's work in the light of his Biblicism and of the Augustinian/Calvinist tradition—have found no such evidence that Edwards secretly cast off his Reformed orthodoxy in pursuit of metaphysical truth, nor indeed would he have needed to.[12] In fact, Thomas Schafer's subsequent dating of Edwards's manuscripts has shown that Edwards conceived of the bulk of his ideas before he ever read Locke's *Essay Concerning Human Understanding*. Edwards was not the intellectually isolated child prodigy Miller had believed him to be.[13]

In fact, Edwards grew up in a New England of bibliophiles such as the Mathers who strove to remain in close connection with developments in Continental science, philosophy, and theology; as a youngster he had access to both his father's and grandfather's pastoral libraries, and while attending Yale, he was one of the students paid to sort the controversial Dummer collection of more than eight hundred books on a wide variety of subjects, some of which had been contributed by Isaac Newton and Richard Steele from their own libraries. (The collection was infamous for containing a number of "heretical" latitudinarian books that inspired some of his classmates to abandon Reformed theology for Anglicanism. Edwards read these books avidly but seems not to have been tempted to follow their example.)

At the time of his death, Edwards had amassed a respectable library of his own, many items of which he lent to fellow clergy and laypeople; in addition to his own borrowings and buying of books from Boston, he received contemporary reading materials from Europe, most especially from the Scotsman John Erskine. Edwards's reading tastes were extremely varied. In addition to the Bible commentaries and aids that one would expect to find in the library of a minister, Edwards also read widely the works of and responses to theological controversies of his day, including those of Deists such as John Toland, Anthony Collins, and Matthew Tindal. He was interested in science and math (especially optics, astronomy, and "the infant science of electricity"), foreign language dictionaries, grammars and etymologies, religious poets such as Milton, Elizabeth Singer Rowe, and Edward Young, and the novels of Samuel Richardson (Thuesen, Editor's Introduction 95). Moreover, as the editor of *Catalogues of Books,* Peter J. Thuesen, reports, Edwards enjoyed not only Locke and Newton but also Addison and Steele. He read many representative texts of the "various emerging genres of the eighteenth-century culture of exchange known as the 'republic of letters.' These new genres included literary periodicals, encyclopedic works, conduct books, epistolary novels, newspapers, and other compilations" (*WJE* 26:95, 75).

Adding to the complexity of delineating the influences on Edwards's thought is the fact that throughout his life, he meticulously recorded his theological and metaphysical musings in a vast series of indexed, cross-referenced working notebooks. The sheer volume of Edwards's idea notebooks is staggering; their contents range from short entries to essay-length dissertations, and their size alone offers an explanation for the difficulty scholars have had in taking in the whole of his (we now know) remarkably consistent thought.[14] Concerning his methodologies as a scholar, in *The Theology of Jonathan Edwards,* Michael J. McClymond and Gerald R. McDermott have pointed out that "to a greater extent than previously recognized, Edwards's theology was the product of a distinctive approach to study"; these study methods include Edwards's proclivity for considering multiple topics at the same time and for constantly writing and rewriting the pros and cons of disparate positions such that when his treatises were published, "they were often based on reflections gathered from five, ten, or even twenty or more years" (10).[15] Continuously seeking new ideas and reading voraciously, Edwards used writing as a means of thinking; he characteristically doubled back in his meditations in processes McClymond and McDermott name "concatenation" (the "search for connections among ideas that might ordinarily be thought of as disconnected") and "subsumption" ("the ways in which Edwards's insights were absorbed into ever-expanding and more general categories") (11).

Despite Edwards's habit of problematizing as many sides of an idea as he could before offering public thoughts upon it, however, his voluminous private notebooks show him to be neither emotionally nor intellectually conflicted over differences between modernity and his faith. While Edwards's notebook entries, sermons, and treatises explore natural typology and the new sense in his typical polyglot mixture of scientific, philosophical, and theological language, his core notions of what the new sense is and how it functions in the lives of the redeemed must first of all be attributed to Edwards's thorough reliance on—and orthodox interpretation of—the King James Bible. That is to say, although Edwards's depiction of nature as a vehicle through which God speaks to the believer was an *extra*-biblical extension of his Calvinist theology, it was not necessarily an *un*biblical one. The idea that God communicates to humanity through natural revelation despite the fact that the earth was corrupted at the Fall is as old as the Judeo-Christian Scriptures themselves. The creation narrative in Genesis details God's pronouncement of the natural world as "good" and delineates Adam's work of careful stewardship. The Psalms repeatedly allude to the connection between the beauty of the earth and the majesty of God's character. In the New Testament, Christ affirms God's connection with and concern for even the "sparrows" and repeatedly instructs His disciples to observe the natural world in order to understand spiritual principles (Matt. 10:29; see also Matt. 6). Pauline theology reaffirms this idea that "the invisible things of him from the creation of the world are clearly seen, being understood by the things that are made, even his eternal power and Godhead," even though "the whole creation groaneth" to "be delivered from the bondage of corruption" stemming from the Fall (Rom. 1:20; 8:21 and 22).

Furthermore, Edwards did not interpret the Bible from within a cultural and historical vacuum, of course, but instead participated in the long hermeneutical traditions of Augustine and Calvin, theologians whose strands of thought resonate down the centuries of American letters. Chief among these formative theological concepts is the belief that God is so entirely Other and so distinct from the situation and suppositions of humankind that only by divine and supernatural intervention may human beings be in relationship with God and grasp the essential, core truths of the triune Godhead. As McClymond and McDermott and many others have noted, Augustine's formulation that "the mind needs to be enlightened by light from outside itself, so that it can participate in truth, because it is not itself the nature of truth" is a conception itself built on Platonic ideals and the New Testament writings of the Apostle John (*Confessions* 4.15.25, in McClymond and McDermott 381); *crede ut intelligas*—"Believe that you may understand"—was not only key to Edwards's formulation of the "new sense" but also foundational in helping him "resist the Arminian tendency to see conversion as the gradual development of a person's God-given but natural abilities. Instead, the new birth took place by God's immediate action, without the mediation of human powers" (382). This credo helps promulgate a worldview in which the dichotomy between divine alterity and human limitation is extreme, and thus adds alacrity to the desire for some comprehensible place of communicative overlap between the two realms. The created natural world becomes a logical and fecund middle ground for this counion, making the natural type inherently relational in its work.

Concomitantly, Edwards's depiction of nature as a vehicle through which God speaks to the believer without nature itself becoming deified or merging with the identity of the viewer was distilled through Augustine's heir Calvin, who called the natural world a "theater" of God's glory yet warned that one needed the "spectacles" of Scripture through which to understand it.[16] As Susan E. Schreiner explains:

> In Calvin's theology, the restoration of the imago Dei allows nature to regain its revelatory function. In fact, the ability to study nature profitably (without falling into idolatry) is a part of this restored image. . . . [T]he natural, fallen mind, directed only by the light of nature, was quite competent in the "investigation of lower things" such as astronomy and the other sciences. Scripture, then, does not function to make nature more knowable in a scientific way. Scripture only allows the contemplation of nature to become again a legitimate religious activity. . . . As order in the Soul is gradually restored, the mind is once again able to perceive the order and beauty still present in nature and, once again, to refer this "theater" back to God. (106)[17]

That Edwards's tradition was alarmed neither by science nor by differing registers of meaning is further borne out by the fact that Augustine and Calvin espoused a doctrine of inspiration termed "accommodation." Believing the Bible to be neither "inerrant" nor "infallible" in the nineteenth- and twentieth-century senses of the terms, these early theologians held that the authority of the Scriptures rested in their supernatural ability to change lives rather than in an absence of all types of error. God "accommodated" the spiritual truths in Scripture to limited human language and understanding; thus, while it did portray historical events, the Bible itself wasn't subjected to the demands of entirely literal or scientific accuracy. Differences or discrepancies among the various books of the Bible were attributed to the necessarily human vantage points of the writers and were not viewed as a threat to the revealed truth of the message of salvation.

This tolerance for ambiguity also predisposed the Reformers toward the practice of looking for broad patterns of meaning suggested by the disparate elements in biblical texts—texts that were themselves assumed a priori to be in dialogue with one another. Chief among their hermeneutical strategies was the employment of typological interpretation. In his seminal work *The Eclipse of Biblical Narrative: A Study in Eighteenth and Nineteenth Century Hermeneutics,* Hans Frei has identified the typological mode as a way of reading what he asserts is the Bible's unique narrative style, a style akin neither to myth nor to an early magical realism. Instead, he writes, in typology,

> believable individuals and their credible destinies are rendered in ordinary language and through concatenations of ordinary events which cumulatively constitute the serious, sublime, and even tragic impact of powerful historical forces. These forces in turn allow the ordinary, "random," lifelike individual persons, who become their bearers in the crucial intersection of character and particular event-laden circumstance, to become recognizable realistic "types," without thereby inducing a loss of their distinctively contingent or random individuality. (15)

In other words, Frei is saying, typology allows biblical characters such as Joshua to exist fully as humans acting with their own volition at their own moment in history even as they indicate and enact divine, prophetic, or atemporal realities beyond themselves. Hence, Joshua exists both as the leader who brings the children of Israel across the Jordan River into their Promised Land and as a type of Jesus (whose Hebrew name is an alternate form of the name Joshua), rescuing his people and bringing them through death into the New Covenant. In addition, by reading biblical texts with this typological mindset, Frei continues, exegetes such as Calvin saw meaning as embodied and embedded in the telling of narrative itself, rather than as something the text referred to outside itself.[18] The Bible was thought of as a unified whole, then, with its layers of historical, typological, and doctrinal meaning conceived as mutually reinforcing its messages, which were ultimately to be enacted in the lives of believers.

Edwards also joined his tradition in embracing "the customary Calvinist tenet that scripture interpreted itself" and the assertion that "all scriptural doctrines had to flow from scriptural exegesis," as E. Brooks Holifield summarizes in *Theology in America: Christian Thought from the Age of the Puritans to the Civil War*. Edwards's hermeneutical practices were consistent with the belief that "to understand difficult passages, the interpreter had to read them in the light of clearer ones." Yet by the time Edwards's New England predecessors held sway, Holifield continues, "this maxim produced a primary reliance on what they called the literal or 'historical' reading of the text. Unlike the medieval exegetes, who also read the Bible as an allegory, a repository of hidden moral truths, and a catalog of references to the New Jerusalem," the New England divines stressed the historical mode, along with commenting on "exemplary . . . patterns for imitation" and, of course, typology (29–30). Perhaps, indeed, it was this narrowing of figurative layers to the chiefly historical that inspired Augustine's and Calvin's eighteenth-century heir Jonathan Edwards to open a figural window on the Bible, so to speak, and to revivify the typological tradition by extending it to the elements of the natural world Edwards loved.

Along these lines, insightful work has been done reestimating Edwards's relationship with his immediate predecessors, the New England Puritans, whose works he would have studied as a boy in his father's and grandfather's libraries. In *Orthodoxies in Massachusetts: Rereading American Puritanism,* Janice Knight convincingly asserts that the Puritans were far from monolithic in their conceptions of the ways God communicates with humankind. She conjoins Edwards with an alternate orthodox Puritan tradition that she names the "Spiritual Brethren," or Cambridge circle, and traces through Richard Sibbes, John Cotton, John Preston, and John Davenport. Basing her argument on the notion that it is the victors who write the histories, she contrasts the Cambridge group with the lineage of "Intellectual Fathers"—William Ames, Thomas Hooker, John Winthrop, and others—who won the political and rhetorical battle for the colonies. Among other theological differences between the two groups, Knight finds that the more mystical, Augustinianly inclined Cambridge circle believed that "God is a communicating being whose happiness is realized in dissemination"; consequently, in the writings of Sibbes and his heirs, "the phenomenal world provides the emblems by which human beings may understand both this conjunction of being with communication in God's nature and secondarily in its outflowing to the creature" (135, 136). Thus, according to Knight, Edwards, who read both Sibbes and Cotton (as well as the "Intellectual Fathers"), was in fact well within the bounds of a previously defined orthodox Reformed tradition in the development of "the new sense" and his system of natural typology that flowed from it.

These predilections are also manifest in the work of two English Puritan divines whose emblematic devotional writings were immensely popular in Edwards's New England: *The Saints Everlasting Rest* (1649) by Richard Baxter (also a favorite source of Marianne Moore) and John Flavel's *Husbandry Spiritualized* (1669).[19] William Dyrness, whose excellent *Reformed Theology and Visual Culture: The Protestant Imagination from Calvin to Edwards* confirms and advances Knight's insights, particularly singles out Flavel's book as influential in this regard. Flavel instructs his readers not only to consider the work of husbandry as valuable labor but also to understand that its deeper meanings are "coded, visible only to those who wear the proper spectacles. These alone are able to see that

God's creatures and the responsibility for their larger care are a part of a larger narrative, and that believers find their place, indeed their very identity, in working out this narrative of redemption and restoration throughout the warp and woof of their lives" (Dyrness 268–69). Not surprisingly, Edwards was highly appreciative of both Baxter and Flavel, citing in his "Catalogue" six different books by Baxter and making numerous references throughout his writing to seven different works by Flavel.[20] Consequently, although we rightly associate Edwards with the New England Puritans, altering our conception of the Puritans to include a group whose rhetoric emphasized the benevolence of God and the sign systems of the natural world affirms how the notions of "God as a communicator and saint as recipient of spiritual knowledge" in Edwards were not aberrations but markers of a tradition he consciously passed forward from his parents' generation (Knight, *Orthodoxies* 207).

Yet while these elements in Edwards's thinking clearly delineate his position in the orthodox Reformed family tree, emphasis on his debts to Augustine, Calvin, and the Puritans alone has also served, perhaps, to relegate him to a past safely distant from the intellectual milieu of the Continental eighteenth century. In truth, for all his continuities with these earlier theologians, Edwards's thinking was influenced at least as much by his reading deeply in the line of their intellectual successors—Edwards's own contemporaries or near contemporaries—as it was by study of their primary works. While Edwards most likely read a great many of Augustine's treatises, for instance, he lists only the *Confessions* in his "Catalogue" of books and refers to Augustine only briefly in *Religious Affections* and *Freedom of the Will.* Likewise, he cites Calvin directly only three times in his vast writings, each in *Religious Affections.* Although he certainly would have read Calvin's *Institutes* and major commentaries, as his biographer George Marsden observes: "'Calvinism' is and was an imprecise term. . . . New Englanders did not often use the word nor concern themselves much with the precise teachings of John Calvin. Rather they saw themselves as the heirs to what they considered the truly biblical outlook of 'the Reformers.' That tradition included Puritan, Presbyterian, and continental 'Reformed' authors and came in many varieties" (86). Indeed, one of the chief facets of the new Edwards scholarship is that he is finally being considered alongside the thinkers and writers of his own era whose works constituted the bulk of his reading; this development calls for a recalibration in the mental associations we make with Edwards. He is properly neither a "Puritan" nor a "Calvinist" in the seventeenth-century senses of those terms.

In both his extensive work as editor of Edwards's "Catalogue" and in his bibliographic article "Jonathan Edwards and the Transatlantic World of Books," Peter J. Thuesen has cohesively elucidated how "Edwards's theological native language" was not the Puritanism of old but rather contemporary or near-contemporary "scholasticism of post-Reformation Reformed orthodoxy"; this strain includes authors of importance to Edwards such as Peter van Mastricht, Francis Turretin, John Owen, and Matthew Poole ("Jonathan Edwards" 45). Like Edwards, the post-Puritan Dissenters and other British Nonconformists were not only classically trained to read Greek, Hebrew, and Latin, but also were keenly aware of translation problems with the King James Bible and of higher critical challenges to traditional hermeneutical practices by such figures as Benedict Spinoza, Thomas Hobbes, and their followers. The works Edwards cites with the greatest frequency, as Stephen J. Stein's introduction to Edwards's private scriptural commentary, *The Blank Bible* (2006), makes clear, are three sets of synoptic commentaries by writers within this post-Reformation tradition: Matthew Poole's five-volume *Synopsis Criticorum* (1669–1676), which Edwards cites 792 times; Matthew Henry's six-volume *Exposition of the Old and New Testaments* (1708–1710), which he cites 205 times; and his contemporary Philip Doddridge's six-volume *Family Expositor* (1739–1756), which he cites 303 times.[21] (Douglas A. Sweeney reports that, in turn, "Doddridge was an Edwards fan" who read both Edwards's *Faithful Narrative* and his *Life of Brainerd*) (247).

Edwards was also particularly fond of John Locke's commentaries on the Pauline epistles: *A Paraphrase and Notes on the Epistle of St. Paul to the Romans* (1707), *Corinthians* (1706), and *Galatians* (1708). Although the juxtaposition of Locke with the names of the great orthodox Reformed commentators of the eighteenth century might seem jarring from our twenty-first-century perspective, such was not the case in Edwards's time. As Sweeney notes: "On the ground, few participants in eighteenth-century trends would have understood their purposes in anti-Christian terms. Most were Christian. None of them even used the English word 'Enlightenment'" (265). Instead, British thinkers and writers saw their work as

> a modernizing movement that was cautious, led by clergy (not exclusively, but largely), brimming with biblicism, ardent supernaturalism, and faith. Even Newton, Locke, and Priestley spent more time interpreting Scripture than experimenting with nature. Most shared Edwards's combination of Christian orthodoxy, guarded optimism regard-

> ing moral and scientific progress, eagerness to apply human reason to current challenges, earnestness in pleading for genuine virtue in the world, and intercourse with kindred spirits near the north Atlantic. Many also shared his interest in Isaac Newton and John Locke, Thomas Chubb, Hugo Grotius, Francis Hutcheson, Andrew Michael Ramsay, Matthew Tindal, and other major stars in the age of lights. (266–67)

Indeed, Edwards likely viewed his own speculations on science, metaphysics, and philosophy as situating him within what would later be called the Enlightenment conversation and not in opposition to it.

For instance, Edwards's envisioning of a material and spiritual cosmos held together by forces of relational "consent" is notable for its subsumption of Newtonian physics within orthodox theology. Newton's first law of motion—objects in motion will tend to continue in motion until they are externally prevented from that motion—revolutionized the Aristotelian physics in which it was assumed that objects remain at rest unless acted upon. For his part, Edwards recognized "the inadequacy of the old metaphysics of substances and substantial forms to function as the intellectual framework in an age that was increasingly thinking of reality in terms of motion, power, and relational laws" (Lee, *Philosophical Theology* 10).[22] In his early scientific paper "Of Atoms," for example, Edwards analyzes the attractive force that holds atoms in alignment yet keeps them from collapsing into one another; he deduces that atoms "can never again be separated by any finite power," while at the same time there "must needs be an infinite power that keeps the parts of atoms together." Edwards attributes this infinite power to the direct action of God, and since all things consist of atoms, "it follows that the constant exercise of the infinite power of God is necessary to preserve bodies in being" (*WJE* 6:214). By divinizing the model of the atomic bond that holds atoms apart yet together, Edwards created a version of reality that rests not in essences of forms but in a "system of law-like dispositions and habits" (Lee, *Philosophical* 246). A few years later, in his philosophical notebook "The Mind," Edwards would press the concepts of physics into the service of theology in describing a spiritual force similar to the attractive/repulsive atomic bond; he names it "being's consent to being," and the model becomes the foundation of his relational ontology (*WJE* 6:336).

Edwards was also born into a world in which Newtonian science, with its emphasis on motion, force, and the observable physical laws of the universe, had fueled a new empiricism. Seminal works such John Locke's *Essay Concerning Human Understanding* (1690) reversed the order in which humankind was thought to receive and process information about God and the universe. Instead of presuming that nature should be read through divine revelation and a priori, innate ideas placed in the mind by God, natural reason suggested that knowledge of the cosmos and the Creator must come first through what was immediately perceivable by the experience of the senses. And while Locke himself believed that rationality and Christian belief were mutually inclusive (as the title of his 1695 treatise *The Reasonableness of Christianity* declares), Deists such as Matthew Tindal found reason and supernaturalism far more inimical.

Edwards, as has been previously noted, immensely enjoyed Locke's writing and made liberal use of his empiricist language in the description of his own supernatural "new sense." Yet he by no means accepted Locke's thinking entirely nor uncritically. Edwards agreed with Locke that the mind lacked innate ideas and that "religious belief must conform to the principles of reason, but [he] tempered it with the belief that divine, not human reason was the ultimate standard of judgment" (Chamberlain 28). Concomitantly, Edwards seems to have relished making use of Locke's vocabulary and reasoning style as suited his own theological purposes, often taking Locke's principles as starting places for argument rather than resting on his conclusions. For instance, in *Freedom of the Will* (1754), that formidable treatise which produced such angst in his nineteenth-century theological heirs Henry Ward Beecher and Harriet Beecher Stowe, Edwards's reasoning often proceeds in dialectical disagreement with Locke concerning his own central assertion that it is impossible to "will" anything that one does not also "desire." In short, as Robert Brown has explicated at length in *Jonathan Edwards and the Bible*, "Edwards did not need Locke to convince him that sensations produce ideas; this was a commonplace in his scholastic and theological heritage. . . . Edwards's interest was not to show that religious ideas were sense ideas, and therefore empirical, but rather to show that (religious) sense ideas were knowledge, and therefore rational" (28). So "his use of Locke," Brown continues, "was a serious attempt to give philosophical expression to the self-evidential nature of the experiential religious knowledge characteristic of Puritan and Reformed religious psychology" (40).[23]

Thus, while Edwards applied and interacted with Locke in a multiplicity of ways, he did not, as Perry Miller had phrased it, use his ideas as a secret springboard for "an exaltation of nature to a level of authority coequal with revelation" (Editor's Introduction 28). Indeed, as McClymond and McDermott note in *The Theology of Jonathan Edwards*, "the major authors on Edwards from the 1960s onward seemed to have only one thing in common—dissent from Perry Miller" (645). Or, as the cultural historian Joseph Conforti puts it more bluntly in his devastating critique of Miller at the conclusion of the seminal *Jonathan Edwards, Religious Tradition, and American Culture,* Miller "was unable to see beyond Holmes and Parrington or, one might say, beyond the history of Harvard. He reacted to the Unitarian and Progressive derision of Edwards, the only enduring Edwardsean tradition in American culture that he seemed to recognize." In his haste to create a unified tradition of American letters, Conforti argues, Miller constructed a false connection between the Great Awakening and the Revolution and "saddled a generation of scholars" with "highly problematic interpretations of the modernity of Edwards and of the theologian's links to transcendentalism" (193–94, 195).[24]

After generations of writing off Edwards's "new sense" as Enlightenment philosophy recast in the outdated language of Puritanism, we American literature scholars have missed the opportunity to plot his thinking as one point along the historical continuum of the Augustinian Reformed thought that richly informed writers before and after him. The resulting errors have not only simplified our view of Edwards's thought but also skewed our understanding of the history of American ideas. The Reformed hermeneutical traditions have played a role in shaping broader understandings of language, and religion and science have historically informed each other for longer than they have been perceived to be at odds.

In our defense, it must be remembered that the story of Edwards's legacy after his demise is nearly as complex as the sources of his inspiration. After his early and sudden death in 1758, the "appreciation and appropriation of Edwards's ideas" by his immediate theological successors, the New Divinity, were "selective and necessarily so," as McClymond and McDermott put it (622).[25] Given the immense volume and diversity of his public and private writings—and the fact that Edwards had in no way prepared most of it for publication—much of his work was unavailable for decades after his death, including most of his biblical writings and idea notebooks containing his thoughts on typology, moral ontology, and the Trinity. The philosophical sea change at Princeton also took its toll on Edwards's influence. As Stephen D. Crocco points out:

> In the years that followed his death, Edwards's sophisticated theological system struggled to take root in Princeton. Any shallow roots remaining following the premature deaths of his immediate successors were ripped out of the ground by President John Witherspoon, who

> favored the Scottish philosophical tradition—a tradition that Edwards thought ultimately minimized the role of God in morality. Princeton remained interested in revivalism and Edwards's writings on this topic were always valued. However, as a comprehensive intellectual system, Edwards was replaced by the Scottish Realist tradition. (232–33)

Later, when antebellum evangelical leaders such as Lyman Beecher and Edwards A. Park were reintroducing Edwards to a mass audience, it was this revivalist strain that was evoked as a popular icon and institutionalized as cultural authority for the Second Great Awakening. Conforti has argued that this particular strain of Edwardsean thought was a carefully selected creation that involved "canonization of key Edwardsian texts, such as the *Personal Narrative*, the *Life of David Brainerd*, and the *Religious Affections*" (20). Edited copies of these works were published by the Tract Society and other organizations; according to Conforti, the "'improvements' of Edwards restrained the quietistic, aesthetic, mystical and Calvinistic elements of the *Religious Affections* and accentuated the activist, practical, pietistic, and Methodistical side of Edwardsianism" (34). Yet these texts, ones that Emily Dickinson was undoubtedly familiar with, also carried with them the germs of Edwards's own Augustinian Reformed inheritances: the explications of divine and supernatural light that illuminates the believer from outside yet through the natural world.

In the sense of an American literary heritage, then, Edwards's typological imagination situates him upstream of a shared American metapoetic which finds significance in the natural world as a second kind of text that complements the King James Bible. Such a stream veers away from a desire for "oneness" with creation, however, by its emphasis on differentiation and meaningful relation with the other-as-other, a core proclivity that is rooted in the embrace of differentiation and ambiguity in concepts of religion, language, and scientific thought. Later partakers of this stream, such as—as will be examined in this book—Emily Dickinson and Marianne Moore, were neither embarrassed nor intellectually crippled by their own iterations of this religious (and specifically Reformed and Trinitarian) set of beliefs. Rather, they worked both within and against the American typological imagination, using their nature poetry as evocative meditations on the mystery of revelation from a source outside the self, on the roles of desire and ethics to put one into relation with what one perceives, and on consent to life as a kind of being-as-becoming.

2

Beauty and the Eye of the Beholder

Being and Desire in Jonathan Edwards's Natural Typology

"The devil," Jonathan Edwards informed a 1752 Presbyterian synod, "is orthodox." Elaborating in a vein calculated to amuse his audience of fellow Harvard and Yale alumni who spent much of their time examining applicants for church membership, Edwards explains that the devil "believes the true scheme of doctrine; he is no Deist, Socinian, Arian, Pelagian, or Antinomian; the articles of his faith are all sound"; this is because the devil was "educated in the best divinity school in the universe, viz. the heaven of heavens," and consequently had a front-row seat from which he was a "spectator" at the very creation of the world (*WJE* 25:614–15, 617). The sermon, "True Grace, Distinguished from the Experience of Devils," is one of the many treatises, sermons, and meditations Edwards penned throughout his career to help audiences differentiate between the state of authentic Christian selfhood and the self-deluded, false selfhood of the damned.[1] The topic of spiritual identity was a perennial favorite among Reformed ministers and one that, it can be imagined—especially after the debates during the Great Awakening about how to discern a true work of God—still caused considerable angst among laity and pastors alike.

Being a re-created self in a state of true grace, Edwards declares here by way of negation, is not something that is denoted by merely intellectual, or "speculative," knowledge of the Bible or its doctrines; that is objective information that even the devil and his minions have mastered.

Neither, however, is this state of being indicated by having a guilty conscience, a desire for salvation, a fear of God's wrath, nor even "a very great and affecting sense of many divine things" on one's "heart" (626). Rather, Edwards states, what is "most fundamental" in saints and distinguishes them from devils and the damned is "an apprehension, or sense of the supreme holy beauty, and comeliness of divine things, as they are in themselves, or in their own nature" (i.e., without reference to self-benefit) (633). Edwards goes on to assert that "this sense of divine beauty is the first thing in the actual change made in the soul, in true conversion, and is the foundation of everything else belonging to that change" (636).[2] God's "holy and infinite beauty and amiableness" is of such significance to Edwards because he considers it to be not merely *one* of God's many attributes; instead, divine beauty "is all in all, and without which every other quality and property [of God] is nothing, and worse than nothing" (634). For Edwards, the moment in which the self begins to be transformed into a new state of being is when it becomes supernaturally endowed with the specific "apprehension" of the divine aesthetic—a conversion that involves both the mind and the emotions as a place from which the essential reality of God is perceived and acquiesced to.

By contrast, "the wicked, at the day of judgment, will see everything else in Christ [e.g., his power and wisdom] *but* his beauty and amiableness" (634, emphasis added). For those who lack this divinely given "sense of divine beauty," the merest intimation of God's true nature "appears, in their eyes, furthest from beauty" and is experienced by them as a threat to the very existence of the self. With its power to redirect the subject from self- to Other-referentiality, the divine aesthetic triggers "opposition of the heart" in these unfortunates, and "the greater their sight is of his holiness, the higher is their hatred of him raised" (634–35). For the chosen, by contrast, "one glimpse of the moral and spiritual glory of God, and supreme amiableness of Jesus Christ, shining into the heart, overcomes and abolishes this opposition, and inclines the soul to Christ, as it were, by an omnipotent power: so that now, not only the understanding, but the will, and the whole soul receives and embraces the Savior" (635–36).

Having begun his address by foregrounding the devil as the consummate educated "spectator" who is nonetheless blind to the aesthetic aspects of God's true design and nature, Edwards ends the sermon with a series of biblical and natural images that convey the unfolding of a believer's selfhood-as-one-who-sees-God's-beauty. Deeming the

Christian's new life "an immortal seed," Edwards concludes that this state of being is

> the dawning of the light of glory. 'Tis "the day-star risen in the heart" that is a sure forerunner of that sun's rising, which will bring on an everlasting day [2 Pet. 1:19]. . . . 'Tis something from heaven, is of a heavenly nature, and tends to heaven. And those that have it, however they may now wander in a wilderness, or be tossed to and fro on a tempestuous ocean, shall certainly arrive in heaven at last, where this heavenly spark shall be increased, and perfected, and the souls of the saints, all be transformed into a bright and pure flame, and they shall shine forth as the sun, in the kingdom of their Father. (640)

As the culmination of "True Grace, Distinguished from the Experience of Devils," Edwards means for these aggregated biblical and natural types to lift his listeners out of the confines of linear and temporal thought into an affective experience of the now and not yet of Christian eternity. The dual sun/Son that has "risen," is "rising," and "will" rise in the first four sentences of this near prose poem mirror the way the new self, having come "from heaven," teleologically "tends to heaven." By the same token, in an allusion to the second chapter of Acts, each of the saved souls is a "heavenly spark" destined to "shine forth as the sun" and so illuminate "the kingdom of their Father." Yet the individual saint is not extinguished by God's greater identity when "transformed into a bright and pure flame." Rather, saints are "increased and perfected"—fulfilled and completed—retaining their ontological distinction from God even as they "signify" (another favorite word of Edwards's that he uses elsewhere) Him. The natural image of the spark turned to flame becomes God's phenomenological language to spell out how intimate perception of God's beauty is both the "foundation" of a new subjectivity and the trigger for a new "inclination" of desire that functions like a divine compass until "the whole soul receives and embraces the Savior" (635–36).

In this chapter I demonstrate how, reenacting the connective energy of a line of poetry or prose, Edwards's construction of subjectivity is relationally based and desire-driven and intricately linked to his notions of perception and the aesthetic. In both his sermons and idea notebooks, Edwards uses the natural types as a literary device that first enacts his ontological notion of what he terms "being's consent to being"—that is, being-as-relation-to-the-Other—and, second, woos readerly participation into the same, that is, into the ongoing lovers' conversation between

God and the created universe that occurs in the communicative relations between natural type and supernatural antitype (*WJE* 6:336). While Edwards uses terminology from a variety of eighteenth-century discourses to shed light on his vision of the universe as inherently relational, it is in his language of images, natural typology, that we find the key to consideration of the way he makes use of the fundamental qualities of language itself to play out his conception of relational being.

As a discrete unit, at the level of individual entries in his "Images of Divine Things" and "Miscellanies" notebooks, Edwards's typology functions as far more than a figural device for allegorizing nature. It creates what might best be understood as a metonymical, semiotic relationship among the three positions of perceiver/reader, natural type, and divine antitypes. Furthermore, I argue that "Miscellanies" entry no. 108, "Excellency of Christ," serves as a template in which Edwards teaches us how to read his typology in the light of the subject's desire to perceive and become relationally united with what is aesthetically pleasing. Finally, I assert in this chapter that when Edwards employs this literary device in another context, that of his sermons, natural typology accomplishes what didacticism could not: it affords his listeners affective, phenomenological knowledge of the things of God while inviting them to participate in the divine language of creation that his images unveil. In this sense, his sermons depict being itself as a kind of metonymic selfhood. The mutually signifying relation between types and antitypes models a larger relational ontology in which congregants themselves are spoken units in the ongoing conversation among the Trinity. Indeed, as I suggest at the end of this chapter, Edwards's insistence on the Trinity—both as a metaphysical reality and as a conceptual building block for his broadest ontological arguments—would help to hold open a space for the figural in eighteenth- and nineteenth-century hermeneutics that would resist contemporary and later strands of Deist and then Unitarian thought. Deism, Unitarianism, and what would later be termed Princeton Scholasticism—with differing motives—would greatly flatten biblical interpretation by calling for the privileging of the rational and literal senses over the metaphorical and typological.

Along these lines, the work of the philosophers Emmanuel Levinas and Jean-Luc Marion provides a suggestive vocabulary that helps unpack Edwards's construction of a relational selfhood, an ontology that is modeled in the types' integral connection of the natural and supernatural realms without collapsing the one into the other. According to Levinas, the maintenance of such firm boundaries stems from an insistence on the final alterity of the Other (divine or otherwise) from the self; this is a positive and ethical phenomenon, for it both makes possible the independent existence of the self and "calls into question," as Levinas phrases it, the self's assumptions. Marion extends Levinas's argument by describing the significance of the *intention* of the gaze at the Other. For Marion, "every pretension to absolute knowledge" of the Other amounts to self-reflexive idolatry (23). Levinas and Marion, both building on a Judeo-Christian theoretical framework, offer a phenomenological lens that helps illuminate the interconnectivity between Edwards's constructions of knowing as divine revelation, seeing as aesthetic perception, and being as signifying relation. In this sense, as I pursue in later chapters, Edwards's paradigm serves as a literary precursor for other writers in the American Reformed tradition (namely Dickinson and Moore) who would similarly employ typological semiotics and metonymy in their poetic depictions of relations between the natural and supernatural realms.

As literary creation, Edwards's system of natural typology might be described as a cosmological, semiotic drama of connectivity that celebrates desire for relationship, a desire that Edwards's texts present as simultaneously fulfilled and deferred in the mystical moment of reading the language of images. From the standpoint of dominant interpretive paradigms of the past two centuries, however, the paradoxically dual radicalism and conservatism of Edwards's typology have both been obscured. That is to say, Edwards works in an interpretive hermeneutic that moves beyond the rather formulaic or allegorically reductivist notion of typology that our critical emphasis on nineteenth-century literary conceits have schooled us to locate and dismiss. (One remembers here Poe's lambasting of Hawthorne's allegorical short story "The Celestial Railroad" for being hopelessly didactic.) Moreover, in classical typology, the complexity of figural relations arises in great degree from an emphasis on temporal relations rather than on the spatially oriented juxtapositions that visual modernism has taught us to privilege. A brief outline of the elements of classical typology in Edwards's work serves as a way in to the complexity of his typological innovations as they pertain to subjectivity and desire.

As outlined in chapter 1, there is now general agreement among religious scholars that Edwards consistently remains faithful to the sharp delineations between Creator and creation found in the Reformed theology he inherited from the lineage of Augustine, Calvin, and the typological handbooks of immediate predecessors such as Samuel Mather. In this early (1728) entry in his "Images of Divine Things" notebook, for instance, the relationship between earthly flower and heavenly antitype is quite different from a fusion of vehicle and tenor or from an extended metaphor in which an earthly image is evoked merely to stress a higher, spiritual principle:

> Roses grow upon briers, which is to signify that all temporal sweets are mixed with bitter. But what seems more especially to be meant by it, is that true happiness, the crown of glory, is to be come at in no other way than by bearing Christ's cross by a life of mortification, self-denial and labor, and bearing all things for Christ. The rose, the chief of all flowers, is the last thing that comes out. The briery prickly bush grows before, but the end and crown of all is the beautiful and fragrant rose (no. 3, *WJE* 11:52)

First, this is orthodox typology in the classical mode; that is, the chief characteristic that distinguishes it from symbolism or allegoric correspondence is that types (briers and roses) and antitypes (Christ's cross and glory) are considered to be real. Moreover, as Janice Knight has thoroughly described, there is no inherent conflict in Edwards's writing between the types drawn from the Bible that look forward to historical, prophetic fulfillment and the types drawn from nature that indicate the ontological connections between God and the created world ("Learning").[3] In both biblical and natural typology, (1) the spiritual antitype serves as the teleological end and fulfillment of the type, (2) both members of the pairing are ontologically distinct entities that nonetheless come into being by means of their mutual relation, and (3) both function as historical personages or events within the framework of linear time. This last distinction, however, is complicated by the fact that type and antitype are also always read sub specie aeternitatis, in the ongoing, atemporal light of eternity.

In "Images" no. 3, these factors are at play in two ways: first, there is a material quiddity, or "thingness," to the roses and the thorns and a concomitant presumed reality of their spiritual antitypes; and second, the flowers have a teleological, threefold aim toward (1) the believer's immediate and immanent "life of mortification, self-denial and labor, and bearing all things for Christ"; (2) an atemporal "Christ's cross" (as well as implied resurrection and glorification); and (3) a future transcendent "true happiness, the crown of glory" for the believer. The order of the passage, moving as it does from a rose to indicated spiritual antitypes and then returning to a description of the physical, time-bound characteristics of the flower, reiterates, in fact, the importance of the earthiness of the plant to the relationship Edwards is trying to delineate. Rather than negating the mortality of the rose, Edwards's typological construction depends on it. Only as the rose and its growth process exist distinctly from God as His creations can they be viable partners in the reflection of a particular part of God's glory—in this case, the incorporation of time into eternity. In turn, the rose itself is affirmed by the antitypes that lend their eternal significance to its material existence.

Consequently, unlike the sort of moral exemplum found in Cotton Mather's *Magnalia Christi Americana* (1702) (what Paul Korshin has termed more specifically "correlative typology"), Edwards's natural types are ontologically distinct entities that are also teleologically and eschatologically positioned. They point toward and are fulfilled in both a historical Christ whose birth, death, resurrection, and second coming are one-time events and an eternal Christ whose effects on the universe are preexistent and ongoing. Edwards's insistence on the simultaneity of these dual time schemes—horological and chronometrical, as Sacvan Bercovitch has most famously dubbed them—distinguishes his thinking from that of John Smith, Henry More, and the other Cambridge Platonists, a group of philosophers whose language Edwards sometimes borrows. Consequently, Edwards's types never revert to Platonic correspondence.[4] Instead, whether they foreshadow a one-time event or an ongoing spiritual state within an eternal schema, his natural types are always fulfilled in a specific antitype that, as Edwards wrote, "is the very substance, and is the true thing" ("Images" no. 45, *WJE* 11:62).

Edwards's natural types fall within the realm of orthodox typology, then, insofar as his figural relations are depicted in terms of both temporal juxtaposition and metaphysical contiguity, in which the boundaries between the material realm and the spiritual are affirmed rather than collapsed. A further close reading of the entry illustrates how the types themselves function not only typologically but also, I would argue, *metonymically* within the text and, in so doing, as microcosms of Edwards's broader relational ontology. Two different critical approaches to Edwards's textual operations unlock the textually based aspects of his conceptions of subjectivity. First, considering the semiotic complexity of the mutually "signify"-ing relationship between rose and antitypes in "Images" no. 3 underscores Edwards's definition of existence as a state in which beings exist *only* as they come into relation with other beings. Second, Levinas's understanding of ethical relationship as one in which neither party claims complete knowledge of nor representational mastery over the other (a "relation with a total alterity irreducible to interiority, which nevertheless does not do violence to interiority—a receptivity without passivity, a relation between freedoms," as he puts it) offers a helpful model for understanding how the believing perceiver experientially participates in the discursive play of the types without rendering them symbolic representations of the individual ego (*Totality* 211).

In order to mark these aspects, it is necessary to navigate the types alongside the larger backdrop of Edwards's metaphysics. As many scholars have noted, individual significance and meaning in Edwards's universe are found not in an ontology of being, or essence, but in an ontology of relational action, a state that Edwards often expresses in the language of typology as "signification." As he explains at length in "The Mind" nos. 1 and 45, true existence consists of living in the right ("proportionate") relationship with all other things; this relationship of gesturing away from self and toward the other is being itself, and the only state in which humans may find true happiness. Throughout his writings, Edwards attempts to delineate this relational ontology by describing it in the terminology of a variety of disciplines—geometry ("proportion"), aesthetics ("beauty"), moral philosophy ("excellency"), metaphysics ("being's consent to being,") and theology ("love"). These terms, although not exactly synonymous, all help to illumine various aspects of this relational universe, the centerpiece of Edwards's metaphysics.[5]

"Excellency," one of Edwards's chief adjectives to describe this ontological state, "consists in the similarness of one being to another" (*WJE* 6:336). Furthermore, he cites as "an universal definition of excellency: The consent of being to being, or being's consent to entity. The more the consent is, and the more extensive, the greater is the excellency" (336). The "similarness" that Edwards lauds here is not one of straitjacket sameness but rather a spiritual like-mindedness or "consent" in preferring the other to the self.[6] The alternative, "one alone, without any reference to any more, cannot be excellent," for that would be to assert existence as apart from inherent relation to other beings (337). Edwards's frequent use of the verb "to signify" to describe the manner in which type and antitype jointly point toward and, in their mutual "consent," complete each other is felicitous. The word denotes the way in which the type is simultaneously a functioning sign, a proclaiming agent and prophetic indicator of the antitype, and a marker of the antitype's ultimate pull on and semantic completion of the type.[7] His material, yet multi-referential, types "signify" or "show forth" in a discursive sense their spiritual antitypes in an unfolding semiotic chain of the divinely spoken universe.

Edwards's meditations on the relations between signifiers and their referents in the service of his metaphysics were not unusual for his day (the Royal Society had classified semiology as a science in 1641), and his interest in sign systems (including those found in Chinese and the Kabbalah) may be traced throughout his idea notebooks. In "Miscellanies" no. 782, for instance, Edwards ruminates on the imprecision of language, explaining in great detail how the mind must generally rely on "thinking by signs" instead of by the actual ideas themselves. He uses the example of a mind at work reading to point out that "if in order to [have] an understanding of what was contained in that page we must have an actual idea of everything signified by every word in that page, it would take us up many hours to go through with it." Although this process naturally leads to much imprecision, the time spent "taking in all the ideas that are either directly signified, or involved in relations that are signified by them" would be prohibitive (*WJE* 18:457).[8] Moreover, for Edwards the inherent slippage between signifier and signifieds is indicative neither of the consequences of the Fall from man's Edenic state nor of what later theorists building on *Paradise Lost* would term the "Fortunate Fall" into a state of differentiation necessary for language itself. Rather, "Edwards bases the possibility for existence itself on God's will that things be [both] differentiated from and related to one another," in a manner similar to semiotic relations (Daniel, "Edwards as Philosopher" 177).

In this sense, Edwards's philosophy of semiotics differed significantly from those of his equally famous near contemporary Cotton Mather. In "The Eschatology of Signs in Cotton Mather's 'Biblia Americana' and Jonathan Edwards's Case for the Legibility of Providence," Michael P. Clark delineates what he terms Mather's "eschatological semiotics." Mather believed that the disjuncture between signifiers and their referents would be repaired at the return of God's kingdom in the millennium. In the meantime, for Mather and for Puritan poets such as Edward Taylor and Anne Bradstreet, Clark argues,

> the temporal deferral of spiritual significance [in material signs] . . . has a crucial counterpart . . . in the destruction of the material sign by which that significance is rendered legible in the present. That destruction enables us to treat visible things as signs, as Augustine would say; or, in Mather's terms, to look away from their literal and historical meanings and to look toward their spiritual significance. (425)

In contrast with Edwards, whose "emphasis on . . . ontological continuity" allows him to read the typological sign system as an affirmation of the materiality of nature in service of God's ongoing communication to His children, "Mather is always 'looking away' from nature, as he would put it, deferring the significance of the sign to an apocalyptic future in which the epistemological problems associated with scriptural exegesis will be resolved ontologically in the experience of a new bond between flesh and spirit" (434–35).

In Edwards's thinking, in contrast with Mather's, the similarity between the mutually signifying relations of type and antitype and the semiotic relation between signifiers and signifieds serves to reinforce the goodness of creation as separate from and thus in relation to its Creator. Chiefly, this principle has been elucidated by Stephen H. Daniel in *The Philosophy of Jonathan Edwards: A Study in Divine Semiotics*. Using the poststructuralist semiotics of Kristeva, Peirce, and Foucault to explicate Edwards's belief in a universe based on "consent" and discursive exchange between God and creation, Daniel asserts that in the Edwardsean universe, types and antitypes exist in a state of what might be called "immanent transcendentality" (43).[9] In the network of semiotic relations that is the ground of being, Daniel observes, "the type marks the thing as in need of fulfillment. . . . Always pointing beyond itself to the displacement of itself as an image of another, each thing signifies its own completion in signifying its own fulfillment in its other" (48). Consequently, "the type signals its own transcendentality, [and] the antitype instantiates the otherness of signification" (51).

Building on Daniel's groundbreaking work, literary analysis elucidates the way the metonymic relationship between the types and the perceiver mimics this semiotic, relational ontology. To return to "Images" no. 3: in a kind of literary consubstantiation, Edwards tells us in the first line that the separate lives of plant, believer, and Christ are momentarily unified in the share of each in an overlapping quality of mortal life in which "temporal sweets are mixed with bitter." Instead of having an allegorical correspondence based on an implied similarity of individual essence or on a stable, noun-based metaphorical equation of "this is to that," type and antitype metonymically signify each other through their shared qualities. This dynamic, other-directed juxtaposition of qualities characterizes the ongoing relational "being-ness" of the passage. The contiguous lines of metonymic energy engage the perceiving believer as well; the believer participates in the language of images not by *having* briars but by making an empathetic connection of his or her own experiences of pain first with the piercing attributes of the uncomfortable thorns, then with Christ's suffering on the cross. In turn, Edwards construes this shared emotional space as the jumping-off point for another felt or affective experience that comes from observing the qualities of the "beautiful and fragrant rose," this one prophetic: Edwards suggests that Christ's implied crown of thorns becomes "true happiness, the crown of glory." This is a future state for the believer, but one he or she may momentarily enter into in the present through the relational, experiential connection to Christ established in the earlier commiseration with his pain. Finally, Edwards metonymically conjoins the earthly rose, the Christic Rose of Sharon, and the mortal/immortal life of the believer in the final sentence of the image, which refers equally to all three: "The briery prickly bush grows before, but the [chronological and teleological] end and crown of all is the beautiful and fragrant rose" (*WJE* 11:52). Thus, individual subjectivity according to Edwards's typology might be textually understood as a kind of metonymic selfhood in which entities both come into being and are intimately unified through their signification of each other.

As the close reading of the entry also demonstrates, the affective, experiential nature of the types is as important for Edwards's typological hermeneutics as are the discursive aspects. Through empathetic connection, the believing perceiver enters into the metonymic dynamic portrayed in the type relationship; at the same time, the discursive, mutually signifying "consent of being to being" inherent to the typological structure protects the types from being converted into symbol and so subsumed into the ego of the perceiver. For Edwards, as he writes in a notebook entry, "all existence is perception," or, all things take on existence as they are imagined as relational entities by a mind or minds (*WJE* 6:398). Emmanuel Levinas, for whom "ethics is an optics" of relation as well, elucidates the phenomenological experience of a perceiver who enters through empathetic imagination into something like the discursive play of Edwards's types (*Totality* 23). For Levinas, what preserves the ethical relation with the Other (which he describes as a relation with the infinite) is the essential "strangeness of the Other, his irreducibility to the I, to my thoughts and my possessions" (*Totality* 43). To enter into the type-antitype relationship of mutual "consent" would mean in Levinas's terms to assent to a relation of "respect" in which neither self nor the Other is obliterated; instead, one relates by "commanding a being to command me. This reference of a commandment for a commandment is the fact of saying We, of constituting a party" (*Entre* 35).

The mutually respecting "We" of Levinas's "responsible subjectivity," while it lacks the metaphysical dimensions of "being's consent to being" in Edwards's relational ontology, is still a "heteronomy" in which individual "consciousness, subjectivity, no longer has first place in its relation to the other" (*Righteous* 172). According to Levinas, in the realm of human relations, "responsible subjectivity" or "heteronomy" functions like "Speech" itself, which he defines as "a relationship between freedoms who neither limit nor deny one another, but reciprocally affirm one another. They are transcendent in relation to one another" (*Entre* 35). In a similar dynamic, the mutually indicating, discursive transcendence of Edwards's textually based types invites the one who reads his depiction of the images to be a self-forgetful signifier in the mutual conversation of "responsible subjectivity" as well. Key for both thinkers in the maintenance of such a relation, however, is the management of human desire. For Edwards, human connections remain an ethical "relationship between freedoms" (to use Levinas's phrase) when desire for the other is directed beyond the immediate person and toward "being's consent to being" in general; in this sense, persons may transcend the bonds of individual subjectivity and avoid the dangers of a too narrowly focused duality as well.

Indeed, while fine scholars such as Paul Ramsey have underscored how Edwards's notion of love or "true virtue" is the fullest culmination of "being's consent to being," I would argue that critical attention to the text-based operations of the types offers further insights into the phenomenological role desire itself plays in Edwards's system of relational subjectivity. For Levinas, desire is conceived of as "the idea of the Infinite. . . . It paradoxically consists in thinking more than what is thought and maintaining what is thought in this very excess relative to thought—entering into a relationship with the ungraspable while guaranteeing its status of being ungraspable" (*Basic* 55). Accordingly, the metonymic, discursive function of the types enacts the way desire for the Other becomes a kind of typological longing for the divine which reifies the typological bond rather than circumventing it; instead of repressing desire, in fact, the typological dynamic both creates and redirects desire toward the ethical and the infinite rather than toward selfish dimensions.

Edwards's utilization of human desire in the service of discerning and developing spiritual affections is not an aberration in Protestant spirituality. Rather, as Michael McClymond and Gerald McDermott explain in their compendium of Edwards's theology, his view of desire "situates him in an Augustinian-voluntarist tradition that characterized the human self more in terms of its desires and choices than its thoughts and concepts" and asserted that the self by necessity will always follow its deepest desires (314). This strand of thought is especially prevalent in the writings of John Calvin, for whom "a focus on the adoration of God's glory and the centrality of union with Christ form the core of . . . the spiritual life"—not the doctrine of election that later internecine debates would highlight (Lane, "Calvinist Spirituality," 162). Calvin's understanding of the world as a theater of God's glory that whets all creation's appetite for Him, for instance, is typified in his explication of Romans 8, where he asserts that Paul's personification of the created natural realm as groaning in earnest expectation for God to redeem all things shows "how immense is the price of eternal glory, which can excite and draw all things to desire it" (*Epistles*, 172).

This Augustinian and Calvinist strain of "longing" was carried forward into the New World by a group of American Puritans exemplified by Richard Sibbes and John Cotton, who, as Janice Knight writes, "transform the *imitatio christi* from an anguished self-discipline to an effulgent expression of agape. . . . Theirs was a God whose mercy was a fountain flowing without limit; a God who was a lord but, more importantly, a lover; one who melted the heart instead of hammering it" (*Orthodoxies*, 82–83). Although Edwards was deeply familiar with and influenced by the Ramist logic and faculty psychology used by divines such as Thomas Shepard, John Winthrop, and William Ames, as Andrea Knutson has carefully delineated, his emphasis on the role of desire "radically disrupts the prevailing notions of how the mind works according to faculty psychology. Whereas in faculty psychology, an idea enters the mind through reason so it can be judged good or evil and reacted upon appropriately through the will . . . for Edwards, an individual is introduced to an idea and then one's desire can determine the direction the soul takes, constituting a significant break from Shepard's doctrine" (62).

Edwards's allegiance to the Augustinian understanding of desire may be traced throughout his career. In the early "Miscellanies" entry no. 108, "The Excellency of Christ," Edwards lays out his theories of the interconnectedness of subjectivity, imaginative perception, and desire in the signifying work of natural typology. In this notebook entry, his chief rhetorical strategy consists of establishing a hierarchy of desire by constructing analogous moves from physical human beauty, to the natural world, to the beauty of Christ. He does so in relation to a further metaphysical backdrop—that of his own brand of idealism, in which rightly perceiving an image is coeval with spiritual experience. As he describes it, imaginatively entering into an apperception of and desire for "proportionate" "mental beauty" is the way into an experience of relational subjectivity as well. Such "mental beauties" represent the most desirable aesthetic component of Edwards's relational ontological equation and indicate the signifying, "proportionate" relationship of one entity to another that constitutes being itself.[10]

In "Miscellanies" no. 108 Edwards begins with the physically immediate—our experience of the body, of the gaze, and of desire: "When we behold a beautiful body, a lovely proportion, a beautiful harmony of features of face, delightful airs of countenance and voice, and sweet motion and gesture, we are charmed with it; not [however] under the notion of the corporeal, but a mental beauty" (*WJE* 13:278). Indeed, he continues in the next sentences, should we be confronted with a Pygmalion-like statue, "we should not fall entirely in love with the image, if we knew certainly that it had no perception or understanding." This is because, Edwards explains, "when we love the person for the airs of voice, countenance and gesture," it is "because there is an analogy" between them and "those excellencies of the mind" they represent. Moreover—and here is Edwards's most salient point—we cannot think of the cherished aspects of the person without at the same time experiencing the emotions those ideas excite.[11]

While a statue fails to engage the relational dimensions because of its lack of "perception and understanding," he continues in the next paragraph of "Miscellanies" no. 108, the human experience of natural beauty does seem to denote a substantive Personality behind the world's structures: "There is really likewise an analogy or consent, between the beauty of the skies, trees, fields, flowers, etc. and spiritual excellencies; though the agreement be more hid and requires a more discerning, feeling mind to perceive it than the other." Finally, Edwards concludes at the end of paragraph three, since Christ "by his immediate influence gives being every moment and by his Spirit actuates the world, the beauties of nature are really emanations, or shadows, of the excellencies of the Son of God"; to apperceive them is to experience within one's own mind the person of God (279). Such a rhetorical move is possible because in Edwards's universe the imaginative perception of ideas is more real than a physical encounter with material things. Edwards believes *all* existence is mental; what we perceive as the real world is in fact a stable idea in God's mind. God "supposes" things into existence, and even what we perceive as the resistance and solidity of physical bodies is a specific kind of exertion of God's power within His mind; as Edwards wrote early on in "Of Atoms," God is that unknown something that makes solids hold together.[12] Consequently, since all existence is made up of ideas in God's mind, having a perfect idea of a thing—that is, seeing how it appears in God's mind—is the same as having the thing in actuality.[13]

If we have followed Edwards's tutelage and become astute readers, the space we enter into in the prose poem of paragraph four of "Miscellanies" no. 108, then, functions itself as a sort of Venn diagram in which the qualities of the natural, material realm (here given through the surrogate of written text rather than experienced directly for ourselves) metonymically overlap with the character qualities that he associates with the person of Jesus Christ. The paragraph reads, in part, "When we are delighted with flowery meadows and gentle breezes of wind, we may consider that we only see the emanations of the sweet benevolence of Jesus Christ; when we behold the fragrant rose and lily, we see his love and purity" (279). Edwards's language here, seeking as it does to re-present both natural fecundity and the ultimately inexpressible "infinite joy" of the Son of God that the physical types indicate and are indicated by, has a tone of joyful celebration that is reminiscent of the later Transcendentalists yet lacks the self-reflexiveness of the Emersonian transparent eyeball. Rather than casting a material world whose boundaries are collapsed into a romantic, divine selfhood that mirrors the gaze of the viewer, Edwards attempts to prevent his language from being metaphysically end-stopped. Instead, the aim of his language is to enact the way all things point beyond themselves, casting light along the path of the divine matrix of being as relation-to-the-other so that all things appear in a loving and graciously acquiescent process of signification that is "being's consent to being."

Consequently, becoming the literary critic that Edwards's text calls for does require a "more discerning, feeling mind," as he puts it in the second paragraph of this "Miscellanies" entry. In order to make meaningful a juxtaposition such as "when we behold the fragrant rose and lily, we see his love and purity," the reader is required to summon his or her own memories and affective responses to nature in order to then guess a corresponding emotional imagination of what Christ's concomitant "love and purity" might be like (279). Through making the affective leaps these repeated textual concurrences demand (roughly ten in this paragraph, depending on how you count), the reader is schooled in how to interpret the semiotic, emotionally charged images of divine things in the natural realm.

These moments of unity and fulfilled relational desire for the divine, however, are as partial and incomplete as the semantic capacity of language itself, Edwards reminds us in his closing corollaries. Only in heaven will believers have the "capacity" truly to read "the proper images and communications" of the joys of Christ and the fellow saints (280). With his added corollary no. 112, Edwards ends the "Miscellanies" entry by transforming the saints into the teleological object of Christ's own love and desire: "What beauteous and fragrant flowers these will be, reflecting all the sweetnesses of the Son of God! How will Christ delight to walk in this garden, among these beds of spices, to feed in the garden and to gather lilies!" (281). Evoking the Song of Solomon, Edwards envisions a heaven in which the saints become the garden; they are the perfected language of images, types that "reflect" and in turn are "delight[ed]" in by their aim, the Son of God. The human gazer now becomes that which is gazed at, the desirer, the one who is desired.

Edwards's habitual correlation of the gaze with the engenderment of holy desire, intimacy, and mutual signification (though not possession) of the other is in keeping with what Debra Shuger has outlined as "ocular eroticism," a model she locates in medieval and Renaissance literature as distinct from the later libidinal model of sexual desire (178). As she explains, in both sacred and secular literature before 1650, "the movement of eros is always inward and down, so that sexual desire is an inflection of erotic longing, not its origin or essence; by contrast, in the model that privileges genital sexuality, movement takes place outward and up, via cathexis and sublimation" (178). What might be termed the gaze-driven, "sacred eroticism" of Edwards's ecstatic language and spiritual longing at the conclusion of "Miscellanies" no. 108 marks for him the human response to God-initiated "communications" that are received through the realm of human visual ability to read natural images (Shuger 181; *WJE* 13:280).

In the Renaissance model, as Shuger relates, there is "no necessary physiological or affective difference between sacred and secular desire. One is not 'spiritual,' the other 'bodily,' but each engenders the same sense of lack, the same longing constriction of the heart, excited apprehension of beauty, alternations of joy and desolation, desire for presence, and lachrymose pain" (181). Writing in the eighteenth century, Edwards, by contrast, distinguishes between a kind of sacred eroticism in response to a transformative force perceived as originating outside the viewer and a more self-referential desire that operates by seeking to project an essentializing sameness outward. While both types of desire come from a "sense of lack" of the sort Shuger describes, Edwards depicts sacred desire as producing a type of self-forgetfulness as it gives way before the mystery of its relation to the Other. Non-sacred love in Edwards's writing, to the contrary, seems to fall well within a Freudian model of focusing on possessive subsumption and immediate gratification by locating an image of self within the other. As Edwards writes in a "Miscellanies" entry from the 1730s, humans naturally love that which "they conceive of . . . as in itself tending to their pleasure. . . . A natural [man] may love others, but 'tis some way or other as appendages and appurtenances to himself. But a spiritual man loves others as of God, or in God, or some way related to him" (Misc. 821, *WJE* 18:533).[14] Consequently, Edwards's heaven is a place where vision, desire, and intent are perfectly married: in heaven, where total apperception indicates complete relational concert with God, "everyone shall have his cravings filled" (Misc. 822, *WJE* 18:533). What concerns Edwards about earthly life is whether the aim of desire (which he frequently terms one's "disposition" or "inclination") tends toward loving "others as of God, or in God" or recursively circles back upon itself as its own goal. The aim of spiritual love, in other words, is ultimately God-directed, and it resists becoming fixated on its own image in the other by finding pleasure as an incidental outcome rather than seeking it as a primary one.

In this sense, Jean-Luc Marion's phenomenological distinction between the "idol" and the "icon" is helpful for understanding how Edwards's constructions of this sort work. Unlike the symbol, which functions as an "idol" in the sense that it attempts to represent the unrepresentable without suggesting the limits of its own mimetic qualities, Edwards's types, by contrast, like Marion's "icon," "summons the gaze to surpass itself by never freezing on a visible" (Marion 18). According to Marion, "valid as icon is the concept or group of concepts that reinforces the distinction of the visible and the invisible as well as their union, hence that increases the one all the more that it highlights the other. Every pretension to absolute knowledge therefore belongs to the domain of the idol" (23). In contrast to the "idolatrous," then, Edwards's typological desire seeks to establish an ethical yet positively detached link between the perceiver and the Other. Even in heaven, his saints do not become conflated with the Christ whom they gaze upon, although they "reflect . . . all the sweetnesses of the Son of God," as Edwards writes in "Miscellanies" no. 112 (*WJE* 13:281); rather, on earth and in heaven, natural types become an iconic window through which one might momentarily catch a glimpse of the desired eternal.

Finally, in its model of mutually completing and ethical fulfillment, the antitype-type relationship is a figural device in Edwards's work for the generative space where the meaning-making exchange between the gaze and the beloved, subject and object, signifier and signified takes place. Keeping in mind that for Edwards it is this relationship of active being that is the ground of existence itself (as opposed to individual parts working in isolation), typology in this sense marks the place where the energy created by the gaze of love drives such connectedness, as well as indicating the kind of non-fixated mutual signification that occurs in holy love. Impelled by desire, typology is shorthand for the longer equation of being that Edwards sometimes thinks of in grammatical terms as a transitive verb. As he delineates in another "Miscellanies" entry, synonymous with being's consent to being, "transitive . . . acts"—in fact, transitive *being*—might be understood in both its grammatical and philosophical senses: as opposed to an immanent or self-referential state, the transitive being that the types concretize is composed of actions that rely on direct objects of desire to give the sense of existence; ontologically, one comes into being only as one is drawn out of oneself to be completed by one's effects upon the other (Misc. 819, *WJE* 18:531).[15] According to Edwards's theology, believers under the New Covenant are thus judged by the aim of their desire as much as for their overt actions. This aim is manifested in their supernaturally endued, metonymically inflected "moral and natural qualities," which indicate the underlying "inward principle and exercises," themselves the inner actions (dispositions, inclinations) that are being itself (i.e., "the being of those things lies more or less in them").[16]

As the transitive verb in the subject-object relation, typological desire points in both directions as the human wish for "fulfillment" and the divine wish to "communicate" Godself for the perception of divine glory, to use Edwards's homiletic terminology. In this equation, Christ's beauty creates a desire in the perceiver to be "filled" in the same way that human lack instigates Christ's desire to "communicate" Himself for humankind's perception of His glory. Furthermore, the dynamism of typological desire initiates a process of type-antitype phenomenological and iconic transformation in the believer that begins even before heaven, as he affirms in sermons such as the 1723 "The Pleasantness of Religion." Since Christ is the antitype and mutually reflecting fulfillment of the Christian's state of future, perfected beauty, he explains, believers "may rejoice" in earthly life to see the partially mirrored "image of God upon their souls, to see the likeness of his dear Jesus. . . . If they delight to see the loveliness of Jesus Christ, it must needs be a matter of delight to see that Christ has communicated of his loveliness to their souls" (*WJE* 14:108). The intimacy of perfect sight that Christ "communicates" is seeing self as coming into being through difference from and relation to the truly Other. Attention to the textual markers in typology reveals that for Edwards, sacred seeing is always seeing-as-self-in-relation-to.

At the level of his sermons, then, natural typology furnishes Edwards with a repeated semiotic pattern through which to teach his audiences how to become signifiers themselves of Christ in the divine discourse. Edwards frequently focuses on directing his congregation's mental gaze toward their typological relationship with Christ, prioritizing the direction, or "disposition" and "inclination," of human desire as the seat of moral and immoral behavior. Natural typology brings its transitive function to bear in these sermons by operating underneath the theological palimpsest to mark the emotional and ontological deep structure of the discourse. In so doing, it supplies the transitive verb to the grammatically nominative roles played by the audience and God. Hence, following the typology in many of Edwards's sermons uncovers an underlying pull or tension in the argument that only partially resolves itself in the final aim of Edwards's addresses: the immediate, albeit incomplete, experiential realization for listeners of the personage of Christ.

In a 1741 communion sermon, "Like Rain upon Mown Grass," for example, Edwards metonymically aligns his listeners' identities with the natural type of cut grass: both are completely dependent on the antitypic sun and rain for refreshment and renewal. Expounding on the New Testament doctrine that "the old man must be crucified and killed" before experiencing new life in Christ (Gal. 2:20), the sermon offers a typological reading of Psalm 72:6 with the doctrine *"Christ, in communicating himself and dispensing his benefits, does, as it were come down as the rain on the mown grass"* (301). Edwards assures his listeners that "Christ comes down from heaven in the saving influences of his Spirit on the hearts of men" to bring about spiritual resurrection to a self abandoned to God (*WJE* 22:303); as in the typological relation of mown grass to the sun and rain, "so it is with the soul of man. Its prosperity depends wholly on the influences of the Sun of righteousness and on spiritual showers" (304).

Throughout the sermon, Edwards freely intersperses biblical, historical, and eschatological time frames, merging the believer's story of self with a continuing recursion of the atemporal story of salvation. In the doctrinal section, he delineates multiple theological instances in which the believer and Christ participate in the typological relationship of mown grass to sun and rain (and vice versa). By the application section it is apparent that Edwards's purpose in creating a typological nucleus that evokes a sense of available sufficiency and plenty is so that the sermon will bring his listeners to turn willingly from a "disposition" toward "lusts" that would ultimately leave individuals seeking "self-exalting" and self-referential pleasures and to move them toward other, divine-centered foci; in other words, to function as types that signify others rather than self. Consequently, the unifying theme of the typological junctures throughout the sermon is to evoke an "inclination" that "delights in self-abasement . . . as being self-empty" yet is paradoxically made full in its signification of the divine Other (314).

In what amounts to the emotional center of the sermon, Edwards relies on natural typology rather than theology or biblical narrative to explain that the self-as-receptive-mown-grass "must be willing to be thus cut down" (316). He asks his audience to reflect upon whether they have ever been brought into a typological "sense of things, and to such a frame and disposition of heart, that your soul became as the mown grass" and whether they have had a further "experience" of "the refreshing, reviving influences of the Spirit of Christ upon your hearts, as of the rain on the mown grass" (313, 315), He goes on:

> Have you had those discoveries of Christ, or that sense of his excellency or sufficiency and wonderful grace, that has refreshed and rejoiced your heart, and revived it as it were out of the dust, and caused hope and your comfort to spring forth like the tender grass springing out of the earth by clear shining after rain? Has there been light let into your soul, as the light of the sun pleasantly breaking forth out of the cloud after a dreadful storm, or as the sweet dawning of the light of the morning after long wandering in a dark night, or the bright and beautiful day star arising with refreshing beams? . . . Have you tasted that in Christ that has turned the stream of your affections that way and filled you with longings after more of him? (315)

Here, as in Edwards's notebooks, typology works as a kind of mystical and metonymical alignment between natural object, believer, and divine antitype. In quick succession, Edwards presents four different divine images (grass and sun and rain, sunshine after storm, dawn after night, and the rising of Venus) designed to give his listeners a "sense of his [Christ's] excellency or sufficiency and wonderful grace" (315). By participating in his language of images through their own memory of the affective components of the these natural phenomena, the congregants' understanding of the phrase "light let into your soul" contains an overlay between material and spiritual light, between chronological and teleological time frames, and between the identity of the listener, the natural type "light," and the antitypic affective and communicative presence of Christ.

Since, in Edwards's meta-narrative, the idea of the thing *is* the thing, the sustained effect of these juxtapositions points listeners toward an experiential place from which they might jump beyond language toward a mystical and signifying being-ness that Edwards's images imply. Edwards's types are "readerly" in the sense that they depend upon his listeners' participatory inward and imaginative examination of themselves and the material world so that they might experience a momentary lifting of the veil that covers the "more spiritual, noble and real world" (*WJE* 11:70). The typology in "Like Rain upon Mown Grass" invites a listener to gain affective, experiential knowledge of what it might mean "to deny or renounce his own sufficiency and excellency, and to deny his own sinful desires and inclinations" (*WJE* 22:316). Acquiescence to transitive being is indicated by a concomitant change in the direction of desire in which Christ "turned the stream of your affections . . . and filled you with longings after more of him" (315).

Edwards understood language to be more complex and unsettled than earlier, decontextualized literary readings of his works seemed to indicate. Acutely cognizant of the multiple referentiality of language, Edwards was a sophisticated apologist who was adept at using the terms and principles of contemporary theological and philosophical discourse to prove the adequacy of his own typological theory of the world as interpretable text. As he wrote in his typology notebook, Edwards wanted his system of natural typology "to show how there is a medium between those that cry down all types, and those that are for turning all into nothing but allegory and not having it to be true history" (*WJE* 11:151).

Philosophically, that meant Edwards wished to engage the assertions of contemporary Enlightenment rationalists such as Hobbes, Locke, Berkeley, Hume, and Kant, who were asking epistemological questions that challenged the very way educated persons thought about themselves as perceivers of the natural world (or, indeed, if it were possible to know anything of an external world apart from viewing it as a projection of the mind). Edwards also wanted to challenge contemporary English Deists such as John Toland, Anthony Collins, and Matthew Tindal, who were denying certain knowledge of anything except what might be absolutely known through scientific observation. Concomitantly, these English Deists argued that natural reason—not appeal to special revelation—should govern biblical hermeneutics as well. Only the literal mode of interpretation ought be trusted, they insisted (and if biblical texts were found to be untrue at the literal-historical level, any metaphorical or spiritual applications were to be considered equally suspect). Consequently, in the Deists' reasoning, even the New Testament writers erred in their understanding of the ancient Hebrew Scriptures because "the [Old Testament] prophecies plainly pointed 'in their obvious and primary sense, to other matters' than those to which the New Testament writers made them refer," that is, Christological fulfillment (Holifield 161).[17]

Consequently, Edwards's apologetic debate with the Deists was as much a battle over assumptions about the role of figural representation as it was about theology. And he faced a similar disagreement closer to his doctrinal "home" in the writings of contemporary anti-Trinitarians within the Anglican and Dissenting movements. In their haste to defend the Bible from the Deists' arguments from natural reason, authors such as Isaac Watts in *The Christian Doctrine of the Trinity* (1722) and Hubert Stogdon in *Seasonable Advice Relating to the Present Disputes about the Holy Trinity* (1719) "condemned giving the status of fundamental doctrines to '*Unscriptural Terms and Phrases*' . . . arguing that only what is 'plainly reveal'd' in 'express Scripture' is necessary to salvation" (Stogdon, *Seasonable Advice* 23–24, quoted in Schafer's notes to *WJE* 13:256). Edwards was aghast that his fellow Christians would be so willing to embrace literalism at the cost of the levels of spiritual meaning and experience outside the realm of literal interpretation and to cast aside one of key tenets of the faith, the Trinity, merely because the Bible did not specifically coin the term. As he wrote in one of his idea notebooks in 1723:

> There has been much cry of late against saying one word, particularly about the Trinity, but what the Scripture has said; judging it impossible but that if we did, we should err in a thing so much above us. But if they call that which necessarily results from the putting [together] of reason and Scripture, though it has not been said in Scripture in express words—I say, if they call *this* what is not said in the Scripture, I am not afraid to say twenty things about the Trinity which the Scripture never said. There may be deductions of reason from what has been said of the most mysterious matters, besides what has been said, and safe and certain deductions, too, as well as about the most obvious and easy matters. (*WJE* 13:256–57, emphasis added)

Thus, "in an age that was allergic to what it considered 'metaphysical riddles,'" as McClymond and McDermott observe, "the young theologian thought the real error was in failing to take seriously the implications of scriptural statements—a failure that under the cloak of scholarly caution extracted the guts from true religion" (201, 193).[18]

Edwards's numerous references to the Trinity throughout his notebooks, sermons, and treatises are indicative of the importance of the doctrine to his Reformed theology and of his ease with the figural and spiritual modes of biblical interpretation that some of his nineteenth-century Reformed heirs would not share.[19] Furthermore, Trinitarian thought—the concept that the oneness of God mysteriously consists in the relationship of three distinctive Persons—is also the basis of his ontological suppositions concerning being's consent to being. Within the Trinity Edwards located his relational model of being based on the mutual love of the Father, Son, and Spirit for one another. The elements in Edwards's universe, including his understanding of language and natural typology, mirror this Trinitarian mutual affection, deference, and signification. Thus, the nature of Edwards's cosmos is such that, as Stephen Daniel has argued,

> terms are meaningful not as independently intelligible elements that combine to form a language but as functions whose meanings are determined only because of their differences from and associations with one another. As such, the Trinity and the Book of Nature are not *comprised* of entities; rather, the persons of the Trinity, things in the world, and creation as a whole are entities in virtue of their Trinitarian and communicative character. ("Edwards as Philosopher" 165–66)

Edwards's reasonings, of course, did not silence what would become the Unitarian objections to the Trinity, nor the Deist arguments for reading the Bible only in its "natural" or "plain" sense. After Edwards's death in 1755, American Deists like Thomas Paine, Ethan Allen, and Thomas Jefferson were, in the words of E. Brooks Holifield, "relentless simplifiers . . . . intent on debunking . . . [and] exposing the 'absurdity and contradiction' in the complicated Christian scheme of theology and replacing it, in Paine's words, with a religion of nature 'which every man can read'" (163). In particular, Holifield continues, "Paine and Allen thought . . . that the defenders of revelation had never considered the relativity of language and meaning. How could the meaning of a revelation given in one language be preserved over centuries of linguistic change?" (167).

Yet it was Edwards's own understanding of the Trinity—and his insistence on more than the literal-historical mode of interpretation—that led him to locate a typological rather than a pantheistic or romantic sense of the divine in the natural world. His metaphysical conception of the world as a discourse of divinely spoken images gave rise to an ontological theory of language in which his types are neither allegorical nor the "fused sign and referent" that Perry Miller saw as the forerunner to Emerson's "Nature." Instead, the boundaries between natural type and supernatural antitype are held in a tension that ensures both their separateness and their continued "desire" for each other, a connection that evokes an "iconic" rather than an idolatrous response from Edwards, to use Marion's aforementioned term. By the same token, Edwards's understanding of sacred desire as moving ever outwards toward the infinite is characteristic of his broader notions of subjectivity as a kind of "transitive" relation to other beings rather than existing as an independent, self-contained essence. At the textual level, Edwards conveys this by employing typology as a series of metonymic and semiotic juxtapositions instead of stable metaphor. At the affective, phenomenological level, typology becomes a device by which his audiences might imagine the unimaginable, a jumping-off place from language into an experience of cosmic, emotional intimacy.

II

EMILY DICKINSON

3

Immersed in the Reformed Hermeneutic

Origins of Dickinson's Typological Imagination

Jonathan Edwards makes exactly one cameo appearance in Emily Dickinson's writing. In a tongue-in-cheek letter to her nephew Gilbert, Dickinson contrasts the cleric's stern reputation with the inclusivity of Jesus (the quotes are actually from Revelations 21:8 and 22:17, respectively): "'All Liars shall have their part' –/Jonathan Edwards –/'And let him that is athirst come' – Jesus" (L712).[1] If it is true that, as Marianne Moore would say, "omissions are not accidents," then the overt omission of Edwards from the rest of Dickinson's writings was certainly not by accident, but neither was it from ignorance. Given that Amherst and its vicinity were a nexus for such famed Edwards advocates as Edward Hitchcock, Mary Lyon, Edwards Amasa Park, and others, it would have been nearly impossible for Dickinson to have escaped an education in nineteenth-century Edwardsean views. Her humorous appropriations of terms such as "Change of Heart" and "awakening" indicate a comfortable familiarity with the popular-culture version of Edwards as well.[2]

Currently, Dickinson scholarship is enjoying the fruits of a renewed interest in situating the poet aright amidst the intellectual, historical, literary, and cultural contexts of her times; books by Cristanne Miller and Faith Barrett, as well as two superb essay collections—*Emily Dickinson in Context,* edited by Eliza Richards, and *Emily Dickinson and Philosophy,* edited by Jed Deppman, Marianne Noble, and Gary Lee Stonum—have significantly advanced our understanding of Dickinson's intense interactions with her own time and place.[3] Thanks to work by these and other scholars, Dickinson will never again be construed as a poet disconnected from the cultural and intellectual currents of her day. This chapter speaks to this conversation by highlighting the fact that Dickinson's considerations of contemporaneous literature, science, and philosophy took place not in a primarily secular milieu but in an intensely religious one. Furthermore, she lived in both an environment and a historical moment in which leading thinkers viewed the world through overlapping religious, philosophical, and scientific lenses, envisioning human life as an amalgam of sacred and secular experience in which most perceived no inherent conflict. Whatever degree of personal faith Dickinson may or may not have held at any given moment, her proclivity for thinking about the ways nature might fill the gap between heaven and earth was indelibly marked by the discourses of the Reformed typological tradition.[4] These discourses were not only the primary wellspring of the chief philosophical mode of her girlhood, Scottish Common Sense philosophy, but also the normative base from which Dickinson would have formed her first assumptions about language, ontology, and perception. Through Amherst First Congregational Church and its social environs, through her friendships and schooling, and through books in her own family library, Dickinson's world was awash in the basic rhetoric and tenets of the Reformed hermeneutic.

To begin with, Dickinson's assimilation of Reformed suppositions about language certainly came through her many quotidian experiences in church services and midweek church gatherings. From the onset of her childhood until she stopped attending church in her late twenties or early thirties, Dickinson would first have heard much Edwardsean theology and typological illustration from the pulpit. During her lifetime, nearly all Amherst First's ministers were trained at either Yale Divinity School or Andover Theological Seminary, the two nineteenth-century institutions that particularly prided themselves on being *the* heirs to the Edwardsean evangelical traditions (as opposed to Princeton, which remained "Old School" Presbyterian during Dickinson's lifetime and, while paying due diligence to Edwards, was resistant to the neo-Edwardsean theologies developed at Yale and Andover). Nor were the connections between the Dickinsons and their church merely formal. Throughout the years, the Dickinsons maintained warm relationships with their pastors and their pastors' families. Edward Dickinson, as a member of the parish committee, played a key role in hiring Amherst First's ministers, and the poet herself carried on affectionate epistolary relationships with several ministers' families long after she stopped attending.

The Reverend Aaron Colton (pastor at Amherst First from 1840 to 1851) occupied the pulpit for the eleven years during Dickinson's girlhood and early adulthood when she would have been attending church most faithfully. As Jane Eberwein and Alfred Habegger have observed, given the number of sermons Dickinson must have absorbed during those years, Colton's preaching likely exerted a formative influence on her use of language and perceptions of God.[5] A graduate of Andover Theological Seminary, Colton was no doubt familiar with seminary president and professor of sacred rhetoric Ebenezer Porter's best-selling and long reprinted *Young Preacher's Manual.* This historical compilation of the "best treatises on preaching" in "cheap and convenient form" instructed young ministers that references to typology, along with Bible history, "may be used, but sparingly[,] . . . always consulting good sense and taste," and warned them to avoid "well-known types, [such] as the Israelites' passage through the Red Sea," which would bore their listeners with excessive familiarity (Porter, *Manual* v, 221, 219). Although there are no extant sermons preached by Colton during his years in Amherst, we can assume that by the time he ascended the pulpit at First Church, typology had become such a familiar trope in Reformed circles as to be considered truism unless presented in some new light or context. Indeed, typology was a familiar enough trope to Dickinson and her friends that she sometimes jokingly makes up her own typological relationships, such as this one in an 1877 letter to Elizabeth Holland: "There is a Dove in the Street and I own beautiful Mud – so I know Summer is coming. I was always attached to Mud, because of what it typifies – also, perhaps, a Child's tie to primeval Pies" (L492).

Subsequent pastors at Amherst First Congregational were equally schooled—and even more enmeshed—in the typological and Edwardsean traditions. Edward Strong Dwight, the next pastor installed after Colton (at Amherst First from 1853 to 1860), was a Yale Divinity School graduate and a great-great-grandson of Jonathan Edwards. Yet he would have received even more notoriety in his day for being the grandson of Yale president Timothy Dwight, a man who carried forward his grandfather Edwards's theological legacy in such a way as to become one of the most influential religious leaders of Dickinson's parents' era (and whose engraved picture, along with those of Edwards, Lyman Beecher, and other illuminati, appeared in the front pages of the William Jenks *Companion to the Bible* in the Dickinson library). Dwight was followed in Amherst by Henry L. Hubbell (1861–1865), an Andover graduate who had been advised to come to First Church by the renowned Edwardsean theologian and Andover faculty president Edwards Amasa Park himself.

Finally, Jonathan Leavitt Jenkins (at Amherst First from 1867 to 1877) was a Yale Divinity School graduate who became such good friends with the poet's sister-in-law and brother that Jenkins and his wife named their youngest son Austin after him. Although Dickinson herself had long stopped attending church by the time of Jenkins's tenure, she was on friendly terms with the Jenkins family, and he is the pastor who famously pronounced Dickinson's faith "sound" in an interview that the poet seems to have undergone for the sake of her father's conscience late in his life. (As Eberwein notes, by the early 1870s, when the interview would have taken place, the 1869 manual for church membership had become so broad that nearly anyone who was interested could be received as a member) ("Calvinist" 73).

It is important to note that the softened brand of Calvinism espoused by the theologies at the seminaries where Amherst First's pastors were trained (respectively, the New Divinity at Andover and the New Haven at Yale) would have seemed extremely Arminian to their more rigorously Augustinian forebear Jonathan Edwards. In brief, the theologians at these seminaries revised the traditional Calvinist view that, because of the fall of Adam, the guilt of sin was imputed at birth; instead, merely the *choice* to sin was inevitable (a small but important distinction to both the Reformed traditionalists and the progressives). By the same token, Dickinson's pastors would have preached that all had equal opportunity to repent, even though some people would choose not to (an inevitability that God foreknew and consequently foreordained). Instead of focusing on predestination, Congregationalists of this persuasion would emphasize the power and responsibilities of their auditors to choose repentance, a practice evidenced in Amherst by the numerous evangelical revivals that occurred at First Church and the nearby Mount Holyoke Female Seminary during Dickinson's lifetime. At the same time, however, the New Divinity and New Haven seminarians considered their theologies at a far remove from that of the more affective, sense-experience-based Methodists. Revivals were staid occasions, and seminarians remained highly influenced by Scottish Common Sense philosophy. These practitioners "saw themselves as rigorously empirical, loyal to the facts of both scripture and consciousness"; most "could not imagine any contradiction between biblical revelation and human reason" (Holifield 355). In short, the sermons and religious culture Dickinson would have been exposed to at Amherst First Congregational would have been orthodox, evangelical, neo-Calvinist, and oriented toward the nineteenth-century version of Edwardsean (rather than Methodist) spiritual revivals. These revivals were perceived as divinely initiated, yet also ones in which—in some mysterious way—human consent played a role in individual choice to respond to the offer of divine illumination, deepened perception of beauty, and participation in the divine ways of being.

At the same historical moment—and without contradiction—church, civic, and educational leaders at Amherst Academy, Amherst College, and Mount Holyoke prized logic, intellectualism, and the progress of science. This love of science was not at loggerheads with the highly religious nature of the education that Dickinson received; rather, intellectual curiosity, systematic inquiry, and a habit of thinking of the natural world as related to its Creator in some fashion were a deep part of the poet's Reformed and even specifically Edwardsean inheritance. (Consider Jonathan Edwards's lifelong practice of amateur science.)[6] Amherst Academy (which the poet attended between 1840 and 1847) and Mount Holyoke (which she attend for the year 1847–48) were both highly devout and intellectually rigorous institutions, founded and taught by men and women firmly ensconced in the Congregational and New Divinity persuasions. In Dickinson's Amherst, the social, spiritual, and intellectual realms were inextricably intertwined. Edward Hitchcock, for instance, the president of Amherst College during Dickinson's formative years, was a renowned geologist, and an enthusiastic promoter of Edwards's legacy. He was also an influential benefactor of Amherst Academy and Mount Holyoke and supportive of both progress in the sciences and ongoing revivalism. The children of the Hitchcock and Dickinson families were friends; Dickinson read his books and textbooks on natural theology, geology, and botany; and in all likelihood she attended his lectures during her years as a student as well. Dickinson's biographer Richard Sewall and others have noted the influence of Hitchcock on Dickinson's own love of science, on her scientific vocabulary, and on her appropriations of and responses to his Christian apologetics and natural theology (as will be discussed in further detail in chapter 4).

Edward Hitchcock and his wife were great friends and supporters of another famed Edwards booster and member of the New Divinity clan in the Connecticut Valley—the educator Mary Lyon, founder of Mount Holyoke Female Seminary, where Dickinson studied for a year. Lyon lived with the Hitchcocks for a time, and Edward Hitchcock wrote her hagiographic biography shortly after her death in 1849 (a volume found in the Dickinson library). Lyon was an adult convert to Congregationalism who sold subscriptions to Edwards's typological interpretation of history, *A History of the Work of Redemption,* at the same time that she was raising money for Mount Holyoke in the 1830s. In the words of the historian Joseph Conforti, Lyon was "steeped in Edwards's works and evangelical techniques," as was evidenced in the school's frequent revivals (95). By the time Dickinson entered Mount Holyoke in 1847, it was considered the sister school of Andover Theological Seminary and was a respected training ground for teachers and for future spouses in the joint work of church ministry or in the mission field. As such, it often presented sermons and lectures by visiting Edwardsean scholars such as Henry Boynton Smith (whom Dickinson mentions favorably in a letter home during her year there). Had Dickinson—a near impossibility given her environs—managed to squeak through her first seventeen years without ever having read any of Edwards's popular treatises or sermons, she surely would have done so at Mount Holyoke. Lyon regularly read aloud from *A History of the Work of Redemption* to her student body and assigned other readings from Edwards during Dickinson's time there as well—probably those texts dealing mostly with mission work and "disinterested benevolence" (a designation invented not by Edwards but by his successors).[7]

Dickinson would also have been instructed in Edwardsean views of revelation, perception and the interconnectedness of the self, and the natural and supernatural worlds by her school textbooks on mental and moral philosophy.[8] Mental and moral philosophy was a nineteenth-century field of study that focused on quantifying and ordering the workings of the mind into distinct empirical categories. Since the workings of the human mind were designed by God, it was believed, understanding them would also yield a rough blueprint of the mind of God. The discipline was greatly influenced not only by Scottish Common Sense philosophy but also by the earlier speculative philosophy practiced by Jonathan Edwards in treatises such as *The Freedom of the Will.* Edwardsean metaphysical assumptions especially permeate Thomas Cogswell Upham's *Elements of Mental Philosophy,* an Amherst Academy text which Dickinson began to study in 1845. (The author was himself a graduate of Andover and a product of the Reformed knowing/seeing/being traditions.) In her study of Dickinson's textbooks, Rowena Revis Jones points out how Dickinson's manner of blending psychological and theological categories "strongly invite[s] several correlations with words and topics examined by Upham, suggesting that he indeed may have helped stimulate her to speculate on connections of the mind with the material world; [and] the nature of sensation and perception as sources of external knowledge" ("Preparation" 308). More recently, Jed Deppman and Melanie Hubbard have both argued in a similar vein for the influence of Upham's *Moral Philosophy* on Dickinson's thinking and work—particularly and extensively in terms of the larger role of mental and moral philosophy in the Amherst intellectual community and the importance of Scottish Common Sense philosophy in the poet's general education.[9] Any examination of Upham's highly influential work that doesn't acknowledge his indebtedness to Edwards and the Reformed tradition tells only a partial story, however. Upham's routine treatment of such Edwardsean-inspired concepts as love to being in general or "the beauties of proportion . . . [that] justify what has been said, that Providence designed, and that it has established an intimate connection between the soul and the material world" illustrates the high degree of religious and philosophical cross-pollination in Dickinson's era, so much so that it is probably impracticable to insist on a closer delineation between the two (Upham 59–60). And in Dickinson's Amherst world, laypersons and scholars simply did not.

Finally, in addition to what Dickinson would have been presented with daily in her formal education, what we know of the poet's family library indicates how deeply ensconced the Dickinsons were in the evangelical neo-Calvinism of their era. As was usual for educated middle-class families in the Reformed tradition, the Dickinsons owned several Bible study aids for the purpose of individual study of the Scriptures, an important part of their Christian practice. Among these aids, the most scholarly and comprehensive is the 1838 *Companion to the Bible,* a nearly seven-hundred-page reference compendium bearing the signature of Edward Dickinson and dated 1845. The *Companion* was compiled by William Jenks (1778–1866), a Congregational minister and renowned biblical scholar out of Harvard who founded the American Oriental Society and was a professor of Oriental languages and English literature at Bowdoin College. The book followed hard on the heels of his six-volume *Comprehensive Commentary on the Holy Bible* (first published between 1835 and 1838), a very popular reference set in Reformed circles that sold more than 120,000 volumes and was republished in multiple editions through the 1870s.

The Dickinsons' copy of Jenks's *Companion to the Bible* is quite representative of the sort of then-cutting-edge Bible help that was becoming extremely sought after in middle-class homes: it offered a wealth of engravings, charts, maps, and interpretive strategies from the Reformed perspective; it also made widely available to laypersons manuscript scholarship designed to bolster apologetics for the historicity and authenticity of the Bible. As archaeological and historical proofs for biblical narratives were becoming an important part of the early nineteenth-century response to European textual criticism, orthodox hermeneutical practices began to take into account not just how to read the written texts of Scripture, but also how to utilize illustrations that were meant to demonstrate the Bible's historical accuracy, as well as to encourage readers to have a deeper understanding and mental picture of biblical life and times. As Paul C. Gutjahr sums up in *An American Bible: A History of the Good Book in the United States, 1777–1880,* illustrative engravings and maps "made the truth of the Holy Land 'materially' accessible to the visual sense of the reader. Since [according to Scottish Common Sense philosophy] the senses could be trusted, what was seen could be accepted as truth" (69).

As an all-in-one study volume designed for the home, the *Companion to the Bible* also contains excerpts from the larger commentary series, including a "Guide to the Reading and Study of the Bible" (with Reformed-minded "biblical criticism, interpretation, and theology") and a "Geographical and Historical Index" that links biblical events and places with the Middle East of the nineteenth century. There is also a "Biography of Biblical Writers and Others Quoted in the Comprehensive Commentary" with extensive entries on such famed Reformed commentators as Calvin, Luther, and Edwards, as well as on Edward Hitchcock and Timothy Dwight.

Although Jenks does not include Edwards's "Personal Narrative"—one of the most ubiquitous of the nineteenth-century Edwards reprints—should Dickinson ever have had an occasion to look him up in the family's chief Bible study aid, she would have found a great many autobiographical details taken directly from the "Narrative." The elements of Edwards's conversion—hearing God's voice from outside the self in the natural realm, having his apperception of the world radically altered, and undergoing a concomitant change of heart that redirects his conceptions of selfhood, in short, the elements of knowing, seeing, and being—are all outlined in this section, which reads in part:

> Again and again the still small voice, in ineffable kindness and love, speaks, and at length effectually. It strikes him there is something exquisitely sweet and beautiful in the idea that *God* should reign, that *He should be God*—and do his own will in all places of his dominion. It fills

> him with a hitherto unfelt delight, that it is so. Unspeakably precious now to his seeing eye, and right affectioned heart, is God in all his works—in day and night; in sun, and cloud, and storm; in fields, and brooks, and trees, and all living and inanimate creation. A divine sweetness—an ineffable delight—a peace, unperturbed, but full of joy, fills his bosom, which his tongue labors, and is utterly unable, to express. Also the excellent glory of the chiefest among ten thousand has dawned upon him; nor can he tell, or begin to tell, the excellency, beauty and preciousness of this bright and morning star. (Jenks 79)

The 1838 biographical entry offers a more comprehensive overview of Edwards's thought than depictions of Edwards written later in the century that would feature, nearly exclusively, Edwards as preacher of missions, revival, and moral benevolence. Instead, the Companion's entry stresses that Edwards was not only a highly learned divine and successful pastor of the Great Awakening but also a man with early scientific, philosophical, and mystical leanings who had a "transcendent metaphysical genius" (81). One wonders what Dickinson would have made of this description of Edwards's awe-filled encounter with God in nature should she have chanced to read it some idle Sabbath afternoon.

Moreover, as a nascent poet, Dickinson would have been sensitive to what the Reformed tradition believed to be the Bible's chief literary mode: typology. While we cannot know for certain, of course, whether Dickinson read the *Companion*'s extensive description of typology, the entry is representative of the understandings of her community-at-large of the interpretive strategy as a dynamic model of language linking past, present, and future. Jenks presents a very traditional explanation of types as Old Testament foreshadowing of the New Testament Christ, along with stern interpretive warnings to stay on the Reformed hermeneutical path. His definition of typology reads in part, "The term is usually employed to denote a pre-figurative action or occurrence, in which one event, person, circumstance, is intended to represent another, similar to it in certain respects but future and distant" (52–53). Including sections titled "Rules for Interpreting Types" and "Analogical and Moral Application," the entry warns that true types must have evidence of "*previous design*" and "*preordained connection* which constitute the relation of type and antitype" (52–53). In looking for typological levels of Scripture, one should neither indulge in "a morbid longing for ingenious explications, mystical meanings, and forced resemblances" nor "discard . . . as irrational and uncritical, all spiritual and allegorical interpretations whatsoever" (54). Thus the *Companion* tries to strike a cautious balance between accepting as types only those things that the Bible specifically labels as such and allowing for some interpretive freedom in which there might be certain extra-biblical spiritual realities that might be cautiously but legitimately interpreted at the level of the individual believer. In general, however, Jenks's *Companion to the Bible* seems anxious to warn its lay scholars against what Jonathan Edwards would have called a "Romanish" tendency to over-allegorize what should be taken as a literal level of meaning. Readers should remember that with "sobriety of judgment and purity of taste," the "analogy between the type and antitype must not be pushed beyond the point to which revelation has extended it" (53).

Dickinson would have met with just such circumspect deployments of typology as the *Companion* suggests in her later readings of the sermons of the Reverend Charles Wadsworth, the well-known Presbyterian pastor whom the poet once called "My closest earthly friend" (L765).[10] Dickinson first came into contact with Wadsworth during a visit to Arch Street Presbyterian Church in Philadelphia in 1855, and his sermons were regularly sent to her by friends.[11] Though she appears to have met with him on only two or three occasions, she corresponded with him for more than twenty years, most likely through her friends the Hollands, and she was distraught over his death in 1882. Like other pastors before him in the Reformed tradition, Wadsworth reads the Jewish ritual sacrifices in the Old Testament as "not only a true and thrilling type of Christ, but a graphic forthshadowing of the spiritual worship of the heart that worships in spirit and truth" (*Sermons* [1905] 115). Likewise, Wadsworth cautions his listeners to be very circumspect in their typological interpretations. As he explains in a sermon published in 1869:

> In the use of all such scripture we are to bear in mind these rules of symbolic interpretation—that frequently there is more in the type than in its antitype—and that in the study of parables and symbols, we are not to look for too minute an accommodation of their every part to the spiritual truth they inculcate. The Hebrew Exodus is undoubtedly an emblem of a Christian's condition in this world in progress toward heaven. And yet, if examined too curiously, a thousand incongruities will appear, which must not be insisted on. Here, as elsewhere, the figure is designed to illustrate some particular truth, and there are many things in the type which will not be found in the antitype, and as well, many things in the antitype which are not set forth in type. (*Sermons* [1869] 92–93)

Jenks's and Wadsworth's admonitions were probably typical of the Scripture-reading advice Dickinson would have heard in her milieu.

Individual interpretation of the Bible was encouraged and even essential for the practice of the Reformed Christian faith. Nevertheless, valid interpretations needed to follow a set of given interpretive rules: typological interpretations were legitimate as long as they followed "common sense" and orthodox interpretations of the timelessness of Christ's Person and the foretelling nature of the Old Testament. Yet within these rules Dickinson would have found a structure and form for exploring teleological aim and ontological integrity; she would also have found a way to imagine the bounded interconnectivity of signifier and signified, observer and observed, and the temporal and eternal realms from within which aspects of the unknown might also be explored.

Conversely, while Wadsworth's typological methodologies were of a decidedly traditional turn (as will be discussed further in chapter 4), another resource in the Dickinson library where the poet might have encountered the Edwardsean typological mindset of knowing/seeing/being was in the writings of the much more progressive and controversial Horace Bushnell (1802–1876). Pastor of North Congregational Church in Hartford, Connecticut, for nearly his entire career, Bushnell was at heart a preacher and not a systematic thinker. Yet through his popular and academic lectures, articles, and books, he became a well-known critic from *within* circles of orthodox belief of the highly rational (what Edwards Amasa Park called with pride the "scientific") hermeneutical methods of the New England Reformed theologies.

Like several of the Dickinsons' pastors, Bushnell was educated in the New Haven theology at Yale Divinity School; there he was a pupil of and chafed under the intensely logic-driven, Baconian methods of leading theologian Nathaniel William Taylor. (The teacher would later distance himself from his pupil, saying that Bushnell knew nothing.) Though Bushnell was considered for a Harvard presidency and was instrumental in finding the site of what would become the new California College in Berkeley, he and his congregation were nearly dismissed from membership in the larger Congregational Church body for Bushnell's then radical views about language and Scripture. Indeed, Bushnell's call for a reinterpretation of biblical language as living revelation speaking through metaphor rather than as a set of propositions and arguments was more dismissed by his Congregational contemporaries than followed. As his biographer Robert Bruce Mullin writes, Bushnell "noted that both the orthodox and the Unitarians in their own ways had succumbed to the errors of logic. The orthodox seized on some images in the Scriptures, such as Christ's death upon the cross as the slain lamb, and logically worked out a system of soteriology based upon the principle of penal substitution. The Unitarians, in turn, reduced the mystery by domesticating it" (146–47). Bushnell, in other words, felt compelled to open the battle lines of scriptural interpretation on several fronts: against the traditional Reformed practitioners such as Jenks and Wadsworth he leveled the argument that they had simplified some figurative language by turning it to the service of making propositional arguments; against the Unitarians he claimed they had flattened and literalized the allusive nuance of figurative language altogether. Despite the resistance from the professional theologians in his own time, however, historians credit Bushnell as having been instrumental in pushing the mid-nineteenth-century theological pendulum away from adherence to Common Sense philosophies and back toward personal, felt experience in biblical explication.

Alfred Habegger, Jed Deppman, and a number of other Dickinson scholars have noted how Dickinson's poetic response to New England Common Sense philosophies shares affinities with Bushnell's own theories of language—especially as Bushnell develops his thoughts in *God in Christ* (1849) and *Nature and the Supernatural* (1858). The three Bushnell books in the Dickinson library, however—*Sermons for the New Life* (the 1860 sixth edition), the child-rearing manual *Christian Nurture* (1863), and the 1880 *Life and Letters of Horace Bushnell* (a hagiographic biography written by Bushnell's daughter)—were popular rather than academic texts. And examining Bushnell the popular preacher reminds us that his theories of language were at least as informed by Jonathan Edwards as by Samuel Taylor Coleridge. Indeed, as a boy, Bushnell had experienced the presence of God in nature in ways very similar to what Edwards reports in his "Personal Narrative." Like Edwards, Bushnell believed that "'the whole outward world' was 'analogical to thought and truth'" ("Revelation," unpublished 1839 address to Inquiry Society at Andover Seminary, quoted in Holifield 458). Moreover, he asserted that God uses types and metaphors to reveal these truths only to a divinely inspired human mind: "'An ox grazing on the burning bush,' he noted, 'would have seen all that Moses saw . . . but it would have been a fire in his eye . . . not the type of an invisible God'" ("Revelation," quoted in Mullin 61). And like the metaphysical Edwards who had been rejected by his nineteenth-century theological heirs, Bushnell was known for "his insistence that God continually intervened in the world miraculously. In the circles of academic theologians, he stood alone in his readiness to find the world still filled with divine miracles" (Holifield 465).

In the volume of sermons in the Dickinson library, Bushnell's typological vision is particularly evident in his repeated emphasis on the believer's immediate knowledge of the mind of God, of the change of perception that follows this knowledge, and of the quality of the corresponding regenerate life that signifies God through this transformational process of knowing and seeing. Bushnell's God is one that communicates not just words but *being* directly to the human soul. And it is his confidence that believers are given "a nature capable of receiving the inspiration of the Almighty"—an ability that, he says, "is the greatest of all distinctions—superior to free will, to conscience, to reason, and to every other gift or faculty of human nature"—that leads to his theory of biblical language as living metaphor which can and must be understood through affective, experiential understanding rather than propositional logic and doctrine (Bushnell 42).

Consequently, in *Sermons for the New Life,* Bushnell speaks to his congregation over and over again of the totality in which Christian believers are "to be penetrated and lighted up from within by the mind of God, to have the understanding of things unseen by the inspiration of the Almighty," of the believer's privilege of "knowing God as revealed in his [or her] inmost life, by a knowledge that is immediate," and of the faith that "gives you God, fills you with God in immediate experimental knowledge, puts you in possession of all there is in Him, and allows you to be invested with His character itself" (34, 37, 102). Echoing Edwards's distinction between "notional" and "affective" knowing, Bushnell explains that this knowledge of God "is not mind dealing with notions, or notional truths. It is what can not be a proposition at all. But it is being trusting itself to being, and so becoming other and different, by a relation wholly transactional" (94). Here is Edwards's ontological being's consent to being nearly verbatim: being is transitive and "transactional," with self coming into being in the action of attributing signification away from itself and toward the divine Other. Also like Edwards, and like Dickinson's own faith community, Bushnell asserts that conversion is the moment when the acquisition of the typological perspective, "the spiritual sense, or the power of divine apprehension," takes place (167). "Life proceeds from a new center," he asserts in the sermon "Regeneration," "of which God is the rest and prop. The Bible is a new book, because there is a light in the soul by which to read it. Duties are new, because the divine love the soul is in has changed all the relations of time and the aims of the life. The saints of God are no longer shunned, but greeted in new terms of celestial brotherhood. The very world itself is revealed in new beauty and joy to the mind, because it is looked upon with another and different love, and beheld as the symbol of God" (121).

The presence of Bushnell both in popular culture and in the Dickinson library indicates the continuity and pervasiveness in the poet's day of the old Augustinian and Edwardsean vision of conversion. In this process of "Regeneration," external revelation leads inward to transformation and to the believer's ability to read the signs of God in "the very world itself." Dickinson was fluent in this same nomenclature of conversion. She records such a change in perspective as Bushnell describes in her close friends and her sister Lavinia during an 1850 revival in Amherst and its surroundings. She wonders to her schoolmate Jane Humphrey:

> How strange is this sanctification, that works such a marvellous change, that sows in such corruption, and rises in golden glory that brings Christ down, and shews him, and lets him select his friends! . . . It *certainly* comes from God—and I think to receive it is blessed—not that I know it from *me,* but from those on whom *change* has passed. They seem so very tranquil, and their voices are kind, and gentle, and the tears fill their eyes so often, I really think I envy them. (L35)

Although it has not been widely remarked on by her critics, Dickinson herself records a brief conversion experience that occurred at some time in her revival-influenced teen years before her time at Mount Holyoke. Writing to her school friend Abiah Root in 1846, she recalls:

> I think of the perfect happiness I experienced while I felt I was an heir of heaven as of a delightful dream, out of which the Evil one bid me wake & again return to the world & its pleasures. Would that I had not listened to his winning words! The few short moments in which I loved my Saviour I would not now exchange for a thousand worlds like this. It was then my greatest pleasure to commune alone with the great God & to feel that he would listen to my prayers. I determined to devote my whole life to his service & desired that all might taste of the stream of living water from which I cooled my thirst. But the world allured me & in an unguarded moment I listened to her syren [*sic*] voice. (L11)

Dickinson mentions here and elsewhere how, after an initial change in the directions of her affections, her interest in what she perceived to be her Christian duties such as prayer and communal gathering waned in the face of the "allure" of "the world & its pleasures." Her youthful letters of spiritual concern during this period demonstrate the Connecticut Valley's New Divinity mix of Calvinist and Arminian precepts concerning free will: on the one hand, she attributes her loss of "greatest pleasure to commune alone with the Great God" to her own "folly"; on the other, as she writes in the next paragraph, she acknowledges that the only way her inner proclivities can change is by a supernatural act of God. "I feel that I am sailing upon the brink of an awful precipice, from which I cannot escape & over which I fear my tiny boat will soon glide if I do not receive help from above," she tells Root (L11). Though a native speaker of evangelical culture and terminology, four years later in another letter to Root, Dickinson continues to locate herself outside the mysterious change in perceptions wrought with conversion. Referring to a mutual friend recently converted who is "certainly very much changed," Dickinson writes, "I am one of the lingering bad ones . . . and I ask what this message means that they ask for so very eagerly, you know of this depth, and fulness [sic], will you try to tell me about it?" (L36).

Apparently Dickinson did not receive an answer to her satisfaction, for she never made a public profession of faith, instead forging her own idiosyncratic and heterodox monotheism in which she respected the person of Jesus but had difficulty reconciling suffering and death with the sovereignty of a benevolent God. Yet she continued to see the world "New Englandly," as she put it in one poem, always orienting herself toward conversation with a divine Other or the inscrutable absence left in this divinity's place (F256). As Shira Wolosky has argued persuasively and at length in *Emily Dickinson: A Voice of War,* Dickinson's longing for, and failure to find, a universe that could assure her of coherence and teleological closure gives rise to a set of poems Wolosky terms "blasphemy-as-prayer," an "assault on divine distance" in which "Dickinson condemns God but in doing so invokes him" (118). In her personal relations, however, Dickinson remained supportive of and even at times wistfully inquisitive about the sincere faith systems of her closest friends and family, as her letters to her intimate friends Josiah and Elizabeth Holland and her emotional connection to the Reverend Charles Wadsworth and other pastors indicate. Furthermore, over the course of her adult lifetime Dickinson's outlook does seem to move toward a generally hopeful stance about the person of God and the assurance of life after death, as scholars Jane Donahue Eberwein and Roger Lundin have shown.[12] Near the end of her life she writes to her cousins the Norcross sisters concerning her mother's death: "I believe we shall in some manner be cherished by our Maker – that the One who gave us this remarkable earth has the power still farther to surprise that which He has caused. Beyond that all is silence" (L785). In this conciliatory *credo,* Dickinson has shifted her earlier focus from an either/or choice between a "Saviour" at loggerheads with the "syren" song of "the world & its pleasures" to hope in a "Maker" whose benevolent aspects might be inferred from "this remarkable earth."

Indeed, her fascination with the inscrutability of spiritual affections and the religious sign, be it in the interpretation of written Scripture, in lived experience, or in the natural world around her, continued throughout her lifetime. Whatever Dickinson's belief about the claims of Scripture as revealed truth, there is no doubt that the language, style, rhythms, and narratives of the King James Bible were Dickinson's most formative and lasting literary influences. In *Emily Dickinson's Reading, 1836–1886,* Jack Capps documents that "biblical quotations in her letters and poems far exceed references to any other source or author" and records that the Dickinson home contained nineteen Bibles (30).[13] Her references to Scripture are not limited to familiar passages but are remarkably wide in their scope; in her poems she quotes at least thirteen books of the New Testament (with the synoptic Gospels and Revelation most frequently represented) and at least twelve books of the Old Testament (with Genesis and Exodus predominating). In her letters, the scope of biblical references is even wider.

Dickinson's personal Bible, an 1843 King James Version published by J. B. Lippincott, bears an inscription to her from her father, along with various markings and even cutouts. She copied a poem titled "The Bible" by her deceased friend Jacob Holt on the back leaf. It reads in part, "It is a pure & holy word, / It is the wisdom of a God, / It is a fountain, full & free, / It is *the* book for you & me"—a surprisingly sentimental view for Dickinson to have so immortalized in her Bible, especially given what some critics have interpreted as her categorical hostility to the Scriptures.[14] Yet although Dickinson's attitudes toward the sentiments expressed in the Bible vary greatly, her relationship with the "Old fashioned Book," as she terms it mischievously in one poem, was long and affectionate (F695). Even the poem that has been viewed as her most caustic critique of the Protestant Scriptures, "The Bible is an antique volume," is really more of a satire of those who use them to "condemn" instead of "captivate" than of the book itself (F1577C). Proof texts aside, a broad view of her poems and letters shows that far from despising the Bible, Dickinson achieved a loving mastery of the King James such that she could sound its notes for a multiplicity of her own purposes. These range in tone from angry repartee with the God of Moses, to pastoral comforting of the bereaved, to witty parody of King James phrases by putting them to domestic use for the amusement of her neighbors.

Ultimately, Dickinson's intimate knowledge of Reformed biblical explication, as well as her command of the literal, moral, and typological senses of interpretation that she gleaned from her Amherst upbringing and education, continually fueled her religious imagination. Her immersion in Bible reading, sermon culture, Christian education, and daily life in a religious college town would have exposed her to consistent patterns of reading and interpretation that she couldn't have helped but absorb, whether she was conscious of it or not. Even where she moves well beyond the bounds of Trinitarian Congregationalism in her attempts to reenvision the relation between God, nature, and the self, the Bible and Reformed hermeneutics remain a vital touchstone to her thinking, sine qua non. For Dickinson, as Cristanne Miller has observed, "the Bible's word, like the New Testament's Word incarnate, carries the greatest meaning when it links apparently discontinuous or separate realms: the literal and the figurative, the personal and the universal, earth and heaven" (*Poet's Grammar* 136). It is this notion of finding an effectual mediator between the immanent and transcendent realms that might replace an imperfect Scripture and an absent Savior which drives many of Dickinson's meditations on nature. With nature and typology, Dickinson wonders, is it possible to repair the breach?

4

Reading with "Compound Vision"

Emily Dickinson and the Nineteenth-Century "Paper Wars"

It would be fair to say that next to her writing, gardening was Emily Dickinson's greatest avocation. As a young woman she perused Edward Hitchcock's *Catalogue of Plants Growing in the Vicinity of Amherst* (1829), avidly studied botany at Amherst Academy, and kept a precise herbarium.[1] She tended both an outdoor garden and a winter conservatory from which she frequently sent clippings to friends and family. For Dickinson, the domestic garden became a space far more cordial to an experience of the numinous than the public gatherings at the First Congregational Church of Amherst, which she stopped attending before her thirtieth year. Instead, as she writes in 1861, as an adult she would find the sacred in her earthly version of the Garden of Eden—cultivated nature, "With a Bobolink – for a Chorister – / And an Orchard – for a Dome"; there "'God' – preaches" and "instead of getting to Heaven – at last – / I'm – going – all along!" (F236 B). While "Some – keep the Sabbath – going to church –" is hardly Dickinson's only poem to celebrate divine presence in nature, it is rightly among the most frequently cited, for it clearly shows how much Dickinson valued the sort of spiritual cognizance that is gained through sense experience. Recently scholars have made significant advances toward identifying the influences of Locke and Common Sense philosophy on Dickinson's explorations of perception and knowledge.[2] Such studies, however, have yet to acknowledge fully the nineteenth-century elephant in the room—the enormous influence of Jonathan Edwards's thinking on this topic, an influence that was very present in Dickinson's era in both the popularly religious and the more scholarly theological registers. From this vantage point, Dickinson's thinking also bears the metaphysical imprint of Edwards, who, previous to Common Sense philosophy and independent of Locke, emphasized that a personal knowledge of God must be gained through the experience of enlightened affections beyond rational apprehension, and whose own "Personal Narrative" describes his conversion process through encounters with nature (see chapter 1).

Careful consideration of Dickinson's practice of reading the natural world through the Reformed knowing/seeing/being hermeneutic lens reveals that she engages typology in a far more complex and sustained fashion than has been hitherto acknowledged or examined.[3] As it did for her New England forebears, Nature speaks to Dickinson, though its vernacular is unclear, and supernatural revelation no longer has the more transparent correlation between idea and object that it did for Edwards. Yet, as in Edwards's system, Dickinson's types have both ontological and teleological properties and are in dynamic interrelations with their otherworldly antitypes. By appropriating typological qualities for some of her animals, plants, and landscapes, Dickinson affirms the inherent value of the created world and even suggests the positive significance lent to these figures by their relation to a transcendent realm—all without having to give final assent to belief in a traditionally Reformed version of God or the afterlife.

While she most often preserves the Edwardsean tension that simultaneously connects and separates type and antitype, Dickinson's God is as likely to be known by absence and inscrutability—and His signs as a trace of that inscrutable absence—as by any kind of tangible presence. Consequently, Dickinson's diverse typologies help her to explore a variety of possibilities for how, or whether, earth and heaven might still be in reciprocal relationship. At times, uncertain of what the transcendent plane might be, Dickinson makes use of typological mechanisms in order to reconfigure them discursively, pointing them horizontally toward further, still earthbound types; these yet-to-be types seem, by their recurrence in natural cycles, to indicate a sense of divinity to be found in immanence, if not tangible presence. In other stances, however, Dickinson seems to affirm the likelihood of some transcendent link between earth and heaven, whether that link be between the living and their beloved dead (instead of between earth and a patriarchal deity) or between a haunted nature and a nearly incomprehensible God under erasure.

Moreover, Dickinson's explorations of typological connections between God, self, and nature—in stances that range from the most conventional of nineteenth-century renderings to her own radical and very unorthodox revisions—do not occur in isolation. She writes during a period of ongoing debate within Reformed circles about the viability of traditional and neo-Calvinist scriptural hermeneutics for the nineteenth-century world. Like Dickinson, theologians at nearby New England seminaries wondered about the role of personal experience and propositional or figurative language in the revelation and perception of spiritual truths. In this chapter I consider Dickinson's readings of Scripture and the natural world alongside the thinking of these theologians in order to demonstrate ways in which she was a participant in the nineteenth-century American religious zeitgeist and to attempt to fill a significant contextual gap in our historical understanding of the poet. I then examine two of the most frequent strategies Dickinson uses to revise these traditions and create her own natural typology—"immanent transcendentality" and saints-as-antitypes.[4]

Characteristically, Dickinson's typological imaginations are as varied as her attitudes concerning belief and doubt.[5] In an 1882 letter describing her mother's final hours to Nellie Sweetser, for instance, she would recall: "The last Token but one, on which her dear Eyes looked, was the Grapes from you. The very last, a little Bird, from thoughtful Mrs. Hills. Grapes and Birds, how typic, for was she not on her sweet way to a frostless Land?" (L782). Deeply conversant with the language of nineteenth-century sentimental religion, here Dickinson evokes a broadly typological—or "typic," as she most frequently phrases it—Edenic association between earth and heaven as a kind of religious lingua franca between herself and her neighbor. In her poetry, however, her deployment of the word "typic" indicates that not only was she familiar with the orthodox Reformed usage of the word as indicative of an Old Testament prefiguration of Christ or a New Testament event, but also she was quite willing to expand the typological function to nature itself, and in ways beyond the definitions and exemplars she would have found in Jenks's *Companion to the Bible* or the sermons of her friend the Reverend Charles Wadsworth. For instance, in the 1866 and later versions of "Further in Summer than the birds," Dickinson configures the "spectral Canticle" of crickets as a foreshadowing or "typify[ing]" of some future, if not quite heavenly, "Repose" (F895 C).[6] In "The things that never can come back are several –" (F1564 B), she asserts that, unlike "Childhood – [and] some forms of Hope – [and] the Dead –," "There are typic 'Heres' –."

These "typic Heres" are supernatural "Foretold Locations" that are connected to an earthly "here" by a "Spirit" who exists between the two realms. The word "typic" is also the first of thirteen variants Dickinson lists for the adjective in the line "Had but the Tale a thrilling Teller" in the earliest version of "The Bible is an antique volume" (F1577 C).[7] The list of variants and the stanza itself, which finishes "All the Boys would come – / Orpheu's Sermon captivated – / It did not condemn –," would seem to indicate that connotations of "typic" were both powerful and winsome to Dickinson. Finally, Dickinson overtly refers to typology in "The murmuring of bees has ceased" (F1142). Here, the changing seasons of nature, the "typic mother," take on the distinctly typological ability to exist at once within two time schemata; hence, with "The Revelations of the Book / Whose Genesis was June," the poet finds the "Posterior, prophetic / Has simultaneous come –."

The range of emotions in Dickinson's use of the term "typic" demonstrates how she found typology poetically suggestive and did not necessarily associate it with reductive or allegorical thinking, as some might today. Certainly a number of her poems do show her disdain for completely literal renderings of biblical tropes. In poems such as "What is 'Paradise'" (F241) and "I know Where Wells grow – droughtless Wells –" (F695), Dickinson adopts a childlike tone to question the wisdom of failing to recognize ambiguity and figurative levels of meaning in biblical texts. Giving both biblical vocabulary and common diction the same sort of emphasis by enclosing them in quotation marks ("Do they wear 'new shoes' – in 'Eden' – [?]" the speaker in the former poem asks), Dickinson shrewdly draws attention to the constructed and representational nature of all language. On one level, both poems are directed toward a sentimental Christian hypocrisy that neglects to take care of the poor in one's own nearby surroundings or that privileges idealized comforts in a future world at the expense of celebrating the beauty and mystery of the present one. As the speaker in "I know Where Wells grow" muses at the end of the poem concerning the jeweled heaven of the Book of Revelation and the unending fountain of water Jesus mentions in John 4: "Those Waters sound so grand – / I think a little Well – like Mine – / Dearer to understand."

Yet on another level, the poems indict Christian readers for their contentment with static interpretations that claim mastery over religious signifiers of the numinous.[8] In the Gospel of John, as Dickinson knew very well, Jesus is not describing a literal heavenly well to the Samarian woman but is providing a metaphor for the fulfillment of the human heart in relationship with God. (Indeed, as mentioned in chapter 3, she alludes to this "stream of living water" passage rather earnestly in a youthful letter to Abiah Root describing her own struggles with conversion.) While "I know Where Wells grow" does not mock the sincere faith of devout believers, it does underscore the pretentiousness of claims to absolute understanding of biblical texts, as well as complacent acceptance of simplified interpretations.[9] "I read in an Old fashioned Book / That People 'thirst no more' –," the speaker comments, adding the interpretation "The Wells have Buckets to them there – / It must mean that – I'm sure –." Thus, although Dickinson explores the possibilities of a remaining connection between natural phenomena and divine revelation, in her own renditions of spiritual or religious interpretation she insists on the open-ended and non-self-referential aspects of what it might mean to indicate divinity. As Elisa New underscores in her books *The Regenerate Lyric* and *The Line's Eye,* Dickinson's "commitment to the unknown" is paramount in her renditions of both nature and God. She links Dickinson to Edward Taylor's "interest in divine Unnameability" and finds Dickinson "ushering back into American poetry the Puritan's concern for the warping of Revelation by blunt and corrupt human senses. . . . The problem is idolatry; the way she finds round it, humility" (*Regenerate* 236, 153).

Dickinson's critique of nineteenth-century hermeneutical practices was in accord with contemporaneous debates about the role of figurative language and individual interpretation that were taking place in the Reformed seminaries.[10] In *America's God: From Jonathan Edwards to Abraham Lincoln,* the historian Mark Noll has outlined the rise of a peculiarly American set of assumptions about Bible reading that he has variously termed the "reformed literal hermeneutic" and "evangelical Enlightenment simplicity." Driven by the need for political consensus and social stability, and informed by Lockean and Baconian principles of finding "simple" truths through empirical methods, the post-Revolutionary Reformed churches in America increasingly relied on common sense and individual, private interpretations of their Bibles as the one agreed-upon and easily democratized authority that could be commonly appealed to amidst the changes of the new republic. In so doing, they took several Enlightenment steps away from Calvin, the Puritans, and Edwards, who had read the Bible with greater senses of nuance, both theologically and figuratively, and with less insistence on reason as the final arbiter of interpretation. According to Noll, among the widely held assumptions that fed the reformed literal hermeneutic were the notions that "people could see clearly and without ambiguity what the Bible said, and that this biblicistic knowledge qualified one to judge connections between moral cause and moral effect"; concomitantly, he argues, these assumptions were

> the common person's counterpart to the Enlightenment confidence displayed by intellectual elites who employed learned formal moral philosophy to the same ends. Democratic biblicism undercut trust in traditional interpretations of Scripture with the same force that they were being leveled by a reliance on philosophical common sense. In both cases, confidence in present abilities overmastered confidence in what was handed on from the past. In both cases, a liberated modern self was the starting point for biblical interpretation. (381)

By the middle of the nineteenth century, this proclivity toward the commonsensical and literal levels of interpretation became increasingly problematic for American Christians as they turned to their Bibles variously to approve or condemn the institution of slavery. Did the Old Testament descriptions of the patriarchs as slave owners prove the moral acceptableness of slavery, or were the principles of Christ and urgings of Paul in the New Testament paramount? In the years of Dickinson's childhood and early adulthood, in fact, the most vigorous discussions among seminarians were hermeneutical rather than theological.

The most notorious public figure who argued against this reformed literal hermeneutic was Horace Bushnell, whose volume *Sermons on the New Life* resided in the Dickinson library. For Bushnell, who had "a theory of religious knowledge that he learned partly from the Edwardsean tradition and partly from Coleridge and [French philosopher Victor] Cousin" and a metaphorical "understanding of language that he had taken from his teacher of Greek and Hebrew at Yale, Josiah Willard Gibbs," the language of Scripture was meant to be understood as living metaphor, and theology was more akin to poetry than to science (Holifield 454). His 1848 lecture at Andover Seminary, "Dogma and Spirit," followed closely by his 1849 book *God in Christ,* ignited years of debate among theologians about the roles of language, reason, and individual spiritual experience in biblical interpretation. As difficult as it might be to fathom the heatedness of the controversy today, as Noll explains, Bushnell's ideas were disturbing to his contemporaries because they "questioned not so much the content of specific doctrines but the methods that had become canonical in American theological discourse for writing and speaking about those doctrines" (*America's God* 294).

That is, instead of agreeing that biblical theology was as rational and propositional as one of the sciences, Bushnell wished to draw attention to scriptural paradoxes and irrationalities, believing that "theologians came closest to the truth when they multiplied conflicting metaphors. . . . He found the language of scripture suggestive of multiple possibilities of interpretation, with 'meanings coming out of meanings, and second senses doubling upon first'" (Holifield 459).

The famed "paper wars" that Bushnell's theories ignited took place between 1848 and 1852 in theological journals such as *Bibliotheca Sacra* (Edwards Amasa Park's journal out of Andover) and the *Princeton Review.* Emily Dickinson, growing up in the theological hotbed that was Amherst and South Hadley, rubbed shoulders with two of the four major theologians in these language debates: she heard both Park and Henry Boynton Smith preach on at least one occasion during this period. (The other two main actors were Charles Hodge of Princeton and Bushnell himself.) At stake were accepted notions about the groundings of Christian knowledge and experience, and the substance of these arguments was far more complex and nuanced than literary scholars have given these theologians credit for. Whether they were defending the reformed literal hermeneutic or were more sympathetic toward Bushnell's Edwardsean- and German Idealist–informed position, none of the debaters discounted the importance of spiritual "knowing" and "seeing"—divinely initiated conversion and personal spiritual experience with the Holy Spirit in the interpretation of the Bible. And wherever these theologians fell on the continuum between privileging intuitive and affectional readings of Scripture or propositional and reason-oriented ones, no one (including Jonathan Edwards generations earlier) believed language to be entirely transparent or stable. Rather, they questioned: Given the varying possibilities inherent in human interpretation of revelation via the medium of language (which all parties agreed was highly figurative), by what methodologies might Scriptures best be interpreted?

Charles Hodge, the eminent Presbyterian theologian out of Princeton, was the most vigorous defender of the reformed literal hermeneutic. To Hodge, theology and hermeneutics required a balance of affective and rational interpretation, but logic and the use of inductive reasoning were the ultimate determiners of God's objective truth. Yet even Hodge did not believe that there was no figurative, metaphorical, or extra-rational language in Scripture; rather, as D. G. Hart observes, he asserted that since "the human mind was limited in its ability to understand the ultimate nature and meaning of both the physical and spiritual universe

. . . [t]he goal of natural and theological science was to *describe* and *systematize* the truths that nature and Scripture revealed, regardless of the mind's ability to determine *meaning* or *purpose* of those truths" ("Poems" 318, emphasis added). Hodge worried that the German Idealism that Bushnell and others were being influenced by would ultimately lead to the boundary-less-ness of the Transcendentalists, for whom there was no distinction between God, the natural world, and humanity and between the holiness of God and the depravity of fallen creation.

Such beliefs about the necessity for theologians to rationally categorize truths behind figurative scriptural language were frequently echoed in the teachings of Charles Wadsworth, the popular "Old School" Presbyterian minister whom Emily Dickinson deemed "My Shepherd from 'Little Girl'hood" (L766). A graduate of Princeton Theological Seminary, Wadsworth almost certainly studied under Hodge either at the end of Hodge's term as a biblical languages instructor or at the beginning of his professorship of didactic theology. Wadsworth, himself a frustrated poet, was frequently lauded for the power and beauty of his sermons. Indeed, like other ministers in the reformed literal hermeneutic tradition, he would caution that biblical language could be ruined by attempts to strip it of its literary attributes. "There is unquestionably such a thing as too much exposition of the Sacred Scriptures," he declares in his sermon "The Gospel Call" (*Sermons* [1869] 71). Arguing for figurative expression as part of the Bible's common sense meaning, he complains elsewhere that "a great fault today, alike in our Bible reading, and Bible exposition, is a too ready and too rigid analysis. . . . Alas that this habit should have gone so mightily with us into the sacredness of revelation till every beautiful figure of the Bible is subjected to the same uncompromising analysis, and all the sweet flowers in the garden of God are cut up as specimen" (*Sermons* [1905] 7).

At the same time, however, Wadsworth placed himself firmly on the propositional side of the argument, asserting that ultimately "language is reason, not shut up in secret chambers, but walking forth with tremendous energy amid the vital interests of the race" (*Sermons* [1869] 309). Moreover, as he says in "God's Thoughts," although language is necessarily limited in its abilities to express God's mind fully, it is also an adequate enough vessel to allow mortals to deduce divine truth:

> Certainly in all our attempts to consider God, we must reason analogically from the finite. We can form no idea of any divine attribute except from its miniature in humanity. And we are to regard it not as

> mere figure of speech, that God made man in his own image as well mental as moral. The Divine intellect may be spoken of as the glorious archetype after which finite mind was cast. And although, as bringing infinity into conditions of time and space, all language must express falsehood when concerned with Deity, yet when the Bible speaks of God as in the exercise of volitions and emotions, we are not to regard it as mere accommodation to a false *usus loquendi,* but as true representation. (*Sermons* [1869] 1)

True to form, Wadsworth was such an adherent of the reformed literal hermeneutic that in 1862 he left his pastorate in Philadelphia and moved to a more politically moderate church in San Francisco (where Mark Twain would regularly visit) until after the Civil War. Though a sympathizer with the Union, he could not bring himself to the belief that God had declared slavery to be a sin since there is no chapter and verse in the Bible stating so directly; understandably, this did not leave him in good stead with the ardent abolitionists in Philadelphia.

While Bushnell and Hodge (and the latter's Princeton compatriots like Wadsworth) represented the extreme ends of the metaphorical-propositional spectrum, Emily Dickinson herself came into contact with the two other principal and more mediating figures of the disputation. Henry Boynton Smith and Edwards Amasa Park, both leading Jonathan Edwards scholars, espoused some use of German theology and philosophy, though not to the extent that Bushnell did. In an 1848 letter to her brother Austin from Mount Holyoke, Dickinson mentions a visit to the seminary from H. B. Smith, who was a professor of philosophy at Amherst College at the time: "Professor. Smith. preached here last Sabbath & such sermons I never heard in my life. We were all charmed with him & dreaded to have him close" (L64). The year after, in an address given at Andover in reply to Bushnell's "Dogma and Spirit," Smith clinched his upwardly mobile career path by finding a Christocentric middle ground between reformed literal hermeneutics on the one hand and Bushnell's extreme rejection of all propositional theology on the other. In "Faith and Philosophy," Smith reminds his audience that Jonathan Edwards used both intellectual philosophy and affective, revelatory faith to develop his important theologies. He warns against relying too much on philosophy and against falling into pantheism, and he asserts (echoing Edwards himself a hundred years earlier) that "it is of the very office of language to express what is consciously working in the soul; language is the express image of spirit" (*Faith and Philosophy* 29). While we do not know the content of the sermons Dickinson was so impressed by at Mount Holyoke the year before, it stands to reason that Smith's methods of textual interpretation at the Female Seminary would have been consistent with what he promotes in "Faith and Philosophy." Dickinson was astute enough in her own understanding of the Bible to have gleaned useful insights into alternate methods of hermeneutics from the rising young theologian. As for Smith, largely because of the success of his address in Andover, in 1850 he was offered the chair of church history at the (then Presbyterian) Union Theological Seminary in New York, where he remained until the end of his career.

More has been surmised about Dickinson's impressions of the fourth participant in this language controversy, Edwards Amasa Park. We know from an 1853 letter to Austin that the renowned Professor Park preached on at least one occasion at Amherst First Congregational Church. Dickinson's evocation of the "splendid" sermon's effects on the congregation is the most effusive depiction of a preacher extant in her writings. Describing a church filled with students and seminarians from Amherst College as well as the regular congregation, Dickinson writes: "It was very full, and still – so still, the buzzing of a fly would have boomed like a cannon. And when it was all over, and that wonderful man sat down, people stared at each other, and looked as wan and wild, as if they had seen a spirit, and wondered they had not died" (L142). Amherst First's response to the oratorical style of the wildly popular Park was quite typical of his nineteenth-century rock star–like reception. A memorial of Park written in 1890 reflects that Park's "mere presence in the pulpit was majestic and fascinating, in the weird abstraction, concentration, solemnity of face, voice, mien, and manner"; auditors "hung with an attention that could hardly have been surpassed if trumpets of angels had been sounding above us, and from which we went astonished, humiliated, with excitement in our minds, and shivers along our whole system of nerves. . . . It is impossible to overstate the impression which those sermons made" (Park 12). Of her own experience listening to Park, Dickinson confides to Austin, "I never heard anything like it, and dont expect to again, till we stand at the great white throne, and 'he reads from the book, the Lamb's book'" (L142).

Edwards Amasa Park, named after Jonathan Edwards and married to the great-granddaughter of that patriarch, had taught philosophy in 1835–36 at Amherst College before becoming faculty president at Andover (and later turning down Amherst College's offer of the college presidency the same year Dickinson chronicles his sermon). Schooled in both German and Scottish thought, Park wrote several biographies of Edwards's immediate disciples and was considered by some to be his generation's finest theological mind since Edwards, but he died before he was able to finish writing his own Jonathan Edwards biography and editing the divine's unpublished manuscripts. Ensconced at Andover until 1881, Park trained and established hundreds of seminarians in his own version of what he believed to be the "true" Edwardsean theological lineage—what became known as the "New Divinity," "the New England Theology," or "Consistent Calvinism." This lifelong theological project of Park's amounted to threading the needle between the traditional "Old School" Calvinism at Princeton and the more progressive "New Haven" Calvinism at Yale. Park wished to soften traditional assertions of God's sovereign predestination of the elect and of humanity's innate depravity to make Calvinism more palatable to nineteenth-century sensibilities. In answer to the question of whether God sovereignly foreordained the chosen or in His benevolence allowed all humans complete free will to make their own choice, Park suggested that God did both, all with divine foreknowledge that the non-elect would inevitably fail to choose Him. This approach allowed Park to promote what he asserted to be true "Consistent Calvinism" and evangelical revivalism at the same time.

Park's most famous salvo in the "paper wars" (most of which took place in *Bibliotheca Sacra,* the theological journal he founded) came in his 1850 Boston lecture to the Massachusetts Convention of Ministers, "The Theology of the Intellect and that of the Feelings." In this paper, Park attempts to salvage some aspects of German thought by acknowledging that figural religious language does speak at different moments to both the intuitive and rational faculties; moreover, the theology of the intellect and the theology of the feelings ought to work together to reinforce both head and heart knowledge of God's truth. He warns his brethren not to be overly rational martinets, "intent on the sign more than the signified," when they study Scripture (Park 117). As long as reason and the intellect are the final arbiter of conflicts between head and heart, he asserts, it should be acknowledged that the theology of the feelings as depicted through scriptural metaphor "expresses substantial reality" and is "substantially accurate when not literally so; moral truth when not historical" (86, 87).

Lest he be accused of cavorting with the Transcendentalists, however, Park offers an appendix to his published address: there he states that his orthodoxy, "*the* theology of the heart," should not be confused with the "diseased, perverted moral feelings" of *any* theology of the heart (Park

297). By way of contrast he points to "one of the most graphic descriptions of a theology which is neither of sound intellect nor sound heart, but is alike impervious to argument, reckless of consequences, and dependent of an ill-balanced state of the sensibilities," that is, Ralph Waldo Emerson's thought (297). Park cites a letter from Emerson, who wishes to decline direct engagement in theological battle. Emerson writes:

> I well know, that there is no scholar less willing or less able to be a polemic [than myself]. I could not give account of myself if challenged. I could not possibly give you one of the "arguments" you cruelly hint at, on which any doctrine of mine stands. For I do not know what arguments means, in reference to any expression of a thought. I delight in telling what I think; but if you ask me how I dare say so, or why it is so, I am the most helpless of mortal men. (297)

"One of the amazing maladjustments in human life," Park remarks, "is that in which a pious man has such idiosyncrasies, or has been so miseducated as to believe in a false intellectual system, and to feel an impulsive attachment to it. He is of all men the most incorrigible" (298).

Yet the damage to Park's relations with his more conservative Presbyterian colleagues had been done. The fancy linguistic footwork that Park attempted to perform in his paper—such as allowing that when a doctrine was "devoid of sympathy with our most refined sentiments" then "*somewhere it must be wrong*"—made Park, along with Bushnell, the target of considerable disapprobation from traditional Calvinist theologians like Hodge and preachers like Wadsworth (Park 95). It also aroused fears that seminarians from Andover were introducing not only thinly veiled Arminianism to their Congregationalist churches but also German Idealism. Park's path was a difficult one. One the one hand, as a moderate, Park was certainly enough a part of the reformed literal hermeneutic camp to believe that early church fathers were, in his own words, "the 'Church babies'" because "the ancient church fathers had written 'before the rational processes of induction and the fundamental laws of belief had been distinctly explained' by Bacon and the Scots," as E. Brooks Holifield explains Park's comments (345). On the other hand, however, Princeton theologians charged that "Park undermined his own positions . . . when he repeatedly and sometimes disingenuously invoked the distinction between the theology of the intellect and the feelings to maneuver around any historical doctrine of the New England theology, such as the willingness to be damned, that did not pass the test of commonsense reasonableness" (Conforti 118).

None of these theological wranglings, of course, are what Dickinson was responding to in her letter to Austin when she described the effects of Park's 1853 visit to Amherst First Congregational. In her article "Emily Dickinson and Edwards Amasa Park: 'The Loveliest Sermon,'" Jane Eberwein connects this 1853 letter with another letter Dickinson writes twenty years later that suggests what the content of Park's sermon might have entailed. Park frequently re-preached (and later published) two of his most popular sermons originally written in the early 1830s, "Peter's Denials of His Lord" and "Judas." Eberwein persuasively argues that it is the latter sermon—whether it was in the 1853 visit or at another time (given Park's connections with Amherst College, Dickinson quite likely heard him speak on more than one occasion)—that Dickinson is referring to in an 1873 letter to her cousin Frances Norcross. Dickinson writes: "The loveliest sermon I ever heard was the disappointment of Jesus in Judas. It was told like a mortal story of intimate young men. I suppose no surprise we can ever have will be so sick as that. The last 'I never knew you' may resemble it" (L385).

While at least half of Park's sermon is directed toward enlisting his audience's guilty identification with Judas's self-deceit, Dickinson remembers and empathizes with Park's portrayal of Jesus, whom he depicts as an embodiment of the theology of feeling. In lines that Dickinson's 1865 poem "If I can stop one Heart from breaking/... If I can ease one Life the Aching/Or cool one Pain" (F982) seems to echo, Park says that Jesus "condemned the starveling economy of Judas, and showed that whatever elicits one noble feeling, or soothes one broken spirit, or calms one ruffled temper, or lightens up in smiles one downcast face; whatever honors the Messiah, and glorifies God, and makes religion venerable, that is the highest style of usefulness" (49). Park's Jesus is not surprised by Judas's betrayal but is highly sentimentalized in his response to it: "Your Master loved that mean disciple. He knew the contracted thoughts and the low aims of the traitor, and still he not only bore with the man, but melted in tenderness over him" (54–55). Jesus's chief method of redemption toward Judas is not through proclamation of truth but by trying to reach the disciple's emotions:

> In three hours Jesus was to be betrayed and yet he must try once more to soften down his betrayer and win him back to virtue. Even to the last he longed to sweeten that ascetic spirit. He always will display the magnanimity of a friend toward his thankless foes. Never will he be angry as men count anger, even while he deals the bread of perdition to his enemies. (57)

Like a staid Victorian lady who has never been seen to lose her temper, Park's sentimentalized Jesus bears a striking resemblance to one of Dickinson's renditions of Jesus as the Savior who "must have been/a docile Gentleman" and who privileges feelings and gentle persuasion over propositional argument (F1538).

Indeed, in her most sentimental or conventional modes, Dickinson would seem to have been sympathetic with Park's litmus test for scriptural interpretation: biblical metaphors could be "substantially accurate when not literally so, moral truth when not historical" (although Park restricted his interpretations within the bounds of orthodox theology and Dickinson assuredly did not) (Park 87). Like the Reformed theologians engaged in their "paper wars," Dickinson also attempted to tackle the problem of discerning what was revealed knowledge from a plethora of perspectives, including personal, felt experience and rational inference. She touches on these issues in what is perhaps her most direct (albeit brief) comment on biblical revelation in an 1882 letter in which she thanks her friend Elizabeth Holland for sending a Christmas gift: "The Fiction of 'Santa Claus' always reminds me of the reply to my early question of 'Who made the Bible' – 'Holy Men moved by the Holy Ghost,' and though I have now ceased my investigations, the Solution is insufficient – Santa Claus, though, *illustrates* – Revelation. But a Book is only the Heart's Portrait – every page a Pulse –" (L794). Although the first part of this passage has been cited more than once by critics wishing to show the poet's dismissal of the Bible, the last two sentences restore the section to its broader context of considering the relationship between literal and figurative levels of meaning. To treat metaphorical devices (such as this passage from 2 Peter 1:21 in which "holy men of God spake as they were moved by the Holy Ghost") as a literal "Solution" to questions about the Bible's inspiration, Dickinson says, is a limited and "insufficient" way to go about understanding matters of a metaphysical nature. Yet the "Fiction of 'Santa Claus'. . . . *illustrates* – Revelation": as an imaginary character, he is useful as a figurative indicator of a deep emotional and spiritual truth about the importance of gift giving and receiving. In a similar manner, she surmises, the Bible is revelatory in the sense that "a Book is only the Heart's Portrait – every page a Pulse –." When interpreted with sensitivity, the Scriptures can be evocative of a divine love and generosity beyond the range of human perception. Recalled to Dickinson's mind as she considers the inferential relationship between Holland's Christmas gift, sent in absentia, and the greater dynamic and vital reality of her friend's person, Dickinson's metaphor for "Revelation" and the Bible is both open-hearted and optimistic about a recipient's ability to read the "Heart's Portrait" of a giver, be she natural or divine.

In more pessimistic modes, however, and unlike Park, Dickinson is more determined to address the darker mysteries of religious belief and less likely to feel assured that when a Reformed doctrine is "devoid of sympathy with our most refined sentiments . . . somewhere it must be wrong" (Park 95). It is in her grappling with such unknowns as the character of God, the fate of loved ones who have died, and the meaning of the Christian resurrection that Dickinson's revised and multiform typologies allowed her to insist bravely on the ineffable within the self, nature, and the divine Other. In these moments she often reconfigures the dynamics of typological relationships to eschew emotionally comforting answers to questions of faith; instead she attempts to outline the philosophical circumference of a belief she feels the Bible and the natural world *might* imply but which cannot be validated in the sense of scientific proof. Most often for Dickinson, valid interpretations of the Christian Bible, or the equally mysterious natural world, are those that give place to "uncertain certainty" (F1421).

Consequently, Dickinson's confidence in language as a medium that could yield stable interpretations over time—another concern of the aforementioned "paper wars," is more akin to Bushnell's belief in language as living metaphor than her friend Wadsworth's sense that language is "true representation." On the one hand, Dickinson is aware that both biblical and natural sign systems, once detached from the moorings of traditional explications, are by their very elusiveness and obscurity available for as many interpretations as the human imagination might pose. She does resist, however, the notion that since manifold interpretations are possible, there is, therefore, no prime mover behind and beyond nature. "So," she concludes in "My cocoon tightens – Colors teaze" (F1107), "I must baffle at the Hint / And cipher at the Sign / And make much blunder, if at last / I take the clue divine –." For Dickinson there *is* a sign, and a cryptic universe is not the same as a nihilist one.

The poet's reluctance to offer a totalizing interpretation of nature or Scripture is akin to her larger resistance to what Margaret Homans first conceptualized as Dickinson's refusal of the Adamic authority to name and control; instead, Homans sees Dickinson aligning herself with Eve and her deeper knowledge of language as arbitrary and opaque. Since, as Cristanne Miller has suggested, there remains for the poet "no stable relationship between spiritual truth, the facts of existence, and the terms of language" (*Poet's Grammar* 147), Dickinson must create a poetic in which any apprehension of nature, necessarily mediated through a language of shifting and endlessly deferred signification, will always be partial, deficient, and illusory. Nature as discourse can no more be stabilized or decoded than the written word.[11]

By the same token, when Dickinson considers the possibility of a divinely inspired apperception of the world—through either reason or felt experience—she finds the relationship between observer and observed more troubled than any of the theologians of the "paper wars" seems to express. Thus, she writes in 1865:

> Perception of an Object costs
> Precise the Object's loss – Precise] more oft
> Perception in itself a Gain
> Replying to it's price –
>
> The Object, absolute, is nought –
> Perception sets it fair
> And then upbraids a Perfectness
> That situates so far –] that 'tis so Heavenly far –
> (F1103 B)

Perpetually under erasure, the "Object" of "Perception" is "nought," lost for all conceptual and linguistic purposes to the speaker; in its place is the "Gain" of the flow of language itself. In this poem, différance has the dual effect of creating an idealized, incessantly postponed "Perfectness" and a corresponding existential angst that the play of signifiers "situates so far –." Dickinson's variant for line eight, "that 'tis so Heavenly far –," adds a metaphysical dimension to the text. The unbridgeable distance between the signifier and signified is likened to the gap between heaven and earth. Dickinson explores a similar theme in an earlier poem, "Beauty – be not caused – It Is –" (F654), in which "Deity will see to it" that one can never "Overtake" or grasp the beautiful. In both poems, Dickinson's discursive paradigm seems to undercut any possibility of perceiving beyond this aporia and so approaches a conception of an always postponed transcendental signified.

This position is (fortunately for Dickinson critics, but unhappily for the theologians) an inherently conflicted one. Her experimentation with natural typology configured as a kind of immanent transcendentality is one of her many responses to the problems of language and nature as tempting but slippery texts. By redirecting the typological relation of a natural signifier away from a transcendent signified and toward another natural signifier in poems such as "We should not mind so small a flower" and "When they come back – if Blossoms do –," the satisfaction of the flow of language and the mirroring, circular relation between projecting type and fulfilling antitype, signifier and signified, take the place of transcendent fit or correspondence. These now-and-not-yet types seem, by their recurrence in natural cycles, to indicate a sense of divinity to be found in immanence, if not actual presence. Concomitantly, the textual word becomes nuanced with the life-giving and supporting qualities of the Logos, or divine Word.

As a result, Dickinson sometimes sidesteps the dilemma of perception as "the Object's loss" by creating a closed circuit in which meaning and meaning making cannot be separated, and neither appears to depend on some externally transcendent scaffolding to uphold it. In this typological relation, each signifying type, in its participation in the signified and further signifying antitype, signals a "transcendental (rather than transcendent) sense of the other" (Daniel, *Philosophy* 24); in other words, the Other is located "within the system of discourse as the transcendental component of the sign (the signified) without presuming the transcendence that characterizes the symbol" (25). In the 1859 "We should not mind so small a flower," for instance, a small flower gains enormous poignancy and worth by virtue of its place in the poem as both typic signifier and antitypic signified:

> We should not mind so small a flower
> Except it quiet bring
> Our little garden that we lost
> Back to the Lawn again.
>
> So spicy her Carnations nod –
> So drunken, reel her Bees –
> So silver steal a hundred flutes
> From out a hundred trees –
>
> That whoso sees this little flower
> By faith may clear behold
> The Bobolinks around the throne
> And Dandelions gold. (F82 B)

The typic flower, instead of serving as a conventional spring emblem of the transcendent Resurrection (a symbol of the sort Edward Hitchcock made fashionable in his 1850 *Religious Lectures on Peculiar Phenom-*

ena in the Four Seasons), indicates here its typological fulfillment in a horizontal ability to "bring/Our little garden that we lost/Back to the Lawn again." As dynamically interrelational as Jonathan Edwards's "little white flower" in his "Personal Narrative," the flower indicates the once and future garden that will be its completion (both physically and discursively within the meaning of the poem itself), while the garden, evoked in all its sensual detail in the poem's second stanza, is both the telos of the flower and the affirmation of its materiality. Indeed, like heaven's ebullient glory, the garden's excessive—although tangible, because earthly—beauty exerts a causal pull on the signifying ability of the flower. "So spicy" the garden's "Carnations nod," "that whoso sees this little flower/by faith may clear behold" a vision of a heavenly garden here on earth in which there are "Bobolinks around the throne" and "Dandelions gold." The garden is conceived by the poet as both anterior and prophetically posterior to this particular flower's existence; yet both manifestations are clearly within the realm of finite time and seasonal change rather than transcendent eternity. At the same time, the final stanza gains a biblical cadence and momentum with phrases such as "whoso" and "by faith" and the allusion to the throne of God described in the prophetic Book of Revelation.[12] Yet the "faith" Dickinson evokes here is based on the sensory experience of the garden's presence rather than a belief in transcendent intangibles.

A later poem, "When they come back – if blossoms do," presents an interesting variation on this theme. Dickinson's melancholy tone and biblical allusion serve to overlay the cyclic return of spring with disturbing concerns about the transcendent Resurrection:

> When they come back – if Blossoms do –
> I always feel a doubt
> If Blossoms can be born again
> When once the Art is out –
>
> When they begin, if Robins may,
> I always had a fear
> I did not tell, it was their last Experiment
> Last Year,
>
> When it is May, if May return,
> Had nobody a pang
> Lest in a Face so beautiful
> He might not look again?

If I am there – One does not know
What Party – One may be
Tomorrow, but if I am there
I take back all I say – (F1042)

On the natural level, the poem works as the poet's reflection on the irony that seasons do, in fact, return, while "Tomorrow" is never assured for the mortal life. Yet, although Dickinson begins the poem so as to construct another immanently transcendental equation between typic "Blossoms" and antitypic spring, it quickly becomes evident that the poem is also a meditation on the struggle between faith and that religiously weighted word in the second line, "doubt." The "born again" of the third line, for instance, sets up an early and obvious reference to John 3 and Jesus's conversation with Nicodemus about salvation.[13]

Key in this poem is the rhetorical patterning of the stanzas, which delineates the contours of the speaker's conflicted impulses. The first line of each stanza starts with an adverbial clause that begins to state a proposition, only to be interrupted by a further qualification ("When they come back – if Blossoms do –," "When they begin, if Robins may," "When it is May, if May return," and "If I am there – One does not know"). Lines two through four of each stanza constitute an aside that could stand alone as a complete sentence and that further interrupts the original thought (e.g., "Had nobody a pang/Lest in a Face so beautiful/He might not look again?"). As a consequence, closure for the opening avowals of each of the four first stanzaic lines is postponed until the last line of the poem, "I take back all I say."

This deferral of semantic payoff reveals an underlying anxiety concerning the trustworthiness of a universe run by an unseen God. With the repetition of the word "if" six times in the poem, the speaker's deeper concerns about the Resurrection are displaced onto what would surely be a likelier bet for typological fulfillment, the return of May, robins, and flowers. The doubled "if I am there" in the final stanza poignantly underscores the speaker's trepidation regarding not only the location of an antitypic "there" but also her selection or fitness for it. Wistful, the speaker *wants* to believe she will see the "beautiful" Resurrection "Face[s]" alluded to in the third stanza, yet "One does not know/What Party – One may be/Tomorrow." "Party" carries the connotations of legal sides in a dispute between the groups of the saved and the unsaved and also reveals a deep unease regarding the question of future identity; though we may know that spring returns and, as it does so, it may indeed point toward a supernatural revivification, there is no sign of who or what that resurrection identity will be like. While her logical "if"/then contortions finally bring the speaker to a confession of faith by default (if all of the above are true, she maintains, "I take back all I say"), she is caught between the proverbial devil and the deep blue sea: this natural typology projects forward to either the possible annihilation of identity or personal damnation.

Yet an imagined and indeterminate immortality is not fully satisfying for Dickinson, whose drive toward relationship is oriented toward other *persons,* not just metaphysical states of being. Correspondingly, in other modes the absence of deceased loved ones becomes for Dickinson the last, uncanny typological signifier of a transcendent realm, and the saints in heaven become an antitypical focus of typological fulfillment rather than the heavenly Christ. In a letter to the Norcross sisters after the death of Otis Lord, for instance, Dickinson writes: "Each that we lose takes part of us; / A crescent still abides, / Which like the moon, some turbid night, / Is summoned by the tides" (L817). Here, a type-antitype relationship is constructed in which the speaker is completed in that "part" of herself which exists in the beloved, who now resides, presumably, in heaven. Conversely, in a reversal of natural phenomena, the heavenly "crescent," "like the moon," is itself "summoned by" the earthbound "tides" rather than controlling them; the beloved dead as antitype is held in reflecting relationship to the speaker, recalled by the force of the love-like waves themselves.[14]

The distance that Dickinson construes between the living and the dead in this typological relationship does not posit the speaker and her beloved as more intertwined than they were on earth, but rather situates them in an association that preserves both their connection and their inviolate independence from each other. In the twentieth century, the philosopher Emmanuel Levinas describes such a relationship in ethical terms as one in which neither party claims complete knowledge of nor representational mastery over the other; it is a "relation with a total alterity irreducible to interiority, which nevertheless does not do violence to interiority—a receptivity without passivity, a relation between freedoms" (*Totality* 211). According to Levinas, in this relationship the mysterious alterity of the Other ensures the continued independent existence of the self and at the same time "calls into question" the self's assumptions, keeping the self from presuming that reality is made in its own image.[15] As does Dickinson, Levinas extends the notion of the Other to the idea of the Infinite, which he names Desire. A relation with the Infinite "paradoxically consists in thinking more than what is thought and maintaining what is thought in this very excess relative to thought—entering into a relationship with the ungraspable while guaranteeing its status of being ungraspable" (*Basic* 55). As it appears in Dickinson's letters and typological poems, this alterity is not necessarily despairing; in fact, the alterity undergirds the mixture of distance and intimacy that Dickinson cultivates in her epistolary relations.[16]

Furthermore, in a few poems such as "The Admirations – and Contempts – of time," Dickinson suggests that the alterity of death can, in fact, act in a manner similar to what the postmodern philosopher Jean-Luc Marion has termed the "Visible Mirror of the Invisible": death is a tangible moment intersected by eternity in which the alterity of the Unknown becomes visceral and present.[17] In this poem, the abstracted "Dying" is perceived through an iconic "Open Tomb" that lends the speaker a "Compound" typological "Vision" with which she might see the typic connections between the transcendent and immanent realms:

> The Admirations – and Contempts – of time –
> Show justest – through an Open Tomb –
> The Dying – as it were a Hight
> Reorganizes Estimate
> And what We saw not
> We distinguish clear –
> And mostly – see not
> What We saw before –
>
> 'Tis Compound Vision –
> Light – enabling Light –
> The Finite – furnished
> With the Infinite –
> Convex – and Concave Witness –
> Back – toward Time
>
> And forward –
> Toward the God of Him – (F830)

Dickinson's syntactic inversions in the second and third lines of the poem suggest two nonexclusive alternatives as the recipient of the momentary, profound vision: Is it "the Dying" people themselves who are justly revealed, "Show[n] justest – through an Open Tomb –" to those gathered around the bedside at the instant when heaven's gates are temporarily ajar? Or does "The Dying" of line three refer to the process of dying itself, which "as it were a Hight / Reorganizes Estimate"? In either case, the "Open Tomb," suggestive of the Resurrection of Christ and the atonement reconciling heaven and earth, functions iconically for the speaker as a corridor or window "Toward the God of Him."[18]

By the same token, the "Open Tomb" of the first stanza signals a typological relationship Dickinson will explicate in the second. The "Hight" that "Reorganizes Estimate" through the disclosure of an "Infinite" alterity reveals that the speaker's earthly apperception is "Finite" and fallible. With the view through an "Open Tomb," however, what "We" previously "saw not," we now "distinguish clear" and "mostly – see not / What We saw before –." Here Dickinson rephrases the Apostle Paul's well-known prophecy of the saints' future knowledge in heaven: "Now we see through a glass, darkly but then face to face: now I know in part; but then shall I know even as also I am known" (1 Cor. 13:12). In Dickinson's biblical revision, such knowledge is not withheld until after death but may be glimpsed through "The Dying." The "Compound Vision" shows the equal and opposing forces of "Time" and "Hight," finitude and infinitude, to be held in typological balance. Each signifying and completing the other, "Light – enabling Light – / The Finite – furnished / With the Infinite –," type and antitype mirror each other ad infinitum.[19] They are "Convex – and Concave Witness" which signify "Back – toward Time – / And forward – / Toward the God of Him –."

The poem, one of the most overtly typological in Dickinson's oeuvre, shows that the "Compound Vision" which encompasses both mortality and eternity—not just one or the other—is the requisite perspective for the poet's true "Estimate" of her subjects. The gaze through the "Open Tomb" of the resurrected Christ is Dickinson's reappropriation of Jonathan Edwards's and the Reformed tradition's "seeing eye and right affectioned heart," in which the typological perspective connects myopic human vision with the transcendent (Jenks 79). Jean-Luc Marion's redefinition of the term "icon" is helpful for understanding how Dickinson's revisions of the Reformed notion of "seeing" work. According to Marion, "valid as icon is the concept or group of concepts that reinforces the distinction of the visible and the invisible as well as their union, hence that increases the one all the more that it highlights the other" (23). Unlike the symbol, which operates as an "idol" in the sense that it attempts to represent the unrepresentable without suggesting the limits of its own mimetic qualities, Dickinson's type (in the aforementioned poem, the "Open Tomb") functions as an "icon" that "summons the gaze to surpass itself by never freezing on a visible" (18). If, as

Marion states, "every pretension to absolute knowledge therefore belongs to the domain of the idol," the definition would seem to include the presumptions of theologians such as the Presbyterian Charles Hodge, who understood the role of theology as comprehensively classifying and organizing into systems even what was admittedly beyond human understanding (23). Dickinson's typological revisions, in contrast, seek to establish an ethical yet positively detached link between the perceiver and the Other. Like the converted reader of Edwards's natural typology, Dickinson's saints in heaven do not become conflated with the one who gazes; rather, death becomes an iconic window through which she might momentarily catch a glimpse of their existence, "Somewhere – in silence –" (F365).

In "We miss her – not because we see," Dickinson uses natural typology to construct the same lines of tension between remoteness and intimacy as in "The Admirations – and Contempts – of time –." Dickinson's deletions and syntactical acrobatics convey a difficult and abstract distance between the speaker and the beloved of the poem which nonetheless leaves a tenuous signifying relationship between the two intact via the medium of an iconic gaze.

> We miss Her – not because We see –
> The Absence of an Eye – Absence] Journey
> Except it's Mind accompany
> Abridge Society Abridge] debar – • deprive – • impair
>
> As slightly as the Routes of Stars – Routes] flights slightly] scarcely
> Ourselves – asleep below –
> We know that their superior Eyes
> Include Us – as they go – Include Us] Scan better – • Convey Us –
> (F771 B)

What sort of "Society" can there be among the living and the dead, wonders the speaker. Dickinson's disjointed syntax, deletions, and ambiguous pronouns here force the reader to work through the poem slowly, finding connections as laboriously as a faith that relies on inference for its justification. A paraphrase revealing the complexity layered into the poem might read: "We miss her mind even more than her physical presence because it is with our minds that we are truly present in society. Yet we know that from their advantageous perspective in infinity, the dead more than comprehend and include us, just as the stars in their routes more than encompass the earth."

The two stanzas of the poem balance each other, making a subtle distinction between physical sight and certainty and metaphysical vision and intuition. In the first stanza, the speaker "see[s] – / The Absence of an Eye," while in the second, she is seen by absent yet "superior Eyes," envisaged by the Invisible at a place of intersection between the finite and the infinite. In the first, "Abridge" and its variants emphasize exclusion from human "Society," while in the second the speaker, by no doing of her own, is "Includ[ed]" into a broader, supernatural society that she can neither fully perceive nor represent. Hence, to be ignorant of the whereabouts of the loved one in the first stanza contrasts with what "We know" by intuition in the second.

Such complementary symmetry helps construct the typological relationship Dickinson establishes between speaker, loved one, and stars as well. For the speaker to "miss Her" is to hold open the place of her absence, discursively attesting to and signifying toward the nearly deified "Eye" and "Mind" implied in the second stanza. The ambiguous "their" in the poem's seventh line conflates the majesty and distance of the stars with the dead themselves; both, it would seem, return the gaze to "Include Us" (or "Scan better" or "Convey Us"), albeit "slightly" or "scarcely" "as they go," bringing the gazer and the gazed into a proximate, mirroring relationship. Two of the three variants for the third line, "Include Us" and "Convey Us," give to the conception of being regarded by the dead the added sense of the dead communicating with "Us" and carrying us as they do so, semantically including "Ourselves" or speaking "Ourselves" into the larger dialogue of the universe. Thus, the existentially alienated "We" of the first stanza becomes embraced, "asleep below," by its signified and signifying antitype in the heavens.

Other poems in which Dickinson displaces God as the aim of natural types in exchange for "the saints in Heaven" are less optimistic and offer implied responses to both the Bible and scientist theologians such as Edward Hitchcock. Her chief methodology in searching the natural world for this evidence of life after death was to use the power of inference.[20] The approach is not unlike the one taken by Hitchcock, William Paley, and other authors of Dickinson's school textbooks whose natural theology looked for evidences of divine design and who found numerous emblems of God's promises in the created universe. In "Lain in Nature – so suffice us" (F1309), for instance, Dickinson reconsiders 1 Corinthians 15 (a passage she critiques repeatedly), the Apostle Paul's extended metaphor about the Resurrection in which he likens the body to a "seed" that is "sown [as] a natural body" and "raised a spiritual body." It reads:

> But some man will say, How are the dead raised up? and with what body do they come? Thou fool, that which thou sowest is not quickened, except it die: And that which thou sowest, thou sowest not that body that shall be, but bare grain, it may chance of wheat, or of some other grain: But God giveth it a body as it hath pleased him, and to every seed his own body. . . . So also is the resurrection of the dead. It is sown in corruption; it is raised in incorruption; It is sown in dishonour; it is raised in glory: it is sown in weakness; it is raised in power: It is sown a natural body; it is raised a spiritual body. There is a natural body, and there is a spiritual body. (1 Cor. 15:35–38, 42–44)[21]

The paragraph is important to Protestant conceptions of the Resurrection, and in fact is one of the core scriptural passages of Edward Hitchcock's highly popular *Religious Lectures on Peculiar Phenomena in the Four Seasons*. Hitchcock, whom Sewall describes as having "inspired a whole generation with a love of nature that combined a sense of its sublimity with an accurate knowledge of its parts and processes," was professor of natural theology and geology at Amherst College (and president from 1845 to 1854), an ordained minister, and a practicing scientist who discovered dinosaur footprints in the Connecticut Valley and corresponded with Charles Darwin (342). He was one of the nineteenth century's key advocates for what is now known as the argument from design, and he is credited with creating a modern science department at Amherst that was unparalleled for its time. Dickinson's love of scientific inquiry was doubtless influenced by his example, as he gave frequent lectures at Amherst Academy during the years of her attendance, and Mount Holyoke used several of his textbooks. The Dickinson family owned at least two of Hitchcock's most popular books, *Religious Lectures on Peculiar Phenomena in the Four Seasons* and *The Religion of Geology and Its Connected Sciences*, and the Dickinson and Hitchcock children were friends.

Like his contemporary Edwards Amasa Park, Hitchcock wished for his readers to realize the distinctions between the nuanced and allusive literary language of the Bible and its more direct statements of moral or doctrinal teaching. Neither genre functioned in the same manner as scientific observation, of course, but by using natural theology, one could make reasonable assumptions about the character and promises of God that are confirmed in the Bible. *Religious Lectures on Peculiar Phenomena in the Four Seasons* was originally a series of talks, which it is highly probable Dickinson heard Hitchcock deliver in person, or read for herself, or both. In "The Resurrections of Spring," Hitchcock elaborates on the notion that "spring presents us with numerous examples of life emerging from apparent death." Using an inferential method comparable to Dickinson's in her poem "When they come back – if blossoms do –," Hitchcock reflects, "Had we no experience of the effects of spring, we could not imagine, during the winter months, of such a climate as ours, that leaves and flowers and fruit would ever clothe the barren trees; or a green carpet again cover the earth" (39). "Just so it is," he continues,

> with the resurrection of the dead. Go to their burial-place, and see if, among the great congregation that lie side by side beneath the soil, you can discover any signs of life. You call, but there is no answer; you remove three feet of earth, but you shrink back, horrified at the corruption that riots there upon all ages and all classes. Yet, when the last trumpet shall sound, that whole surface shall become instinct with life, and corruption shall put on incorruption. (40)

This process is all according to divine design, Hitchcock explains, for our understanding that "spring restores to us . . . well-remembered forms of vegetable and animal life" (40) serves to remind us of the surety of God's promise concerning human resurrection. Consequently, we may have confidence about the fate of those who die before us, he assures, because

> if the doctrine of this discourse be true, and if they were the true disciples of Christ, they shall be restored to us in the resurrection morning; and we shall recognize them amid the millions who then awake from the grave, as we now recognize the plants and animals of spring. There shall be a characteristic something in their spiritual bodies that will lead us at once, and with exulting joy, to fly to their embrace. (56–57)

Hitchcock ends the lecture by describing the future reunions between separated parents and children, and between siblings, spouses, and friends. He then instructs his audience to read the Book of Nature as a primer. "Let us look upon the thousand forms of life and beauty, that meet us from day to day, as symbolizations of that nobler resurrection," he adjures, "when forms a thousand times dearer shall start into life from a deeper winter, and put on a verdure that will never decay and a glory that will never fade" (59).

Dickinson once wrote to T. W. Higginson: "When Flowers annually died and I was a child, I used to read Dr. Hitckcock's [*sic*] Book on the Flowers of North America. This comforted their Absence – assuring me they lived" (L573). In her poetry she returns time and again to imaginings of the Resurrection; once in a while, as in "Smiling back from coronation" (F651), she considers what it would be like to be a part of such a triumphant rising from the dead; more often, as in "No crowd that has occurred" (F653) or "I cannot live with you" (F706), she depicts the experience of one excluded from the resurrection of the righteous. "Lain in nature – so suffice us," however, is particularly notable in this context for Dickinson's appropriation of the natural world in a way that seems to be a reply to Hitchcock. In this poem, Dickinson's speaker considers the "missing Seed," or departed body, of 1 Corinthians 15, and finds that absence, or lack, constitutes a disturbing proof of its own that runs counter to the comforting cyclical returns of the natural world. Absence must "suffice," however, and Dickinson draws upon traces of the old typological resonances to enable it to do so.

Lain in Nature – so suffice us
The enchantless Pod
When we advertise existence
For the missing Seed –

Maddest Heart that God created
Cannot move a sod
Pasted by the simple summer
On the Longed for Dead – Longed for] soldered
(F1309)

In contrast with Hitchcock's somewhat morbid reminder that to "remove three feet of earth" from a grave would only cause us to "shrink back, horrified at the corruption that riots there," Dickinson's poem finds nothing either to shudder at or to celebrate in "the missing Seed." As she often does, Dickinson syntactically delays the full revelation of her subject—in this case, who or what is "Lain in Nature" (not lain in heavenly repose)—until the end of the poem. Figuratively buried at the end of the second stanza, these "Longed for" or "soldered Dead" are "Pasted" beneath "sod" that even the "Maddest Heart that God created/Cannot move." In lieu of the dead's presence, the poet foregrounds what must "suffice us": "The enchantless Pod."[22] "Enchantless," the empty seedpod has no magical or divine power but can only suggest the slimmest of typological connections that the Corinthians passage once resonated with. Emptiness seems an absurdly feeble basis by which to "advertise existence/For the missing Seed." In her version, it is only by the poet's textual re-creation of a vacant natural pod whose shape suggests absent seeds that the imagination can possibly "move" the "sod" from the dead in a way the "Maddest Heart that God created/Cannot."[23]

Dickinson's line "Maddest Heart that God created" also echoes a phrase of Charles Wadsworth's that Dickinson may well have read by the time she wrote the extant 1873 copy of "Lain in Nature." Charles Wadsworth's sermon "Progress in Decay" (published in his 1869 volume of sermons) also offers an extended meditation on Paul's metaphor of the temporal body as the seed of the future, eternal body. Yet, unlike Hitchcock, Wadsworth asserts that the heavenly reconstitution of the saints will radically transform their previously earthly relationships. Indeed, the Presbyterian Wadsworth's imagination is much less anthropomorphic and sentimental than the New Divinity Hitchcock's or Park's: should loved ones suddenly appear on Earth in their resurrected state, Wadsworth says, instead of calling them "mother" or "father," "methinks we should shrink abashed from the blinding splendor of that new creature of God!" (364). So wonderful is heaven, Wadsworth continues, "how surpassing, then, the *madness* of an immortal spirit loving supremely these earthly things" (365, emphasis added). It would be characteristic of Dickinson's wry humor here if she were responding to Wadsworth's depiction of the Resurrection as incomprehensible and alien as well as joyous; in so doing she might resonate with the greater mystery of Wadsworth's version and also gently upbraid herself as one of those "Maddest Heart[s]" who lacked the faith to choose God's eternal heaven over her earthly one.

Dickinson's evocations of 1 Corinthians 15, Hitchcock, and Wadsworth in "Lain in Nature" are evidence not only of how the Reformed typological imagination lingered into the latter part of the nineteenth century, but also of the poet's determination to continue to suggest the contours of belief even in the face of scientific and hermeneutic doubt. While she may or may not have known the nuances of the theological debates in the Reformed "paper wars," she clearly responded to and incorporated a multiplicity of prevailing approaches to biblical texts in her own readings of scriptural sign systems. Dickinson understood that, at its heart, the typological impulse is a relational one; to create an earthly type and a spiritual antitype that stand in a mutually completing yet discrete relation to each other is to envision a universe that consists of interconnective yet free relation and in which the bond between the living and the dead may be attenuated but never sundered. While she possessed the genius and skill to subvert notions of the transcendent through a poetics of immanent transcendentalism, Dickinson also longed for an object and a teleological end of her affections that overarched the here and now. Her typology of displaced presence, moving the position of antitype from Christ to the saints in heaven, accomplishes just that, for where she cannot imagine a divine reception and return of her affections, she can imagine a human—though spiritually "translated"—one. Drawing on the Reformed hermeneutic assumptions of knowing and seeing, revelation and perception, Dickinson uses the natural world—or absences in the natural world—to make spiritual inference about the possibilities of such typological connections. As she wrote to the Norcross sisters in 1870, "God made no act without a cause –/ nor heart without an aim –/ Our inference is premature,/ our premises to blame" (F1192).

5

"*Myself – the Term between*"

Dickinson's Typology of Split Subjectivity

Dickinson's oeuvre contains a host of masterly poems dramatizing the experience of the mind observing itself, states of cognition that she explores in a variety of moods—sometimes, for example, with a sense of uncanny fear, as in "One need not be a chamber – to be Haunted" (F407), or sometimes in quiet dread of the fine line that divides sanity from madness, as in "I felt a Cleaving in my Mind –" (F867). In modes more existential than psychological, however, Dickinson locates the source of internal division *externally*. In these poems, the drama of the self's inner conflict is triggered by the impingement of a massive, often supranatural force emanating from locations as banal as a sunset, a summer's day, or a well. In this subgenre of her poems, Dickinson cagily plunders the tradition and terminology from within which she first imagined possibilities of fractured selfhood, Reformed Protestantism—a worldview that formulates the human condition as one that is fundamentally unsettled in its division between the mortal body, or "flesh," and the immortal "spirit."

According to the New Testament theology with which Dickinson was so familiar, this split, for the present, causes "suffering" but also carries the promise of a future wholeness, freedom, and "glory" that will be restored with the second coming of Christ and the believer's resurrection, an event that is foretold by the presence of the Holy Spirit that "dwelleth in you," as Paul writes in Romans 8. The Spirit, Paul continues, gives an inner attestation to the believer of her redemption: "The Spirit itself beareth witness with our spirit, that we are the children of God" (Rom. 8:16). Moreover, according to this familiar passage, even nature mirrors the divide between mortal and immortal, as well as the hope for a promised reconciliation: "For we know that the whole creation groaneth and travaileth in pain together until now. And not only they, but ourselves also have the firstfruits of the Spirit, even we ourselves groan within ourselves, waiting for the adoption, to wit, the redemption of our body" (Rom. 8:22–23). In his theology, Jonathan Edwards envisioned this reconciliation in terms of "being's consent to being," a metaphysical state of being-as-becoming in relation to God, a now-and-future dynamic that can be illustrated in the believer's participation in the divine semiotics of natural typology (see chapter 2).

In Dickinson's nineteenth century, one of Edwards's truest metaphysical heirs, the immensely popular Horace Bushnell, would likewise advance this discussion in his often republished sermon "The Spirit in Man" (found in the Dickinson library's copy of his *Sermons for the New Life*). Here Bushnell asserts that "to be spirit, or to have a spiritual nature, is to be practically related to a *being* in us and about us, who is above all mere abstractions, or principles: viz., to the person of God Himself" (35). While mere religious "ideas can not walk in us, or witness, or begat anew, or seal [us]," he continues, "the living God, communicating Himself to souls, can do this and more—can raise them to his own plane of existence, and make them partakers with him, even in his character itself" (35). Bushnell further expounds upon Edwards's "new sense of things" with what he identifies as "a kind of double sense in which [the believer] takes note, both of God and of himself together, and is, at one and the same moment, conscious of both. . . . In the new sense he has of a composite life, in which God Himself is a presiding force, he is raised into a glorious equilibrium above himself, and set in rest upon the rock of God's eternity" (38).

Nor was Bushnell the only religious thinker in Dickinson's era to be meditating on the notion of a "double sense." Ralph Waldo Emerson also weighs in on what he terms the problem of the "double consciousness." Coming from similar Reformed backgrounds, Bushnell and Emerson shared an insistence on the correlation between the created universe and the spiritual faculties of the mind. Yet Bushnell's emphasis on typological imagery in Scripture and in the world was by no means an endorsement of Transcendentalism. As E. Brooks Holifield describes it, Bushnell's 1858 *Nature and the Supernatural as Together Constituting One System of God* "was an argument against naturalism. Its main contention was that the new naturalistic tone of American thought—he had in mind not only Emerson and Park but also phrenology and mesmerism—wrongly assumed that religious capacities inherent in human nature defined the meaning of religion. He thought that their naturalism overlooked both the human conviction of sin and the need for a supernatural redemption" (464–65). The boundaries between God, the natural world, and humankind, in other words, remained, even in the progressive Bushnell's estimation.

Although Dickinson did not share Bushnell's unswerving belief in the goodness and trustworthiness of God, like Bushnell (and unlike Emerson), she frequently worked within the metaphysical and hermeneutical boundaries that the Reformed heritage she shared with both men had bequeathed her. Such boundaries prevented her as well from embracing the sunnier estimations of Unitarian and Transcendental contemporaries like T. W. Higginson concerning the beneficence of nature or the potential for self-divinity. For Dickinson, the split between the spirit and body/soul is an agonizing, mysterious, and uncertain one. In her thinking, the relationship is akin to what Emmanuel Levinas would posit in the twentieth century as the position of the persecuted subject alienated from itself by the existence of an unintelligible and immutable Other within itself. This "ambiguity within the subject is the trace of the infinite," Levinas explains, and it produces a subject "alienated in the depths of its identity," what he terms "the Other in the Same" (*Basic* 105, 102). Such a formulation sharply contrasts with the joyful assurance of salvation celebrated in the Christian Church (or the joyful assurance of the needlessness of salvation in other circles).

In this chapter I examine Dickinson's considerations of how such an alienated identity might occupy the uncomfortable gap between the now and the not yet, between mortality and eternity. Although Dickinson seems to accept as a given that the self's teleological end and intent is unfixed, unbounded, and eternal, she does not often share in the Reformed hope of an ultimate unification of a selfhood that will remain a unique entity and yet, somehow, be mystically united with God. Instead, as I go on to show, she frequently draws upon the figure of the Old Testament God encountered by Moses, called YHWH in the Book of Exodus, to construct typological equations pointing toward a God outside of known being. This conception of God (what Jean-Luc Marion terms "Gød without Being") becomes the antitype of an uncanny gap or excess in the Book of Nature. Dickinson's type as a trace of this God reminds the poet that she is not a unified subject but rather herself lives on the divide between the natural and supernatural worlds. In these poems, the "groan"-ings of the "whole creation" that Paul describes in Romans

8 become nature as a "Haunted House," alien and shriven of its sylvan charms, which signifies a "Spirit" that is unnameable and unknowable (L554). I also examine Dickinson's typology of split subjectivity within her responses to Higginson's evocation of nature and in contrast with the thought of Emerson, showing how she differs from him in his estimation of nature and the possibility of unified selfhood.

In "How much the present moment means," "The Fop – the Carp" and "the Atheist" have "nothing more" than the present—"a moment's shallow Rim," Dickinson writes (F1420). These allegorical figures are unable to conceive of a metaphysics beyond their immediate perception, or to realize that at "their commuted Feet / The Torrents of Eternity / Do all but inundate –." If, as Marion has surmised, the concept of Being is based on the notion of a closed and reflexive binarism between being and nonbeing, then we can also understand that Dickinson's God without Being would no longer be the conventional "God" at which the poet pokes fun for its function as an idolatrous mirror of the religiously minded; rather it would be a God *sous rature* (under erasure), a "difference indifferent to ontological difference" that "outwits the play of being with Being" and so may not be conceptualized in terms that may be symbolically frozen (Marion 86). The notion of such a God is not entirely outside the bounds of Dickinson's orthodox biblical training, since God is, in the words of the Apostle Paul, "exceeding abundantly above all that we ask or think" (Eph. 3:20). Many of Dickinson's references to the absence of God are typological renditions of a God who falls under no known ontological category of existence, not gestures of entire unbelief. For Dickinson, a God confined to the dimensions known by humanity may quickly fall under the rubric of "God," subsumed into what she perceives as finite, self-referential, or idolatrous conceptions.[1]

Dickinson hints at a conception of God without Being in numerous poems where the speaker longs to escape from the life/death, being/nonbeing binary in which she feels trapped, where "Alternative to die / Is Nature's only Pharmacy / For Being's Malady –" (F887). Outside this matrix, God incomprehensibly contains both being and nonbeing; as she posits in a variation on Paul's assertion that "in him we live and move and have our being" (Acts 17:28): "In Him, Existence serve, or Set / A Force illegible –" (F1113). Moreover, at points in Dickinson's poetry "Eternity" itself comes to stand for a limited conception of eternal life that is modeled on earthly being or existence; in these instances "Eternity," too, can be inseparably caught in the being/nonbeing dualism. Hence, where the poet encounters that which cannot be said, or "mould[ed] . . . into word," it may be taken as a "sign" that "new Dilemma be / From mathematics further off / Than from Eternity" (F1725). At times the speaker's attempt to apprehend a state that encompasses and yet is not encompassed by either being (a reductive "Eternity") or nonbeing ("the Grave") yields an appalling terror:

More than the Grave is closed to me –
The Grave and that Eternity
To which the Grave adheres –
I cling to nowhere till I fall –
The Crash of nothing, yet of all –
How similar appears – (F1532)

Oxymoronically, to "cling to nowhere till I fall –" and to hear "The Crash of nothing, yet of all –" approaches the sense of the absurd that can pitch thought off the scale of this binary opposition, the "adher[ence]" of the "Grave" and "Eternity."

Where Dickinson creates a natural typology in reference to this distant God outside the being/nonbeing binary, she uses words such as "height," "silence," "the abyss," and "awe" in reference to moments and places where nature allows us to "infer, / By it's Bisecting / Messenger –" the "existence" of "Paradise" (F1421). These terms have been linked to Dickinson's interest in the gothic or sublime modes, and Gary Lee Stonum's distinctions here between the "esthetics of the beautiful" and the "esthetics of the sublime" are quite useful. Pointing out that Dickinson prefers "power as the object of cherishing (rather than, say, beauty, truth [or] love)," Stonum contrasts the "object-centered esthetics of the beautiful," which "stresses a fusion of material reality with spiritual ideals," with Dickinson's "esthetics of the sublime," which is "predicated on intensely experienced, anguishing forces that rupture normal continuities of habit and belief" (67, 118). Hence, the alienated and frequently antagonistic relationship that Dickinson draws between herself and this divine Other behind nature is configured along the lines of power, with the poet herself at the receiving end of an uncanny, inexplicable omnipotence. Yet as Jane Eberwein has noted in *Strategies of Limitation*, "awe" and "silence" are also associated with Old Testament renditions of the ancient Israelites' "YHWH," or the "I AM THAT I AM," the name God gave to Moses from the burning bush and which orthodox Jews were forbidden to speak out loud (Exodus 3:14). Neither could YHWH's face be glimpsed, for as He pronounces in Exodus 33:20, "Thou canst not see my face: for there shall no man see me and live." Dickinson seems particularly drawn to Moses's relationship with God, exploring their interactions in several poems, including "No man saw awe, nor to his house" (F1342).[2]

The alignment that Dickinson makes between awe, nature, and a faceless God who reveals Godself by mysterious intrusion from outside the matrix of being/nonbeing is particularly clear in another poem that references Exodus, "My period had come for prayer." Here Dickinson implicitly contrasts a stereotyped "Creator" and "Curious Friend" who "grows above" with an unfamiliar God whose "House was not – no sign had He –" (F525). While the first might be amenable to "Tactics," the second cannot be "infer[red]" by anything visible in the created order, leading the speaker to ask after the fashion of Moses, "Infinitude – Had'st Thou no Face / That I might look on Thee?" In response, "The Silence condescended – / Creation stopped – for me."[3] The speaker is arrested, provoked to move "beyond" the conventional "rudiment[s]" of theology alluded to in the first stanza: "awed beyond my errand – / I worshipped – did not – 'pray' –." Likewise, at moments in other poems this God under erasure and unbound by ontological demands of presence is recognizable only "By his intrusion" (F1481) into the material world through an inexplicable excess or trace found in natural creation. This God "Presents a Claim invisible –" (F698), which demands a human response, frequently experienced by Dickinson's speakers as an excruciating split between body and spirit, mortality and immortality. In "Departed to the Judgment," for instance, Dickinson surmises how troubling this notion of a future and foreign selfhood might be. Locating her identity as an in-between-ness or "Soul" that is neither "Flesh" nor "Bodiless" spirit, she finds herself orphaned rather than (in the words of Paul) "adopt[ed]" in a coming "redemption of our body" on the day of resurrection; instead, Dickinson writes, "The Flesh – Surrendered – Cancelled – / The Bodiless – begun – / Two Worlds – like Audiences – disperse – / And leave the Soul – alone –" (F399). By attributing consciousness and agency to the "Soul," Dickinson envisions having a present identity that survives the cataclysmic Day of Judgment, though she will do so at the price of being "alone." The speaker finds, as she phrases it in "Behind me dips eternity," that she can resist a future rending of selfhood by positioning "*Myself* – the Term between –" flesh and spirit, or "Eternity" and "Immortality" (F743, emphasis added).

Dickinson uses nature to construct a typological relationship with this "Claim Invisible," or *sensus divinitatis,* chiefly in two ways. First, in some poems she celebrates nature as sacramental excess. In these junctures a God beyond Being is inferred as the antitype of a natural, inexplicable phenomenon that, paradoxically, seems deposited into the world from outside the realm of sense experience and functions autonomously without discernible source or motive; this God at the same time demands a response from the observer. Like music, which Dickinson describes as "A fine – estranging creature –," these natural types in excess are "To something upper wooing us / But not to our Creator –," that is, to the conventional notion of God (F1511). Frequently, light itself becomes the signifier of unintelligible speech, or revelation, from beyond nature. She rarely tries to name these experiences; instead, in poems such as "Further in summer than the birds" and "There's a certain slant of light," she delineates their boundaries by relating how this intangible revelation without origins encroaches on the speaker's experience of the world. In "An ignorance a sunset," for instance, Dickinson describes such an encounter with God as a dark revelation that exposes the trace of the Infinite hidden within the speaking subject:

An ignorance a Sunset — ignorance] impotence
Confer opon the Eye –
Of Territory – Color –
Circumference – Decay – — Decay] Array

It's Amber Revelation
Exhilirate – Debase –
Omnipotence' inspection — inspection] Analysis
Of Our inferior face –

And when the solemn features
Confirm – in Victory – — Confirm –] Withdraw –
We start – as if detected
In Immortality – (F669)

As in the better-known poem "There's a certain slant of light," the image of light, normally associated with spiritual and intellectual illumination, becomes an iconic via negativa; it is a window from beyond Being streaming rays of "ignorance" (or "impotence") "Confer[ed]" "opon the Eye." The paradoxical non-"Revelation" of the mysteries of "Territory – Color – / Circumference – Decay –," rather than disclosing a beatific vision of heaven (as in the King James Version's Revelation of St. John the Divine), exposes the speaker herself as the one observed by the Other. "Omnipotence' inspection / Of Our inferior face" lays the speaker bare, helpless before its power to both "Exhilirate" and "Debase." When the "solemn features" of sunset bring the encounter to an end (the agency, whether the verb is "Confirm –" or "Withdraw – in Victory," is attributed to the Other), the subject finds within herself an uncomfortable typological split between signifier and signified, between the finite and the infinite: "We start – as if detected / In Immortality." In this moment, the notion of self as a unified entity is exposed as myth. The speaker, "start[led]" into an awareness of alterity by this trace from beyond being, becomes a signifying subject in process. The epiphany is both "Exhilirat[ing]" in the liberation from self-referential solipsism it promises and "Debas[ing]" in the sense that it overturns notions of the self's intrinsic value as separate from signifying relation to the Other.

In *Lyric Time: Dickinson and the Limits of Genre,* Sharon Cameron contrasts this quality of Dickinson's light with Milton's and Blake's evocations of the same, noting that for the earlier poets, "such meditations on light are visions about source, and they each have embedded in them a creation myth the playing out of which constitutes its discovery" (179). For Dickinson, "captivated by but unable to spell out light's meaning," however, "there is not rhapsodic praise here because there is no understanding. . . . We are shown a landscape struck by a moment of *kairos,* its ordinary meanings razed to the ground, but replaced by nothing; we see the form of revelation without a clue as to its content" (180). Yet Dickinson's baffling and unsettling encounters with light are not completely outside the religious tradition that inspired Milton and Blake. Rather, Dickinson's light harkens back to the same ineffable mystery of the Old Testament God with whom Moses dealt—a God without Being that cannot be equated with anything found in the created order. This is the light she likens to a "Sacrament" in "A light exists in spring" (F962) and that "solemnizes me" in the poem "A something in a summer's Day," causing the speaker to respond in a fashion similar to Moses when he uses a veil to cover the glow coming from his own transfigured face after conversing with God: "Then vail my too inspecting face / Lest such a subtle – shimmering grace / Flutter too far for me –" (F104).

In addition to excesses, Dickinson also finds strange gaps or absences in nature which function like a linguistic and spiritual trace. Her wonder at the natural world's propensity to "Pluck up it's stakes, and disappear," as she phrases it in "I've known a Heaven, like a Tent –," is sometimes playful, but most often expresses a deep anxiety concerning who or what lies behind such sudden disseminations, leaving "No Trace – no Figment – of the Thing / That dazzled, Yesterday" (F257). The trace, a concept Levinas has defined as that which intersects the world and "signifies beyond being," is something that has always "left *before* having come" and is legible only to the careful, for it "remains only for him who would like to take it up. Otherwise, it has already restored the order it troubled" (*Basic* 61, 72, 70). Silence, for instance, is one of the tropes the poet uses to highlight the contours of the "Claim Invisible." While she frequently lauds the signifying power of the spoken Word/word, at other times, utter, unnatural "Silence" is "all we dread"; it is "Infinity. / Himself have not a face" (F1300 B). Resistant to all interpretation or projection, "Silence" can interrupt the discursive play of signifiers from outside the matrix of being/nonbeing, entering an inassimilable particle into existence itself. In "Speech is one symptom of affection," she deems this uncanny "Silence" to be "The perfectest communication," for it "Is heard of none" yet "Exists and it's indorsement / Is had within –" (F1694).

The relationship Dickinson creates between type (an absence, indicated by mysterious "Silence") and antitype (the corresponding "indorsement" from "within" that gestures toward a God beyond transcendence) happily shares the discursive properties of both nature and the written word. Here Jean-Luc Marion's explanation of how a preternatural "gift" signifies even as it erases itself is useful for understanding Dickinson's conception of how God as antitype can enter the natural realm without being contained by it, as would an earth-centered goddess. According to Marion, the "self-withdrawal of the giver in the gift may be read on the gift"; in this fashion, the "gift gives the giver to be seen, in repeating the giving backward. Sending which sends itself back, sending back which sends—it is a ceaseless play of giving where the terms are united all the more in that they are never confused" (104). In other words, gift, nature, and text all bear the untraceable imprint of that which has gone before, and all contain in themselves manifold implications of further significations. They thus stand in typological relation to one another, signifying forward and backward yet never collapsing into one another.

Dickinson seems to be exploring just such a semiotic relationship in "I send you a decrepit flower":

> I send you a decrepit flower
> That nature sent to me
> At parting – she was going south
> And I designed to stay –

Her motive for the souvenir — motive for] object in
If sentiment for me — for me] it be
Or circumstance prudential
Witheld invincibly – [Secreted utterly] – • reserved [utterly]
(F1346)

Franklin identifies the poem as having been written on the flyleaf of her father's copy of *Sketch Book of Geoffrey Crayon*, a book of purported travel sketches, or "souvenir[s]," by Washington Irving which includes his well-known tales "The Legend of Sleepy Hollow" and "Rip Van Winkle," as well as depictions of European scenarios such as "Westminster Abbey." Dickinson's traveling motif of passing on "a decrepit flower" that in turn "nature sent to me" as "she was going south" conflates Irving's book with the poet's word and with natural typology, each part of the signifying chain. That the gift of the flower is "decrepit"—unreadable, already under erasure, and undergoing decay—reminds the recipient of book, poem, or flower that the referent itself is irrecoverable; all that can be done is to receive the gift without regard for origins, for nature's "motive for the souvenir" is "Witheld invincibly" (or "Secreted utterly," or "reserved [utterly]," according to the variants). Concomitantly, the poem suggests that the old typological associations in which God's character could be read transparently on the flower are as old-fashioned and bygone as the simple legends passed on by Geoffrey Crayon; now the natural element is a type only insofar as it indicates a God outside conception or figuration who may not be traced, only received as an inexplicable and ungraspable gift.

Reading the Book of Nature, Dickinson finds, is rife with experiences of ungraspable gifts. The poem "It bloomed and dropt, a Single Noon –," for instance, dramatizes how the inability to recover an overlooked flower becomes a typic signifier of the mystery behind the physical world. "The single Flower of the Earth / That I, in passing by / Unconscious was –" is the missed appointment in which "Great Nature's Face / Passed infinite by Me –," as when YHWH let His glory "pass by" Moses while hiding His face from him in Exodus 33 (F843).[4] In "What mystery pervades a well!" Dickinson performs a similar move, this time using a tone of childlike wonder to contrast with the disconcerting effects of "looking" in "an abyss's face." In the first two stanzas, she depicts the illusion of a bottomless well as an almost sinister phenomenon:

What mystery pervades a well!
The water lives so far –

A neighbor from another world
Residing in a jar

Whose limit none have ever seen,
But just his lid of glass –
Like looking every time you please
In an abyss's face! (F1433, stanzas one and two)

The eerily absent presence that Dickinson's ordinary well indicates is a "mystery . . . from another world" that "resid[es]" in and "pervades" the well without becoming a part of the natural order it traverses, not unlike the God who appears to Moses as a burning flame that does not consume the bush. Whereas Jonathan Edwards's or Horace Bushnell's typology is infused with a joyful assurance of the presence of God, the speaker's encounter with absence—a "limit none have ever seen"—fills her with fear, "awe" (or the variant "dread"), and "timidity" in the third and fourth stanzas, where she further associates the well with the "floorless" "sea."

In the poem's final stanzas, the tone of naïve observation gives way to another of Dickinson's familiar stances, that of drawing experiential conclusions from a position of reflective distance in time and space. The well is no longer a "neighbor" amenable to being gazed upon "every time you please":

But nature is a stranger yet;
The ones that cite her most
Have never passed her haunted house,
Nor simplified her ghost.

To pity those that know her not
Is helped by the regret
That those who know her, know her less
The nearer her they get. (F1433, stanzas five and six)

To "cite" nature, it would seem, is to use the natural world in a "simplified" or symbolic fashion without acknowledging the "mystery" that animates it. In truth, only those with proximate knowledge of the natural world can refuse the temptation of hubristic attempts at totalizing representation. In Dickinson's nature, the trace of the "Force illegible" (F1113) is always in effect, both drawing and repulsing the speaker, erasing itself so that "those who know her, know her less/The nearer her they get." The type-as-trace pointing to a God without Being is finally a "ghost"—holy or otherwise—whose undeniable residence transforms nature into a "haunted house."

Dickinson's conception of a God-"haunted" natural world is further illustrated by a contextual reassessment of her much-discussed assertion to T. W. Higginson that "nature is a Haunted House – but Art – a House that tries to be haunted" in a letter she seems to have written within a year of "What mystery pervades a well!" (L459 A). Examining the comment within the contexts of Dickinson's particular dialogue with the Unitarian Higginson on the benignity of the numinous in nature and the transparency of language in nature writing sheds further light on her conception of the self as bifurcated between the mortal and the immortal realms. To begin with, her statement "nature is a Haunted House – but Art – a House that tries to be haunted" seems to be an addendum to her conversation in the 1876 letter immediately preceding it.[5] In this letter, Dickinson refers to Higginson's 1863 *Outdoor Papers,* a set of five meditative essays describing his firsthand observations of nature. In essays such as "The Procession of the Flowers" (a piece Dickinson mentions by name to him in an earlier letter), Higginson had waxed eloquent on "moments" in nature

> when the atmosphere is so surcharged with luxury that every pore of the body becomes an ample gate for sensation to flow in, and one has simply to sit still and be filled. In after years the memory of books seems barren or vanishing, compared with the immortal bequest of hours like these. . . . No man can measure what a single hour with Nature may have contributed to the moulding of his mind. (52–53)

Concerning his "thought" (presumably on the ecstatic experience of rapture in the natural world), Dickinson writes:

> Of it's Bliss to yourself, we are ignorant, though you first teach us "that which is born of the Spirit is Spirit" –
>
> It is still as distinct as Paradise – the opening your first Book –
> It was Mansions – Nations – Kinsmen – too – to me –
> I sued the News – yet feared – the News
> That such a Realm could be –
> "The House not made with Hands" it was –
> Thrown open wide to me –
>
> I had long heard of an Orchis before I found one, when a child, but the first clutch of the stem is as vivid now, as the Bog that bore it – so truthful is transport – (L458)

Dickinson's contiguous alignment of reading, nature, and a transitory repair of the fracture between immanent and transcendent existence in this passage is framed by two important references to the King James Bible. The first is from John 3:6, part of Jesus's dialogue with Nicodemus (and a conversation which Dickinson cites several times in her poems and letters): "That which is born of the flesh is flesh; and that which is born of the Spirit is spirit" (or, as she calls the Holy Spirit in one poem, "Old Nicodemus' Phantom") (F1218). The second citation, "The House not made with Hands," is taken from Paul's extended discussion in 2 Corinthians of the distinction between the "temporal" and the "eternal" parts of the self:

> For we know that if our earthly house of this tabernacle were dissolved, we have a building of God, an house not made with hands, eternal in the heavens. For in this we groan, earnestly desiring to be clothed upon with our house which is from heaven: If so be that being clothed we shall not be found naked. For we that are in this tabernacle do groan, being burdened: not for that we would be unclothed, but clothed upon, that mortality might be swallowed up of life. (2 Cor. 5:1–4)

Both passages explore the nature of the division between flesh and spirit, confirming their present incompatibility yet teleologically connecting the mortal body ("that which is born of the flesh" and "our earthly house of this tabernacle") with its heavenly antitype ("that which is born of Spirit" and "a building of God, an house not made with hands")—a resurrected, supernatural body.[6] The Pauline passage just quoted at length, moreover, conveys the agony of a self constituted by the fissure between signifier and signified, deficiency and totality. In her letter to Higginson, Dickinson makes use of the nuances of both these passages to situate her celebration of his literary achievement: his elucidation of nature has produced a state of "transport" in which Dickinson as reader finds the gap between the mortal and immortal momentarily traversed and "'The House not made with Hands' . . . / Thrown open wide to me – ."

Furthermore, Dickinson's figuration of nature (mediated through the imagination of the artist) as the vehicle for this liminal experience is evident in her reading of Higginson's "first Book," which she reports to be "still as distinct as Paradise." The term "Paradise" itself refers both backwards and forwards to the prelapsarian Garden of Eden and its antitype in Revelation 2:7, where there is a heavenly "tree of life, which is in the midst of the paradise of God."[7] Indeed, after reconstructing her experience as reader in terms of biblical paradigm, Dickinson reiterates her emphasis on nature as the site of this encounter by supplying a typological illustration of her own: "I had long heard of an Orchis before I found one, when a child, but the first clutch of the stem is as vivid now, as the Bog that bore it – so truthful is transport –." In this anecdote, Dickinson's secondhand instruction in the existence of the exotic orchis is finally fulfilled in a moment of material presence when she grasps the flower for herself; she recalls that the revelatory "transport" of "the first clutch of the stem" is as undeniable as the more earthy and mundane "Bog that bore it." Thus nature itself becomes a figure for the coexistence of the supernatural in the natural, the earthly "Bog" bearing the unearthly "Orchis," the orchis, in return, lending the bog its distinction.

The "transport," however, as Dickinson's past tense indicates, is a transitory one. It is ultimately more pessimistic than Higginson's recollected "immortal bequest of hours" bygone spent in nature because it contains a more overt reference to the dislocation between time and eternity. The "transport" is prior to the letter that Dickinson writes, recoverable to memory but irrecoverable to physical presence; as experience, the same stem can never be precisely re-created and never re-grasped, the same bog, subject to the changes of time, can never be revisited; and because the speaker cannot discursively recover an originary self with which she experienced them, neither can she get to the bottom of an originary myth ("I had long heard") that gave rise to her desire for the orchis. Always prior to an infinitely receding self, the desire and its fulfillment in nature, like the trace Levinas describes, has "left *before* having come" (*Basic* 72). As discussed in chapter 4 with reference to her poem "Perception of an Object costs," nature as experienced through language is an always-bygone-and-yet-to-be encounter with present completion and totality. In this sense, nature reinforces subjectivity as a state of subsistence in the division between memory and anticipation, between flesh and spirit.

Such, indeed, is a theme of a poem included in L459, Dickinson's next letter and the letter in which her comment regarding nature as a haunted house was most likely included. In "The things we thought that we should do," she considers the weight of unfulfilled childhood anticipations. Ostensibly they are significant not for the fact that they are current longings but because desire itself has swerved and betrayed first expectations. Yet the residue of these desires pushes through the language of the poem, particularly in the last stanza, in which the speaker looks with some nostalgia at the loss of anticipatory grace:

The things we thought that we should do
We other things have done
But those peculiar industries
Have never been begun

The Lands we thought that we should seek
When large enough to run
By Speculation ceded
To Speculation's Son –

The Heaven, in which we hoped to pause
When Discipline was done
Untenable to Logic
But possibly the one – (L553, F1279 D)

Again, as in her reminiscence about the orchis in the previous letter to Higginson, the poet is caught between an irrecoverable past that never was and an uncertain future that may never be. The "other things . . . done" are haunted by the memory of "those peculiar industries" that "have never been begun." In lieu of a world of stable correlations between thought and action, word and deed, desire and aim, Dickinson's fractured subject must constitute her identity not through achievements obtained nor desires whose objects may be "clutch[ed]" (to return to the orchis), but through the slippery signification process in which "Speculation" is constantly "ceded/To Speculation's Son –." Therefore, as the speaker projects in the third stanza, the existence of "The Heaven, in which we hoped to pause," or attain wholeness through the complete fulfillment of the signifier in the signified, "When Discipline was done," is likewise "Untenable" to grown-up "Logic." "But," Dickinson concludes, now undercutting our expectations, it is nonetheless "possibly the one" we had "hoped" for. With the word "possibly," Dickinson gives the poem an unexpected tone of anticipation at its close. If, in Dickinson's view, "Speculation" (God the Father) has "ceded/To Speculation's Son" (Jesus Christ)—if there is indeed on earth yet a trace of a merciful Creator—it is possible as well that although "logic" reminds that there is no immediate or perfect fulfillment of desire on earth, such a heaven might exist beyond logic.

Such, then, is the haunting described by Dickinson's phrase "Nature is a Haunted House – but Art – a House that tries to be haunted": nature is a home that is not a home, where one can't "pause," as she suggests in the aforementioned poem about heaven. For Higginson, as he writes in "The Procession of Flowers," the relationship between language, experience, and nature, between "the fragrance of this spray of Azalea beside me . . . which summer insects haunt and the Spirit of the Universe Loves" and the language that fails to capture these intangibles, is less fraught and agonistic than for Dickinson: "The defect is not in language," Higginson writes, "but in men. There is no conceivable beauty of blossom so beautiful as words,—none so graceful, none so perfumed" as the syllables of his idealized language (53–54). With Dickinson, however, "Art" and language are "House[s]" that "*try* to be haunted." Although she does have moments in which she celebrates Higginson's benevolent vision, the role of the natural world in Dickinson's poetry is also very often to be inhabited by the trace of an unknowable God who "Divides abode" within the soul, alienating it from itself, rending flesh and spirit, and placing wholeness, both past and future, out of the poet's reach (F1690).

In her meditations on these once and future "House[s]," Dickinson is by no means the only nineteenth-century writer considering how to reappropriate Paul's typological passage in 2 Corinthians in which one might "*know* that if our earthly house of this tabernacle were dissolved, we have a building of God, an house not made with hands, eternal in the heavens." Ralph Waldo Emerson, though a generation earlier than Dickinson, shared her concerns that scientific materialism and empirically minded theology working in tandem had rendered decidedly inhospitable both of the "houses" (i.e., the body and the natural world) that the old typological tradition had imagined as temporary containers for and signifiers of the transcendent, immortal aspects of the human soul. In his 1836 *Nature,* Emerson had famously extolled the human spirit's progressive, unconfined ability to make a house and "beyond its house a world; and beyond its world, a heaven" (*Essays* 48). And although he had reversed the Transcendental magnetic poles espoused by that younger, more ebullient persona by the time of his 1851 essay "Fate" (in which he claims, "Every spirit makes its house; but afterwards the house confines the spirit"), ultimately (and unlike Dickinson), Emerson remained characteristically optimistic about the unification of the (masculine) self through the representational, appropriative powers of language and the reparative ascendancy of the Ideal over the material world (946).

Given their common preoccupations, it is not surprising that Emerson's family, like Dickinson's, was rooted in Reformed Protestantism. Emerson was a direct descendant of six generations of Puritan and Reformed ministers, and his aunt Mary Moody Emerson, who helped raise him, was a devout Calvinist and Trinitarian who exerted considerable influence on Emerson long after he had chosen the path of Unitarianism and then Transcendentalism.[8] Writing specifically about the challenge of embodiment as it relates to man's failure to transcend nature, Emerson terms the typological split between body and spirit that of "the problem of the double consciousness," a notion he derives from his Gnostic exegesis of Pauline biblical passages.[9] A brief analysis of Emerson's notion of the "double consciousness" in the 1833 sermon "Religion and Society" and in the 1851 essay "Fate" shows that while he and Dickinson shared an anxiety about rapidly developing fault lines between object and representation in the language of nineteenth-century hermeneutics, they are markedly different in their willingness to trust to language or to the intellect to reconnect the divide.

Emerson's 1833 sermon reflects his rejection of the Unitarian ritual of the Lord's Supper, a practice that, when performed as a speech act, functions in the same way typology did as a nexus between the material, textual, and spiritual worlds. The contemporary solution, Emerson asserts, to his posed question "What is *my* relation to Almighty God?"—that is, the relation of a bodied being to the spiritual Ideal—is not to affirm an embodied Christ as enacted in the Lord's Supper but to "recognize the distinction of the outer and the inner self,—of the double consciousness" (*Complete Sermons* 215). Emerson proceeds to redirect typological fulfillment away from an embodied, Christic Other to an earthly antitype, a bodiless self subsumed by its intellect. "Within this erring, passionate, mortal self," he writes, "sits a supreme, calm, immortal mind," a salvific self within a self that Emerson imagines here as the benevolent "face which the Creator uncovers to his child" (215).

By the time of his 1851 "Fate," however, Emerson responds to the rapid demise of the romantic and symbolic uses of nature in the nineteenth century by framing the human connection to the organic world in vocabulary that is markedly eugenic, chemical, and mechanical rather than spiritual and by moving the locus of the battle for external mastery over nature inward. Now the typological "book of Nature is the book of fate," and the question is no longer how an individual might relate to the Almighty but "how shall a man escape from his ancestors, or draw off from his veins the black drop which he drew from his father's or his mother's life?" (*Essays* 949, 946). Gesturing toward Jonathan Edwards's culturally formative treatise on the Calvinist theology of predestination, *Freedom of the Will* (a text he had first referred to in an 1823 journal entry), Emerson writes in "Fate" that understanding "double consciousness" is "one key, one solution to the mysteries of human condition, one solution to the old knots of fate, freedom and foreknowledge" (966).[10] For this older Emerson, the double consciousness is a "stupendous antagonism, a dragging together of the poles of the Universe" between the body, or "elemental order," and the higher "spirit which composes and decomposes nature" (953). The body becomes the repository of all that is degenerate and "effete" and so must be resisted and annulled rather than completed (951). Similarly, the female gendered Fate—"unpenetrated causes" Emerson deems it in one place—is "whatever limits" ambition (958, 952). Yet, he adds, "intellect annuls Fate" (953). Although "men are what their mothers made them"—that is, trapped and specified by an embodiment marked by species selection, racial bloodlines, phrenological imperfections, and unstable temperaments—by wresting perspective from the physical to the spiritual self, Emerson asserts that he can collapse the alien body that might be gazed upon back into the Ideal, merging subject and object, fusing signifier and signified, mending the typological breach between immanent and transcendent worlds (947).

In feminizing and mastering physicality by collapsing and subsuming nature/fate/body into immaterial male spirit, Emerson switches "houses" from a confining and deadly "mother's womb" to a self-fathered, spiritualized set of movable houses that may be successively built and torn down in the realm of the imaginary without reference to bodily containment (947). Consequently, subservience to the fated, mothered body (and a feminized domestic sphere) is temporary; as he writes, "We can afford to allow the limitation, if we know it is the meter of the growing man. We stand against Fate, as children stand up against the wall in their father's house, and notch their height from year to year. But when the boy grows to man and is master of the house, he pulls down that wall and builds a new and bigger" (957). His vision is finally optimistic and even millennial in its imagination of what he deems at the end of "Fate" to be "Blessed Unity," the body subsumed under the gaze of a paternally functioning "Law" which "dissolves persons," "vivifies nature," and "solicits the pure in heart to draw on all its omnipotence" (968).

For both Emerson and Dickinson, then, typological hermeneutics and structures become a way of navigating constructions of the self and the world that foreground language as mediating the inter-space between faith and empirical fact. For Emerson, who writes in "Fate" that "he who sees through the design presides over it, and must will that which must be" (956), returning to the Pauline texts provides a blueprint for an internal human correspondence in the face of an increasingly mechanical and indeterminate external world. In the place of the Christian hybridity of body and soul, the double consciousness eliminates the embodied, material side of the equation, substitutes mirroring mind for matter, and preserves symbolic language in its role as teleological fossil poetry.

For Emily Dickinson, however, who shares Emerson's Reformed heritage and his proclivity for reading the natural world for signs of transcendent meaning, the Pauline "'House not made with Hands' . . . / Thrown open wide to me" conveys the agony of a self constituted by a *permanent* fissure between mortality and immortality, signifier and signified, deficiency and totality (L458). Typological relations retain boundaries and never "dissolve persons," as Emerson writes, and one can never "see through the design," let alone "preside over it." Instead, Dickinson's nature becomes associated with and functions in place of a mysterious, divine Other outside Emerson's dualisms, its unswerving gaze acting as a typological lever to pry apart and disrupt the subject's ability to remain a stable, enclosed entity in a purely material world.[11] Furthermore, in Dickinson's poems the relation of language to self is portrayed less as a matter of gendering a soul female than as a question of the spiritual effects of gendered positionality. The summons of the self beyond itself in signification toward the divine Other renders the speaker as a kind of passive subject in process, the mortal part always divided from but pointing toward that "Immortality" residing at once in the speaker and beyond being/nonbeing. A number of important feminist studies have called attention to the manner in which Dickinson's troubling of the subject position anticipates the work of poststructuralist theorists such as Lacan, Derrida, Irigaray, Kristeva, and Cixous.[12] Yet it is difficult, finally, to ascertain whether for Dickinson speaking from a position of divided subjectivity is a positive or negative circumstance, for there seems ample evidence within her large body of work to support both the idea that the poet's "in-betweenness" is an empowering and subversive stance that undercuts existing power structures and also that it is an inherently conflicted doubleness from which the poet tries, but fails, to escape. Tracing the typological threads in her poetry suggests ways in which Dickinson as poet avoids a number of the uncomfortable either/or dichotomies that her present-day critics have sometimes championed her work for celebrating. In fact, Dickinson explores both immanence *and* transcendence; she posits a self both intimately connected to *and* separate from God and nature; and she constructs a divided subject position that at times has both positive *and* negative effects on the speaker.

More broadly, considering Emily Dickinson's depictions of nature in the light of her typological revisionism illuminates both her reception of the Reformed hermeneutical traditions and the ways in which she departed from those traditions to devise her own idiosyncratic and heterodox constructions of the relationship between God, nature, and the self. Her appropriation of Edwardsean typological thinking and the natural theology of her own nineteenth-century contemporaries demonstrates that she was thoroughly informed in, yet not constrained by, conventional understandings of what it meant to read the natural world for signs of God's existence. Her willingness to confront frightening implications of what she philosophizes as a self permanently fractured with no reliable promise of wholeness—and to consider a God alien to the dualities of conventional human thought—led to brave innovations in her work. In an 1885 letter to an unknown recipient, Dickinson acknowledges the inherent dangers to those who would attempt to read the natural world for signs of the supernatural in ways outside the bounds of received methods. "How vast is the chastisement of Beauty, given us by our Maker!" she writes. "A Word is inundation, when it comes from the Sea – Peter took the Marine Walk at the great risk" (L965). In this allusion to the disciple Peter's decision to get out of his boat and walk on the Sea of Galilee toward Jesus, Dickinson characteristically aligns words and the Word, and the physical world with the spiritual "risk" taken when we are moved by the "chastisement" of nature's "Beauty" to make spiritual surmises. For Dickinson, however, jointly reading the Book of Nature and reading the Book of God are ingrained, reflexive actions that, like the two lenses that focus light in a refracting telescope, operate in tandem when she makes poetry out of the world. As she tells her correspondent earlier in the same letter: "Should you ask my comprehension of a starlight Night, Awe were my only reply, and so of the mighty Book – It stills, incites, infatuates – blesses and blames in one. Like Human Affection, we dare not touch it, yet flee, what else remains?"

III
MARIANNE MOORE

6

Rightly Dividing the Word of Truth

Marianne Moore in Her Reformed Tradition

Born in 1887, a year after Dickinson's death, Marianne Moore came of age at the same time as the dismantling of the old Reformation faiths in the textual meta-narratives of Bible and creed.[1] During her lifetime as a devout Presbyterian, the denomination began to unravel itself in debates over the textual hermeneutics of historical accuracy, inspiration, and "literal" supernaturalism versus materialist or mythic interpretations of biblical events. What began in the 1880s as disagreements over how or whether to revise the Westminster Confession of Faith in the light of discoveries about evolution quickly became focal points of dissension in seminaries and divinity schools. By the time of World War I, the moderate voices in the Presbyterian Church were beginning to be drowned out by rising insistence on taking an inflexible stance either for or against the claims of higher criticism and its concomitant Enlightenment views of historicity. These controversies would culminate with the reorganization of Princeton in 1929 as a more liberal, progressive institution, and with the establishment of Westminster Seminary as the new bastion of what had previously been termed "Princeton Scholasticism." In general, as one church historian recounts,

> the Presbyterian controversy was one major aspect of the wider fundamentalist-modernist controversy of the era. . . . In the intellectual arena, the advent of Darwinism, historicism, higher criticism of the Scriptures, and comparative religion all strained traditional modes of thought. These intellectual changes were aggravated by massive social

> alterations in America. The rise of the city, vast immigration, rapid industrialization, and the gradual secularization of the culture changed the face of the nation. (Longfield 4–5)

One of the most profound issues at stake in these religious debates was the question of the trustworthiness of language itself. To what extent is not just biblical language but all language a reliable vessel of truth or an adequate bridge between the literal and the figural, the physical and the spiritual? Might it still serve as a numinous space where opposite categories can mysteriously overlap, or is language valuable only insofar as it contains a "literal," scientific, or historically verifiable truth? Ironically, as Hans Frei and other biblical scholars have pointed out, both the right-leaning fundamentalists and the left-leaning, Enlightenment-inspired higher critics seemed to agree on one thing: biblical language must be pinned down.

Somewhere in this fray we might locate Marianne Moore, a poet's poet who was no nominal Easter-churchgoing Protestant. As the maternal granddaughter of one Presbyterian minister and the sister of another, she spent much of her lifetime attending midweek Bible groups and Sunday services, actively participating in the community of her local congregations and the tradition of Sabbath rest, and striking up personal friendships with church leaders and their families. As a young child, Moore lived with her mother and brother in her grandfather, the Reverend John Riddle Warner's, First Presbyterian parsonage in Kirkwood, Missouri, until his death in 1894. Two years later the family moved to Carlisle, Pennsylvania, where they attended Second Presbyterian Church for twenty years until her brother Warner, by then a Presbyterian minister himself and later a naval chaplain, was offered a pastorate of his own in Chatham, New Jersey, in 1916; Moore and her mother subsequently lived with Warner at the Ogden Memorial Church parsonage until 1918. After some years of sporadic church attendance while living in Greenwich Village, and after deciding to settle permanently in Brooklyn following Warner's relocation with the navy, Moore and her mother began regularly attending Lafayette Avenue Presbyterian Church in 1935. Although Moore left Brooklyn a few years before she died, she remained close friends with her final pastor there, the Reverend George Litchfield, until her death in 1972. While Moore's letters and writings display a characteristic reluctance to adopt the language of religious rhetoric in an enthusiastically personal way (at least until her later years), the beliefs constantly expressed by the two people to whom she was the closest, her mother and brother, are noteworthy for their religious fervor. Her mother, Mary Warner Moore, was ardently evangelical in her beliefs, publishing a volume of her father's sermons at her own expense in 1895 and viewing her own life and the lives of her two children as marked by God's special calling; her brother John Warner Moore, who at one point in his career served as the chaplain to Admiral Chester Nimitz and the Pacific Fleet, was also deeply pious and often commented in his letters to Moore on the spiritual aspects of her poetry.

Moore's engagement with the Reformed tradition was intellectual as well as cultural and familial. Her notebooks, letters, prose, and poem notes show that she read widely in the works of Christian thinkers from Augustine's *Confessions* and Calvin's *Letters* to the writings of the modern-day mystics Jacques Maritain and Evelyn Underhill and the theologian Reinhold Niebuhr. Moore's eclectic spiritual readings, too many to enumerate here, also include John Bunyan's *Pilgrim's Progress,* Thomas Browne's *Religio Medici,* Edward Topsell's *Historie of Foure-Footed Beastes,* Pascal's *Pensées,* the poetry of George Herbert and Henry Vaughan, Lancelot Andrewes's sermons, and Jeremy Taylor's devotional manuals.[2] In addition to the Bible, of particular influence on Moore's thinking are three works that she quoted prominently in her poetry: Bible commentaries by the Free Church of Scotland scholars A. R. Gordon (*Poets of the Old Testament*) and George Adam Smith (*The Book of the Twelve Prophets, Commonly Called the Minor*), and *The Saint's Everlasting Rest,* by the seventeenth-century Puritan Richard Baxter. This last work, a devotional manual that focuses on the Four Last Things (death, judgment, heaven, and hell), was an extremely popular aid to meditation in its day and is listed by Jonathan Edwards in his own reading catalogue.

The overlap in Moore's strong grounding in the Augustinian Reformed classics with Edwards's own readings a century and a half before is not as anachronistic as it may sound. No doubt Moore's devotional and meditative readings were influenced or directed not only by her mother but also by her early religious leaders. In her formative years, Presbyterian ministers such as her grandfather and the Reverend Dr. George Norcross (Moore's close family friend and pastor in Carlisle until she was twenty-two) had been trained before the 1880s, in the same era as Emily Dickinson's contemporaries, at a time when there was still a strong emphasis on reading the Reformers. (Indeed, Moore's Reverend Norcross and Dickinson's Reverend Wadsworth in all likelihood shared some of the same professors at Princeton, including the renowned propositional theologian Charles Hodge, the arch-nemesis of Horace

Bushnell.) These Civil War– and Reconstruction-era pastors were not only steeped in the Reformed classics but also chiefly influenced by the propositionally based theology that became known as Princeton Scholasticism, a system of doctrines emphasizing the authority of the Bible and a mode of hermeneutics emphasizing the rational, literal, and commonsensical levels of interpretation.

Poised as she was at the end of nineteenth-century religious thought and at the beginning of the twentieth, Moore was enabled by her personal background to draw upon both forward- and backward-glancing predilections to create her poetic milieus. On the one hand, Moore was deeply familiar with traditional Reformed hermeneutics, history, and theology; on the other, she was exposed early on to contemporaneous conflicts in the Presbyterian Church concerning the role and function of scriptural language in relation to scientific discoveries, hermeneutical strategies, and the authority and inspiration of the Bible. In unfolding the theological proclivities of the three pastors with whom Moore most closely associated in her early years (her grandfather Warner, the Reverend George Norcross, and the Reverend E. H. Kellogg, who replaced Norcross in Carlisle after the latter's retirement in 1909), however, I do not mean to argue that their beliefs were synonymous with Moore's. Rather, I wish to show how assumptions about the way language worked in Moore's formative contexts have bearing on her beliefs about the functions of language as a poet. Moore's characteristic equipoise between the natural and spiritual worlds in her poetry might be traced back to blueprints given her in her first thirty years for ways to navigate the conflicts between supernatural, Christocentric interpretive frameworks versus materialist ones, and the tension on the reader reception continuum between literalist and mythic notions of scriptural intent.

Moore's maternal grandfather, the Reverend Dr. John Riddle Warner (1827–1894), trained at Duquesne College (a forerunner of the University of Pittsburgh) and the Theological Seminary of the Associate Reformed Church, and as a young man led several churches in the Gettysburg, Pennsylvania, area in the period leading up to and during the Civil War. He was invited to the First Presbyterian Church in Kirkwood, Missouri, in 1867 after giving a well-received lecture on his Civil War experiences in St. Louis. (Moore never knew her maternal grandmother, who died of typhoid fever after the battle of Gettysburg in 1863.) Moore, of course, could hardly be expected to have remembered any of her grandfather's preaching, but she doubtless read the book of his sermons published by her mother; Moore's biographer Linda Leavell notes that Moore recalls in her unpublished memoirs that, when she was a child, the book seemed to her "as verity itself" (quoted in *Holding*, 37). The sermons are indicative of some of the firmly held family values that manifest themselves throughout Moore's life. For instance, Reverend Warner took very conservative stances against gambling, drinking, and Sabbath-breaking, even to the extent of discouraging parishioners from reading the Sunday paper or traveling by train on that day (since both practices kept people employed on the Sabbath). He frequently urged his listeners to diligence (on non-Sabbath days), and especially to work toward God's specific calling in each person's life; parents are reminded that they are to be sensitive to each child's individual life mission (a tendency scholars have frequently noted in Mary Warner's letters).

Another very formative model for Moore's own understanding of Reformed hermeneutics was the Reverend Dr. George Norcross (1838–1915), pastor of Second Presbyterian Church in Carlisle, Pennsylvania, from 1869 to 1909, the church Moore and her family attended for nearly twenty years, when Moore was roughly between the ages of ten and thirty, until she and her mother moved to New Jersey to join Warner. The Moore and Norcross families were friends, and Leavell's biography documents that Moore's mother and the Norcross's daughter Mary were lovers for a time. Mary Norcross, included in early exchanges of personal family letters, greatly influenced Marianne Moore's decision to attend her alma mater, Bryn Mawr, rather than the more local Dickinson College, and she tutored Moore for the college entrance exams. The Reverend Norcross, whom a 1905 Cumberland County biographical record describes as "eloquent and scholarly" and "a man of acknowledged learning and culture," was a church historian and a leader in the Presbyterian Church at the regional, national, and international levels ("Rev. George Norcross, D.D."). Well grounded in the Princeton Scholasticism, he graduated from Princeton Theological School in 1868 and was recognized for his subsequent accomplishments with an honorary Doctor of Divinity, also from Princeton, in 1879. During his forty years as pastor at Second Presbyterian, the church—like Dickinson's First Congregational Church in Amherst—saw three periods of evangelical revival, when larger numbers of people than usual converted to Christianity: 1875, 1876, and sometime around 1893.

When Norcross retired in 1909, the leaders of the church chose as his replacement the Reverend Edwin Henry Kellogg (1880–1942), a young Princeton academician with whom Moore also became friends and whose 1914 Bible class figures largely in the notes to several of Moore's important poems of the 1910s and 1920s. Moore directly quotes Kellogg or books from the class in at least eight poems, all written or revised between 1915 and 1924, including her two longest poems, "Marriage" and "An Octopus," and the impress of his focus on the Old Testament prophets is felt in many other contemporaneous poems in which she does not directly quote Kellogg or his texts. Kellogg's seven-year tenure at Second Presbyterian (1909–1916), in fact, was the only pastorate he ever held; he left Carlisle to attend Hartford Theological Seminary for his Ph.D. in church history the same year the Moore family departed.

Although more than fifty years elapsed between John Riddle Warner's birth and Kellogg's, owing to their common roots in Princeton Scholasticism, the three pastors shared a remarkable number of affinities in their approach to the Bible. All were the product of systematic Scholastic theological training and common sense interpretive philosophies that were the standard at Princeton and elsewhere for decades. (Where Kellogg, who spent a year at the University of Berlin in 1907, differed significantly from Warner and Norcross is discussed in chapter 7.) One commonality was that they all, as had Presbyterian ministers for centuries, embraced engagement with culture and science. This was because "more so than most other Christians, Reformed believers insisted that God's kingdom was permeating this world. Calvinists declared that because God was sovereign, Christians must labor to bring all culture under his dominion" (Smith, *Seeds* 47). It was not until the fundamentalist-modernist controversies became intensely divisive in the 1920s and 1930s that fundamentalist insistence on the Bible as literal, scientific truth became problematic for the earlier mindset. Until then, like the Congregationalist Edward Hitchcock and the other scientist theologians at Amherst College and elsewhere, Reformed ministers advocated what might be termed "theistic evolution." For instance, in 1868 (the same year Norcross graduated from Princeton Seminary), the Princeton College president, James McCosh, would affirm that "evolution was an organized process, guided by God, working toward one final end"; at the same time, President McCosh "denounced naturalistic expositions of evolution and urged Christians to separate the truth of Darwin's theory from its error" (Smith, *Seeds* 97).[3]

Consequently, Reverend Warner would take occasion to remind his listeners that as long as God is acknowledged as a First Cause, "we must all admit our indebtedness to the researches of science" for creating "instruments of blessing in providing for our comfort and in protecting us from danger" (Warner 203). Such ease in moving between the natural and supernatural worlds can also be seen in Norcross's 1876 New Year's sermon, in which he speaks in the Edwardsean sense of the "book of nature" wherein "all the broad fields of science glow with evidences of divine wisdom to all who are not willfully blind. . . . Human science reaches no point where the divine wisdom has not anticipated its march" (*New Year's* 4, 15). In light of the sermons of both Warner and Norcross, it is clear that Marianne Moore did not grow up in an environment where culture, science, and faith were considered to be at all at cross-purposes.

One reason why Moore's Presbyterian pastors did not feel that scientific advances undermined the authority of the Bible was that, although their theology was chiefly rational and propositional, Princeton Scholasticism still allowed that the ultimate authority of Scripture rested in its spiritual message, not in its role as a final arbiter of scientific or historical truth. This was in accord with the doctrines of Princeton Scholasticism, which asserted that "the Bible was God's written word; it was a genuine product of human activity that could be studied historically; yet the Bible was also the presentation of the most perfect truth in all that its human authors (under the inspiration of the Holy Spirit) meant to affirm; it was effective in doing the converting and sanctifying work of the Spirit" (Noll, "Princeton" 21). As to questions of the precise nature of that truth—how it was originally conveyed to its human authors and how it might be demarcated and so protected from external attack—many ministers of Norcross's generation were still content to leave them as mysteries with somewhat permeable boundaries. The notion of "verbal inspiration" was not codified until the late 1880s, the concept of strict "inerrancy" was not officially embraced by the Presbyterian ruling body until 1910, and the term "fundamentalism" was not stamped with its present associations until 1920 (Longfield). Warner's sermons indicate that he found no need to press the text for absolute historical or scientific truths, and he acknowledges that "'the existence of difficulties,' as it has been well said, is inseparable from any revelation which is short of infinite. All perplexities arise from imperfect knowledge. . . . 'I could not believe the Bible to be the Word of God . . . if it contained nothing but what I could comprehend'" (Warner 79). Or as Norcross phrases it in the 1889 *Centennial Memorial of the Presbytery of Carlisle* (a two-volume work which he both edited and contributed to), "the Bible, as the original source of Revelation, must be the court of final appeal in all cases of conscience" (as opposed to matters of a scientific nature) (412).

Consequently, Moore's pastors modeled a hermeneutic that approached the Bible as a literary whole. It was a text unified by the theme of salvation through the reader's relationship to Christ and self-authenticated by personal experience and by the common threads of this theme located within the disparate individual books of the Old and New Testaments. Such practices developed, in the words of Emily Dickinson, ways of "nimble believing" and reading. Reformed practitioners of this era approached the Bible less from a position of seeking to answer questions of historical veracity and more toward one of generatively locating and unifying aspects of the salvific message and orienting themselves within the broader narratives of that message. In keeping with this tradition, Moore's grandfather Warner declares in one sermon that when the Bible is "read . . . as God gave it to be read," that is, through daily reverential study and meditation, it becomes an important part of the believer's transformational, signifying relationship with Christ; the reader's "very blood, as it were, . . . [becomes] inoculated with divine truth" (44). It is in this notion of reading the Bible as a kind of direct medium of relational communion (and not in the sense of a fascination with the fixed, literal words on the page) that Warner is able to state, "To me the Bible is nothing if it be not, from first to last, all of Christ" (212).

Warner was not a traditional Calvinist in the sense of holding to the old beliefs of predestination (he emphasizes the role of individual choice in conversion, which could be a "marked" or "a gradual process") nor to creedal identity ("the question of the day to us each personally is not, Am I Calvinist or Arminian, ritualist or dissenter? But is, Have I felt sin, and, having felt it before the Searcher of hearts, do I honestly confess it?") (140, 173). ("Sin is a subject on which I am an expert," Moore once wrote in a letter to Ezra Pound in which she recommends the style of Calvin's commentaries and letters) (*Letters* 259). Warner's sermons, however, do show the influence of the Edwardsean strain of emphasis on inner transformation, and even of Edwards's vocabulary, such as when he refers to the "simple, old-fashioned term, 'A change of heart'" and "the heart's affections" (141, 142). Like Jonathan Edwards, Warner stresses the importance of "full, deep experimental knowledge" of God which leads to a kind of spiritual seeing as a type of moral and signifying relation (142). Furthermore, like Edwards, Warner advocates a transformational sort of being-as-becoming that is the ultimate end of these desires. The believer, "renewed in the spirit of his mind . . . [b]ecomes like God, loving what He loves and hating what He hates," so that "the true nature of the great change can be known only by the subject himself from the workings of his own heart. The heart, not the acts of the body, is the seat of all good and evil" (140, 141). Many years later, Moore would find consanguinity on this ground with the Reformed theologian Reinhold Niebuhr, and the two would form similar ontologies of intent and desire (as I discuss in chapter 8).

Moreover, while the Princeton Scholastic theologians strongly emphasized the use of Scriptures as a source of learning right doctrine, unlike some of the later fundamentalists, they did not entirely ignore the earlier Reformed hermeneutics in which questions of literal and figurative meaning were much less likely to be set at loggerheads but were instead read as part of one larger narrative truth. Consequently, typological interpretation in Warner's sermons functions in the same manner as it did for Jonathan Edwards and the ministers in Amherst. For instance, in his sermon "The Christian in the World," Warner explains how, when Moses and the Israelites wandered in the desert for forty years, God "did . . . keep the symbol of the divine presence [the pillar of smoke and fire] where every Israelite could see it. It was at once a guide and a support. What to them was a type is to us a reality; what to them was but a symbol is with us a living, loving, substance" (48).[4]

Moore's notes for Kellogg's 1914–15 Bible class show that his thinking was, like her grandfather's, highly informed by the Edwardsean strains of not only typology but also the transformative spiritual route of the heart from knowing to seeing to being. Moore transcribes Kellogg's allusions to such common New Testament typological constructions and "shadows of divine things" (to quote Edwards) as the casting of Jesus as the "second Adam" and the Hebrews 9 description of the sacrifice of animals by the Jewish high priest as prefiguring Christ's death on the cross: "It is impossible that the blood of bulls and goats should take away sin—those are all shadows in this world of imag[ination] and sense," Kellogg lectures.[5] Furthermore, Moore's notes indicate that Kellogg frequently discussed (as does the Reverend Warner in his sermon about "the heart's affections") a modernized version of Calvin's *sensus suavitatis* (which Edwards terms the "sense of the heart"). For Calvin and Edwards, this was the idea that a person must have a regenerate "heart" (knowing) before he or she can have insight into the ways of God (seeing); this apperception comes by divine revelation rather than natural reasoning and is accompanied by a sense of joy and peace (being).[6] In a remarkably similar vein to Edwards and Warner, Kellogg comments on the importance of a change of heart as well, commenting, "It is only God can give the broken heart—a man can't break his own heart." Moreover, he continues, there is as a "result of this fellowship with God, inward peace and freedom and this peace and freedom [are] reflected in the outward life." Again, in the same vein as Edwards, Kellogg asserts that the "broken heart" and "regenerated reason" applies to the perception of nature as well. In the same spirit that the psalmist recollects the "thunderstorm as the voice of the Lord on earth," and that Isaiah 6 declares that "the fullness of the whole earth is his glory," Kellogg asserts, "we only hear the flood shout glory when our own hearts shout glory."

One area in which Kellogg differed significantly from his predecessors was in his acceptance of the newer forms of biblical criticism. But in taking their earlier stances in favor of the traditional Reformed posture of accepting the divinely revealed internal proof of Scriptures as the best evidence for the Bible's inspiration, both Warner and Norcross were highly aware of dissenting views within their church and acknowledged these tensions to their congregations in sermons. Warner's reverence for the intertextual relationships of the Old and New Testaments as a canonical whole no doubt accounts for part of his distress with what he terms "the criticism of the day" in an undated address to a ministerial association in St. Louis (210). This criticism, "which so insidiously assails the Word of the Lord," Warner declares, "is in the largest part *not modern*. Old theories which have been exploded long ago are revived, newly dressed, and recommended to the religious world" (210). It is unclear what scholarship Warner is specifically critiquing here, but it is most likely the work of late nineteenth-century German higher critics such as David Strauss and Ludwig Feuerbach, whose theories drew upon the Enlightenment thinkers to insist that the Bible must first be interpreted as historical texts making either reliable or unreliable historical claims, and not primarily as narratives. Warner characterizes such critics as too culturally accommodationist; where they see something in Scripture they feel is "beneath the culture of the day; [they] cut it out. You will find as you search it commands which cannot be obeyed, incompatible with our advanced civilization. Cut them out, and what matters it that the knife may go right through the decalogue?" (211). ("An anthology of the Bible is not the Bible," writes Marianne Moore in the *Dial* in 1925) (*CPr* 237). For Warner, "given, as is all the Scripture, by inspiration of God, we cannot use the knife on any part, even of that which, for want of a better term, we call the 'imprecatory Scriptures.' . . . God is the author of all dispensations; the one loving spirit broods over and breathes through them" (212).

By 1909, when Reverend Norcross of Carlisle gave his fortieth-anniversary and retirement sermon, "Forty Years in the Wilderness," the moderate voices in the Presbyterian Church were beginning to be drowned out by rising insistence on taking an inflexible stance either for or against the claims of higher criticism and the concomitant Enlightenment views of historicity according to which, as Gary Dorrien explains in *The Making of American Liberal Theology*, "all claims to truth, in theology as in other disciplines, must be made on the basis of reason and experience, not by appeal to external authority. Christian scripture may be recognized as spiritually authoritative within Christian experience, but its word does not settle or establish truth claims about matters of fact" (1). In 1910 the Presbyterian General Assembly would respond to the growing dissent by affirming "five points" of fundamental (or core) belief to the Presbyterian Church: inerrancy, virgin birth, vicarious atonement, bodily resurrection, and miracles. Addressing these increasing tensions, Norcross says in his final sermon as head pastor of Carlisle:

> We have been passing through a period of theological unrest and many are fond of calling it "a period of transition," but when the fogs are blown away, it will be found that the foundations are standing sure where Christ and his apostles laid them. Being thoroughly convinced of this, your pastor has tried to contend earnestly for the faith once delivered to the saints; and he trusts that none of his flock have wandered away into the bogs of modern scepticism. (*Forty Years* 16–17)

Which "bogs of modern scepticism" might have seemed most dangerous to Norcross can be surmised from several clues in the sermon. At one moment, for instance, he seems to be responding to controversies of authorship, dating, and the textual form of the Pentateuch:

> Some modern scholars, of the sceptical school, tell us that forty years to the Hebrew mind meant a long but indefinite period of duration. However, there is no chance here to pick a flaw in the inspired record. The forty years in the wilderness had seen a generation die and vanish from the earth. Only two mature men of the vast host, which set out from Egypt, passed over Jordan dry-shod and set their triumphant feet in the land of promise. (8–9)

The internal consistency of the story, in other words, convinces Norcross that the story of Moses and Joshua is literal (though not only literal), and not solely mythic.

Although (as will be examined in chapter 7) Moore's second pastor at Carlisle, the Reverend E. H. Kellogg, was far more adept at higher criticism and employed it as a tool for scriptural study, like his predecessors from Princeton before him, he too asserts that internal evidence as revealed to individual and corporate believers by supernaturally given knowing is the greatest proof for the spiritual veracity of Scripture. In his 1933 anniversary sermon celebrating the one-hundredth anniversary of Second Presbyterian of Carlisle, he cites Jonathan Edwards as an exemplar of a Reformed embrace of internal evidence:

> As even that sturdy and stern old Calvinist, Jonathan Edwards, long ago said (whom I believe I quoted to you to this effect when I last spoke to you here sixteen years ago) "the" (Church's) "Gospel of the blessed God does not go about begging for its evidence" (either in Scripture or in argument) "as much as some think. It has," as he said, "its highest and most proper evidence in *itself*." I add to Jonathan Edwards this, that it lives in power in the unity of the universal Church. (Kellogg 8)

Despite the controversies of her era, when Moore writes directly about the Bible in her prose, she is much less interested in questions of scholarship, authority, and inspiration than in the importance of the Bible to sustaining belief and to its formative role in the rhythms of her own thought, life, and poetry. For instance, in a tongue-in-cheek nod to her upbringing, she admits to having "an imagination based on the Child's Bible" in a 1933 review of an art film; late in life she relates that each morning, "whether infirm or not, [she reads] a few lines calculated to counteract infirmity, from the Bible usually, as stabilizing 'the innocency of our lives and the constancy of our faith'" (the quote is from the Book of Common Prayer) (*CPr* 310, 660–61). During her years with *The Dial,* in addition to reviewing Bible helps and literary translations, Moore insists on the importance of accurate references to the Bible in the books she reviews. She sternly corrects Vachel Lindsay for imprecision ("to speak of 'Christ, the beggar,' is inexact since it has never been said of Christ that he begged; he did without") and sharply reproves Maxwell Bodenheim as "self-deceived or willingly a charlatan": "Our anger is stirred by his epitome of Christ's 'mistakes' in emancipating humanity. He says Christ approved the repressing of instinct and that he 'told people to believe with their feelings and let their minds go on a vacation'" (*CPr* 86, 103–4).

In particular, Moore writes several times during her career of how fond she is of the King James Version, and how—for herself—the translation's rhythms and meanings are inseparable. Rhythm was Moore's lifeblood as a poet: as she remarks in a 1938 piece on poetry in the *Oxford Anthology of American Literature,* "I feel that the form is the outward equivalent of a determining inner conviction, and that the rhythm is the person" (*CPr*

645). She reiterates this notion in her 1944 essay "Feeling and Precision," in which she offers the King James Version as one of several exemplary texts that marries "feeling" and "precision": "You don't devise a rhythm, the rhythm is the person, and the sentence but the radiograph of personality" (396). Thus, when she writes in 1960 that she "can scarcely read the Bible without forsaking content for rhythm," as an example of what she calls her own "rhythmic eccentricities," she means not that she read the Bible as poetic form divorced from its substance, but that, as with all poetry for her, the rhythms of the King James had come to signify "the person" and "the determining inner conviction" inextricably tied to and behind the Bible's meanings (518). (In her 1956 University of California lecture "Idiosyncrasy and Technique," Moore says, "The rhythms of the King James Version of the Bible stand forever as writing, although certain emendations as to meaning seem obligatory." Moore follows by obligingly citing her Lafayette Avenue Presbyterian pastor Dr. Alvin Magary, who had recommended the accuracy of James Moffat's translation—then returns to the KJV in the rest of her lecture) (507).

For Moore, faith was less a verbal profession than the actions one undertakes because one trusts that what one believes is true; she consistently lauds the virtues of fortitude, humility, hope, empathy, truthfulness, commitment to others' freedom, and courageous submission of self to God as evidences of deep Christian belief. Consequently, Moore rarely wrote directly and confessionally about the specific contours of her own faith, although throughout her poetry and prose the impress of her Reformed lineage, her years of participation in the Presbyterian Church, and her wide spiritual readings are evident. More specifically, and because of these affinities with the Reformed hermeneutical traditions, she affirms throughout her long oeuvre the same trajectory of spiritual knowing as dynamic revelation, aesthetic seeing as signifying relation, and ontological being as ethical becoming that are found in the typological thinking of not only Jonathan Edwards and Emily Dickinson but also her grandfather Warner and subsequent pastors Norcross and Kellogg. Like her fellow heirs of the Reformed tradition, Moore locates the origin of spiritual knowledge outside herself: "The Bible is a book inspiring a faith which—beyond the power of self-discipline—growing from darkness, leads to the place of understanding; as the Patriarch Job said, 'Behold the fear of the Lord, that is wisdom,'" she writes in a commemoration of the retirement of Dr. Magary (*CPr* 654). Elsewhere, in a church bulletin meditating on "Conscience," she terms this phenomenon "spiritual apperception" and then links the directional aesthetics of desire (seeing-as-signification) with ontological being-as-becoming (*CPr* 651). Quoting her friend W. H. Auden's well-known praise of Grimms' fairy tales as an example of the importance of following the moral conscience, Moore cites that "wishes for good and evil are terribly real"; that is, desires themselves have real spiritual implications and consequences in the direction one chooses to head in life.[7] The hero in a fairy tale succeeds, Auden (and Moore) continue, because he admits to the need for spiritual knowledge outside himself (he has "a humility which admits that he cannot succeed without Divine Grace"), because he orients himself in hopeful relation to the Other ("secondly, a faith which believes that Grace will help him"), and because he chooses to embody the process of relation to the Other through identification with the path the Other chooses for him ("lastly, he succeeds through willingness to accept suffering") (651–52). Moore ends the meditation with her own observation: "To summarize: Choice is inescapable; and with the aid of humility in subordinating self-will to God's will—to the voice of the ages alive in us through Christ—the spirit attains *true* freedom, in which it continues to live and not die" (652).

All this is not to suggest, of course, that Moore's own renditions of the natural world are frankly devotional or even broadly Presbyterian, but rather that the intricate ethical, aesthetic, and philosophical complexities of Moore's poetry reflect a sustained engagement throughout her long career with an equally complex Reformed hermeneutic, a tradition that was in many ways complementary rather than contradictory to the American modernism that she helped to define through her writing, influence, and editorship at *The Dial.* Moore carves out of the basic philosophical framework of the Reformed tradition a conceptual structure of her own on which to hang the elements of perceiver, natural object, and spiritual implication. Informed by the basic sensibilities of a worldview that insists on the distinctions between, yet mysterious interrelatedness among, humanity, the created universe, and God, Moore positioned herself as a detached observer of nature in the face of not only the romantic lyric tradition but also a masculine modernist sensibility in many ways still akin to the Sublime. While, as she writes in "Light Is Speech," "Free frank/impartial sunlight, moonlight,/starlight, lighthouse light,/are language"—perhaps a language akin to divine language of Edwards's natural types—such "Speech" is a hieroglyphic communication available for multiple interpretations, but not appropriation, and only at an artistic remove (*CP* 97).

The work of delineating the deep structure of this philosophical association was started by Elisa New. In the final chapter of *The Line's Eye*, "Work, Works, Working: Edwards, Moore, and Frost," for instance, New traces the connection between the curse placed on the builders of the Tower of Babel for exalting their labor above God (Genesis 11) and thus "divinizing creativity" with Moore's own countercultural construction of a "propriety" that resists the notion of labor for the sake of its own glorification (263). Moore's "propriety," New asserts, "is not . . . a behavior performed or a work executed but rather the essential and dynamic realization of Being in creative action" (293). Throughout her book, New rightly links this dynamism to Moore's association with a philosophical tradition begun with Jonathan Edwards and his idea of being's consent to being, the belief in ontology as harmonious relation rather than solipsistic essence.

Such correspondences between Edwards and Moore, I argue in the following two chapters, come not from Moore's reading of Edwards but from theological and philosophical cognates arising through their shared heritage of Augustinian and Calvinist biblical interpretation. This common tradition may be detected in Moore's own modernist hermeneutics for reading the Book of Nature; her ethical constructions of the relationship between nature, the self, and the moral/spiritual realm have a number of striking affinities with Edwards's natural typology. Considering Moore's depictions of animals and plants alongside the contours of Edwards's philosophically constructed types illumines why neither the label of "symbol" nor that of "emblem" has been a comfortable fit for describing what happens in a Moore poem and why, as numerous scholars have pointed out, her natural world belongs in neither a romantic nor a skeptical universe. We cannot finally pinpoint the conceptual line that separates the material and the ideal or the sacred and the secular in Moore's poetry because she herself made no such distinction. For Moore, all entities, be they natural, cultural, or technological, have the dynamic, semiotic, and spiritual possibility of signifying beyond themselves and, in so signifying, or "surrendering," as she puts it in "What Are Years?," they find their "continuing": "This is mortality,/this is eternity" (*CP* 95). Significance, identity, and meaning in Moore's poetry are created by contiguous relation; in some sense, every part of Moore's universe is connected to every other in a relationship that neither denies individual difference nor sets up an absolute dichotomy between spirit and flesh.

7

"Part Terrestrial, and Part Celestial"

"The Real" and "The Actual" in Moore's Revisionist Typology

Although the times were tragic for her denomination, it was, ironically, felicitous for Moore the poet to come of age during a period of increasing disunity in the Presbyterian Church concerning the function of words and the Word. As outlined in chapter 6, early twentieth-century disputes over biblical criticism ultimately led to hermeneutical schism between the fundamentalists' insistence on the literal mode of interpretation and the modernists' privileging of questions of historical veracity above narrative integrity. Moore's young adult training in these competing strands of the Reformed hermeneutic tradition in fact provided her a set of tools with which she would fashion her in-between poetic spaces—spaces where the biological, the symbolic, and the ideal are held in equal relation. The precise manner in which Moore positions objects in the natural realm between the material and ideal—and the *implications* thereof—has historically been a subject of contention among her critics.[1] The crux of this perplexing tension stems from the way Moore's plants and animals can celebrate the materiality and indeterminacy of the biological world and at the same time gesture toward a codified universal meaning that would seem to bring her spontaneity to a dead-ended symbolism. While Moore freely associates and overlays the natural, physical realm with the conceptual, the citizens of her natural world are reduced neither to allegorical figures nor to timeworn, conventional emblems or tropes; the referents maintain their "thingness" even as they signify a transitory meaning beyond themselves.

In *The Poetry of Marianne Moore: A Study in Voice and Value,* Margaret Holley observes that Moore's poetic is in fact predicated on her decision to reveal the material/ideal pairing as a false dichotomy. She writes, "Moore's project may be preliminarily described as an effort to push past polarization of the factual and non-factual dimensions of our discourse" (80); Moore is able to accomplish this because "meaningful free play depends on conventions of usage as much as on inspired deviation. This meaningfulness of language in use dissolves the dualism of facts versus values by conveying the sense of one through the medium of the other" (99). Specifically, in Moore's animal poetry, Holley finds that "the emblematic equation and the process of behavioral observation are antithetical approaches which Moore juxtaposes as a way of yoking together different dimensions of her subject, the idealized and the real" (129). Holley's observations on the poet's postmodern revisualization of these categories are illuminating, for they point toward Moore's iconoclastic epistemological system that refuses to distinguish between being and doing, and between action and ethic. Likewise, David Kadlec identifies a link between Moore's ethics and her studied confluence of the material realm with the symbolic. Examining Moore's oeuvre particularly in the light of her close reading of William James, John Dewey, and Charles Darwin, he finds that "Moore's poetry is . . . marked by a deliberate effort to adapt the conceptual premises of modern genetics to language and semiotics" (154). Kadlec goes on to explain how "Moore derived from modern genetic theory an aesthetic of wayward semantic leaps that enabled her to uniquely confront the essentialist logic of modern eugenics, or the science of racial engineering" (155). By contriving an "aesthetic of accident" rather than humanly driven genetic selection, he continues, Moore's poetic of "contingency showed her that ethical positions could be powerfully significant not when they were written in stone but when they were adopted as choices" (156, 155).

Robin Schulze, also basing her work on a careful study of Moore's extensive reading of biologists and naturalists, convincingly asserts that Moore's "verse . . . ruminates on the intersection between nature and culture, on the issue of human use and misuse of the natural world and the cost *to nature* of human ignorance and arrogance" ("Imperious Ox" 5). Schulze finds that Moore's Christian beliefs are chiefly expressed in an "environmental ethic" in her nature poetry; while Moore "flirt[s] with the ideas that nature constitutes a legible sign system of the divine mind," Schulze maintains, "the question that drives Moore's . . . [poetry] is *not* the divine order of nature but the order that man hath wrought *upon* nature in the apparent absence of a discernible divinity" (11). Kadlec's and Schulze's astute observations concerning Moore's "aesthetic of accident" and "environmental ethic" offer key insights into the way the poet applied her broadly based scientific knowledge.[2] Yet, as I will show, Moore's affirmation of ethics, ecology, and the modern difficulties of interpreting natural signs is not necessarily in opposition to her equally complex affirmation of the unseen; Moore is no disillusioned Emily Dickinson, writing in a universe where only absence may "ornament/His Absent Character" (F953). The ostrich, the jerboa, the frigate pelican, the pangolin, to name a few, all function within her poems both as signs differentiated from their symbolic contexts by their inherent otherness and mystery in connection to the natural world and as signifiers gesturing beyond themselves toward multiple possibilities of imaginatively constructed meaning, including the spiritual. They are not symbol or Platonic correspondence but something else altogether.

In short, Moore has lifted a metaphysics of Reformed natural typology from its overtly Christian contexts and brought it into literary modernism, an important poetic strategy that her critics have not yet engaged. By foregrounding the signifying and polysemous aspects of language, Moore bifurcates the antitype away from Christ to Judeo-Christian attributes, spiritual principles, and moral truths; by emphasizing multiple subjectivities and metonymic contiguity over metaphor and narrative experience, she shifts our aesthetic experience of the poems away from a revelatory sense of the heart to an epiphanic sense of the ethical. All the while, like Jonathan Edwards's model of the attractive bond between atoms that holds them at once together and apart, Moore's newly revised types retain ontological, semiotic, and epistemological characteristics that prevent either the complete separation of, or the collapse of boundaries between, nature, observer, and the abstract realm of spiritual ideas.

In this chapter I trace the philosophical and hermeneutical fingerprints of what would become Moore's revisionist natural typology to a 1914 Bible class taught by her pastor, the Reverend E. H. Kellogg. The class provided Moore a timely middle way to navigate between the Scylla and Charybdis of nineteenth-century Princeton Scholasticism that she inherited from her grandfather, the Reverend John Warner, and her childhood pastor, the Reverend George Norcross, on the one hand and the new historical and higher criticisms that called many of their assumptions about biblical inspiration and interpretation into question on the other. Kellogg's brand of neoorthodox theology—termed "believing criticism"—offered a return to the hermeneutics of Augustine, Calvin, and Edwards that avoided the polarization of the traditionalist and progressivist camps. In so doing, it made a limited embrace of the new historical and higher criticisms while at the same time shifting emphasis from the Scholastic view of reason leading to faith toward a renewed embrace of the Augustinian *crede ut intelligas,* faith enlightening reason. The connections between Moore, Kellogg, and the believing critics that she studied during the class have never before been uncovered, yet the ontological, teleological, and ethical implications of their hermeneutics color Moore's thinking throughout her literary career. I outline some of Moore's immediate personal and poetic replies to their philosophies, then trace her responses to their fullest expression in her so-called animal poems of the 1930s and 1940s. There, the "Real and the Actual" of the believing critics becomes reified to a "part terrestrial and part celestial" realm of language itself.

E. H. Kellogg's 1914–15 class at Second Presbyterian Church in Carlisle seems to have been a partial survey of the Old and New Testaments with emphasis on the Hebrew prophets, Christian apologetics, and general Reformed hermeneutics informed by some of the principles of higher criticism that were de rigueur in the early twentieth century. Moore retained the notes from Kellogg's class throughout her long life, directly referencing Kellogg and books from the class in at least eight poems written or revised between the years 1915 and 1924: "The Past Is the Present" (published in 1915 as "So far as the future is concerned . . ."), "Picking and Choosing" (1920), "In the Days of Prismatic Color" (her 1921 revision of the 1919 version), "Snakes, Mongooses, Snake-Charmers, and the Like" (1922), "Novices" (1923), "Marriage" (1923), "When I Buy Pictures" (her 1924 revision of the 1921 version), and "An Octopus" (1924). The influence of Kellogg's lectures and texts on Moore's thinking and poetry were manifold and long-lasting. In *Holding On Upside Down: The Life and Work of Marianne Moore,* Linda Leavell notes the importance of Kellogg to Moore, both personally and aesthetically, during their shared time in Carlisle, citing a 1909 letter Moore wrote to her brother in which she called Kellogg "a great marvel" (101). In "Marianne Moore and a Poetry of Hebrew (Protestant) Prophecy," Cristanne Miller has thoroughly outlined the ways in which many of Moore's poems between 1914 and 1924 bear the impress of the Old Testament Bible commentaries and study aids that Kellogg chose for the course. Miller finds that the focus in these books on the voice of the Hebrew prophet as truth-teller, as well as on the rhythmic and grammatical structures of the Hebrew language itself (commentators offered their own translations of the Old Testament texts), appealed both to Moore's poetic ear and to her desire to comment on matters of social justice from a position outside conventional Western norms. As Miller shows, a substantial number of Moore's poems from this era (many of which were left out of *Complete Poems*) "present Hebrew poet-prophecy as a model both for her stance as an ethical speaker addressing issues of contemporary public concern and, secondarily, for the anti-lyrical, prosaic, descriptive, but highly structured and cadenced forms of her poetry" (29).

Moore's ethical and aesthetic affinity with the Hebrew poets and prophets may be directly related to Kellogg's use of what was then cutting-edge biblical criticism in the course. Kellogg himself was a young academician, only seven years older than Moore, who had graduated from Princeton and studied in Germany before coming to serve as pastor at Second Presbyterian Church in Carlisle. Like Moore, Kellogg descended from a line of Reformed thinkers. His grandfather was also a pastor, and his father, Dr. Samuel H. Kellogg (1839–1899), was a renowned Presbyterian minister, theologian, Old Testament scholar, and linguist, who died when Kellogg was nineteen. Kellogg the elder published numerous books on biblical prophecy, a highly regarded translation of the Old Testament into Hindi, and a commentary on Leviticus included in the *Expositor's Bible* commentary set (the same set of commentaries from which Kellogg drew George Adam Smith's volume on the minor prophets for his class). Kellogg spent part of his childhood in India with his missionary parents, and, like his father, attended Princeton for both his undergraduate and seminary degrees (1902 and 1906 successively). He then spent a year studying philosophy of religion on a fellowship at the University of Berlin and another year in India doing mission work before answering Second Presbyterian's call in 1909. During his time as pastor in Carlisle, he seems to have discovered that his true calling was as a college professor; he concurrently taught biblical history as an adjunct professor at Dickinson College and at Wilson College (where he later became a trustee). After he completed his Ph.D. in 1918, he served as an assistant professor of biblical history and literature at Connecticut College and then in 1921 became professor of philosophy and religion at Skidmore College, where he remained until 1938.

Not surprisingly, Kellogg's stance toward higher criticism and notions of biblical inspiration were more modern than those held by Moore's grandfather Warner and the Reverend Norcross, the previous pastor at Second Presbyterian in Carlisle, both of whom had been trained in nineteenth-century historical scholarship. When Kellogg was invited back to Second Presbyterian to give its one-hundredth anniversary sermon in 1933 (a mere twenty-four years after Norcross's farewell sermon warning against "bogs of modern scepticism"), he would speak favorably of the contributions of "modern scholarship" to the Christian understanding of the Bible and caution against the hairsplitting debates the Protestant religion was so wont to get into ("arid scholasticism removed from real world-battles," he calls the nineteenth-century controversy over the imputation of sin) (Kellogg 3, 7).

Yet Kellogg was not precisely a higher critic; rather his writings, sermons, lectures, and choice of study books for his 1914 Bible class indicate that he closely aligned himself with the hermeneutical methodologies of the small group of Reformed moderates who came to be known as "reverent," "devout," or "believing critics." For the first three or four decades of the twentieth century, believing critics (most coming from Scotland and England, where the American fundamentalist-modernist divisions never gained much momentum) advocated an enthusiastic incorporation of the new textual and historical research into biblical studies, as long as it was done in such a way as not to undercut the Bible's trustworthiness concerning spiritual matters or what they believed to be the essential truths of Christ's historicity and the necessity of a Gospel-based faith in the Person of Christ. As the historian Mark Noll explains, these theologians and scholars

> occupied a position that counted as conservative within the academic context, but which represented a more complete accommodation to modern criticism than either British or American evangelicals accepted. . . . What these scholars had in common was a twin commitment to the divine character of Scripture and to the value of an unfettered research. For them, the results of a moderate criticism were given; but this did not entail a commitment to unbelieving rationalism, Hegelian evolution, Spencerian naturalism, or any of the major heterodox assumptions which had played such a large role among the nineteenth-century German critics. (*Between* 81)

This stance allowed a calling into question of the traditional interpretations of some of the miracles of the Old Testament, for instance, while still asserting a sort of "truthfulness" in the ancient manuscripts that was spiritual and poetic, if not always literally manifest in the physical realm. In general, as Noll recounts, they believed that as long as modern biblical research was "not predicated on the denial of the supernatural," such scholarship could "legitimately produce conclusions that overturn traditional . . . beliefs about the Bible," and that, conversely, it was possible that holding on to some notions of biblical inspiration could still be "compatible with reinterpretations of venerable positions" (158). In short, the believing critics sought to make a distinction between the received doctrines, or "dogma" (which was human interpretation of biblical texts and might be questioned), of the Protestant Church and the "revealed" truths of what they still believed to be a divine and sacred text. As Kellogg urged his former congregation in 1933, laypersons and seminarians alike should emphasize the Christ-centered aspects of the faith over the doctrinaire, for the universal church is the "trustee of the one 'dogma' which He is" (Kellogg 5).

Moore's exposure to the middle way of the believing critics came through several of the books she studied as part of Kellogg's 1914–15 class, as well as his lectures. The texts she lists for Kellogg's class are nearly all written by pastors and/or seminary professors in the Reformed Free Church of Scotland who were also turn-of-the-century participants in some fashion in the believing criticism movement. The most respected and well known of these is George Adam Smith (1856–1942). Moore quotes Smith's influential 1890 *Book of the Twelve Prophets, Commonly Called the Minor* prominently in "Snakes, Mongooses, Snake-Charmers and the Like," "Novices," and "Marriage," and no doubt drew upon his scholarly Hebrew translation as inspiration for several of her earlier poems featuring the Hebrew poets. Smith was a Hebraist and professor of Old Testament at Aberdeen who had been educated at Tübingen and Leipzig. His highly influential scholarship, which includes a two-volume commentary on Isaiah (1888) and the *Historical Geography of the Holy Land* (1894), as well as his lecture tours, did much to introduce the uses of historical criticism to laypeople. Like other believing critics, Smith saw little to no conflict between the gains of what modern criticism could reveal about biblical texts and a personal faith that the Bible still constituted a revelation from God; he believed that the Bible contained inspiration but was neither verbally inspired nor infallible, and that, as a text, it ought to be considered within its historical and literary contexts. His commentaries on Isaiah, for instance, which *The Christian Century* lauded at the time of his death as "a monument of the new biblical scholarship," put the chapters in chronological rather than canonical order and offered critical conclusions about editorial choices made by the book's ancient and multiple (as opposed to a single) authors ("Sir George" 373).

Another commentary from Kellogg's class which Moore quotes directly in her poetry ("When I Buy Pictures," "Novices," and "An Octopus" in *Observations*)—a volume that she annotated during the class and retained until the end of her life—is the Reverend Alexander R. Gordon's 1913 *Poets of the Old Testament.* Gordon (1872–1930) was trained in Aberdeen and eventually became the chair of Hebrew at McGill University. He authored several books and was one of the Old Testament editors for the 1941 University of Chicago Press American Translation version of the Bible. Like Smith and other believing critics, Gordon treats the texts in light of chronology and schools of writers rather than in terms of the canonical tradition of individual authorship (recognizing, for example, the impossibility of identifying which Psalms might really have been written by the historical David, a point about which Kellogg quipped in his class, "After all, who cares?").[3] As Cristanne Miller has detailed, Moore seems particularly to have appreciated Gordon's poeticism and his ability to give, in the words of a contemporary reviewer, "sympathetic appreciation of, and insight into, the soul of Hebrew poetry" ("Marianne Moore" 70).[4]

A third book Moore read during Kellogg's Bible class is P. T. Forsyth's 1911 *Christ on Parnassus: Lectures on Art, Ethic, and Theology,* which Moore quotes in her 1923 poem "Novices." Kellogg's theology—both during the years he was in Carlisle with Moore and later when he was a professor of philosophy and religion—seems to have been profoundly influenced by Forsyth (1842–1921), a believing critic and British Congregationalist who has been termed a "forerunner of Neo-orthodoxy" and "a Barthian before Barth" (Rogers and McKim 393). A prolific writer on subjects encompassing theology, homiletics, and the arts—and one whom Noll considers "perhaps the most important theologian in the prewar period"—Forsyth underscored much of his work with meditations on the problems of biblical authority in an age of both higher criticism and dogmatic reactions against the new scholarship (*Between* 81). Kellogg appears to have followed Forsyth's thinking so closely that, as the lecture notes Moore took in his Bible class demonstrate, he quoted and paraphrased from Forsyth's works liberally. *Christ on Parnassus* is highly representative of Forsyth's overarching philosophies. First, Forsyth insisted that Christians should place their faith in the message contained in the Bible, not stress individual words of the book itself. For "the Bible *contains* God's revelation (though in no dissectible way); what *is* the revelation is the Gospel, as some put it, or, as others would say, Christ, or the line of historic redemption. And, as to Inspiration, it is not, strictly speaking, the Bible that was inspired, but the souls of the men whose writings fill it" (*Christ* 243). Rejecting the notion of "verbal, literal infallibility of Scripture," Forsyth distinguished between "inspiration" (a subjective process and subject to the writer's imagination) and "revelation" (an objective and permanent truth) (243).

Second, Forsyth decries what he believes to be the violence done to biblical texts not by modern scholarship but by the "literal and scientific mind of the West" that "thrusts its dogmatic categories" upon poetical Old Testament books (241). When the poetry and prophecies of the Old Testament are read in nonfigural ways, he insists, "must it not mean some, and often much, blunting of sense for their true treasures, and the ruin of their divinest meaning and worth. If we will drag scientific laws from a lyric poem, and future history in its particulars from a passionate wail, what can we expect to leave behind us but debris?" (242). Instead, Christians should recognize the literary nature of the Scriptures and also study the Bible as an organic whole rather than paring it down to certain verses and proof texts. Forsyth believed that the final authority of the Bible originated not from the book itself but from an inward authority of God which a committed believer understands experientially. In so asserting the importance of the individual and his or her Christocentric experience during the process of interpretation, Forsyth was, like his younger contemporary Karl Barth, attempting to wrest biblical interpretation away from the theologians and return it to the hands of local churches, while at the same time encouraging members of these churches to make use of what new biblical studies had revealed.

Moore found empowerment in the ideas of Kellogg and the believing critics at the levels of both personal identity and poetic calling. Throughout his course, she records Kellogg praising the spiritual work of poets and poetry, and not only in connection with the Hebrew prophets. Regarding his course's text on the Gospel accounts of Christ, James Stalker's *Life of Jesus Christ,* for instance, Kellogg points out that the book was "designed to give us a general idea of the whole life" and "is in a sense, a poem" with "much poetic enlargement of the facts." While Stalker made "little or no attempt . . . to answer some of the most persistent and difficult questions that arise in reading the gospels," such as "the sources of the gospels and the dates when written or the points of view of the Evangelists in writing and of the early church," yet "had Mark attempted or achieved such a model biography of Jesus as history [or] science demands his work would have been useless for religion," Kellogg observes. "A maker is a poet," Moore wrote in the margins of her copy of Gordon's *Poets of the Old Testament* next to the sentence "The old 'makers' simply poured forth the feelings of the moment" (24). In particular,

Moore seems to have identified personally with one of the minor poet-prophets covered in Smith's commentary, Jonah, composing "Is Your Town Nineveh?" (1916), a poem that commiserates with Jonah's "personal upheaval" in "the sweltering east wind of your wishes," during or shortly after the class and "Sojourn in the Whale" in 1917 (*Becoming* 183). Indeed, the reluctant and peevish Jonah remained a sympathetic figure for Moore. Reading Calvin's *Letters* in 1921 or 1922, she takes extensive notes on Calvin's thoughts on the prophet, recording such comments as "He wished to die. There is nothing superfluous here, for Jonah shows with regard to his joy and his grief how tender he was and how susceptible of both" (Rosenbach VII:0103).[5] Even in 1956 she takes extensive notes on Jonah in a Bible class led by her Lafayette Avenue pastor in Brooklyn, Dr. Alvin Magary.

Moore was also no doubt inspired by the believing critics' assertion that the language of poetry is a language that *enacts* divine inspiration rather than literally *containing* it. Her notes contain numerous allusions to the distinctions between Greek, Hebrew, and Christian philosophies of art and spirituality, a subject that is also the theme of Forsyth's 1911 *Christ on Parnassus*. According to Kellogg and Forsyth, the Hebrew poets and early Christian writers of the biblical texts were offering a profound alternative to Platonic idealism that is at a remove from the embodied world and to pantheistic submergence of individual identity with the objects of worship. Moore was interested in this model of the infinite expressed in the finite, as well as the spiritual illumination necessary to recognize this relation. To hear "the thunderstorm as the voice of the Lord on earth" and to perceive "the earth as full of the lovingkindness of God" is a supernatural knowing revealed "to those that have eyes to see," she notes. By the same token, Kellogg explains in a paraphrase of Calvin, "you can't *prove* the gospel to the intellect of the natural man" because "the Christian religion is not rational. It is dramatically opposed to the Greek idea 'all things in reason.'" Instead, after conversion, "you know the truth in an immediacy" and find, paradoxically, that "there is no reason which is not the regenerated reason."

"Is Christ Apollo Belvedere in a long vistaed corridor as any cold or academic thing?" Moore records Kellogg asking rhetorically in the midst of this conversation. Seven years later, Moore would famously echo this phrase in the negative, asserting, "Truth is no Apollo / Belvedere, no formal thing," in her 1921 revision of "In the Days of Prismatic Color" (*Becoming* 242–43). The poem, which she had originally published in Bryn Mawr's literary journal *The Lantern* in 1919, had focused from the beginning on the prelapsarian vision of Adam, for whom there was "no smoke and color was / fine" and who was free from the obscuring influences of later, civilized artifice that is "at the antipodes from the initial great truths." The poem is one of many Moore writes during her lifetime about the importance of the genuine in art and the ironic, creatively generative impossibility of completely fulfilling this ideal; such poems dually lament and celebrate the artist's *felix culpa* that, as Bonnie Costello phrases it, "we fall into art, which is by its very character distant from nature and truth" (27).

Moore republished the poem at the bequest of William Carlos Williams and Robert McAlmon, who wished to feature some of Moore's work in their literary magazine *Contact.* (They also republished "Those Various Scalpels" in the same issue.) In her original 1919 version, "Truth" both directly parallels and contrasts with a many-legged creature from Loeb's *Greek Anthology* that represents "Complexity/ . . . that has been committed to darkness." This monster, bearing multiple "feet" as a creature at once mythical beast and poetic line, is

formidable only in the
dark. Truth, many legged and formidable also,
is stationary by choice.
The wave may go over it if it likes; know
that it will be there when it says: I shall be there when the wave has
gone by.

(*Becoming* 242–43)

Moore's revision of the first two lines of this stanza with the streamlined Apollo Belvedere phrase (and preceded by the impatient "To what purpose!") is significant both artistically and philosophically. As critics such as Bonnie Costello and John Slatin have long pointed out, the revision makes a more noticeable break in her own stanzaic pattern than her earlier line had done, thus calling greater attention to a "Truth" that not only resists the monster of excessive and vain complexities but also breaks the mold of all patterns.[6] The line also resonates more directly with the community of artists and writers with whom Moore had begun to socialize and collaborate when she moved to Greenwich Village in 1918, artists for whom, as Linda Leavell has noted in her 2013 Moore biography and elsewhere, Alfred Stieglitz and Wassily Kandinsky's emphasis on recognizing the "inner" or "spiritual necessity" of photography and painting served as a counterpoint for all that had become overtly representational and didactic in Western art.

Additionally, however, Moore's switch echoes the Augustinian and Calvinist views of spiritual perception of "the initial great truths" in which truth is not ratiocinated from propositional theology, nor is it "any" secondhand "cold or academic thing," to quote Kellogg's original phrase. Moore chose to repurpose Kellogg's metaphor for the poem during the peak years when she was mining the Bible class notes and texts (between 1920 and 1924) and, presumably, reviewing the believing critics' claims that the deepest biblical truths are experienced through an individual's own work at literary construction and receptiveness to personal revelation, claims that add further dimensions to the poem's insistence that "Truth is . . . / no formal thing." For the ancient peoples—Greek, Roman, or Hebrew (who were waiting for a kingly Messiah of their own)—to counterintuitively recognize divinity in the frailty of a human and crucified Jesus would have taken an embrace of truth reached through imagination rather than reasoning based on their own cultural expectations.[7] Such a notion of truth as "a moral reality at the core of one's personal life," as Moore's class notes read, was not only populist but also radical and radicalizing in its resistance to external power structures, as the martyrdom of many early Christians suggests.[8] Thus Moore found in her earlier researches within her own hermeneutic traditions a confirmation of her belief in the galvanizing primacy of spiritual perception in art and life, in addition to the role and responsibility of the perceiver.

Furthermore, if Moore shared with the believing critics such as Kellogg, Forsyth, Smith, and Gordon (and with their earlier Reformed ancestors) the belief that perception of spiritual truth was intuitive and innately God-given, and that this truth (whether found in belief or art) was resistant to changing fashions of interpretation ("Know that it will be there when it says: 'I shall be there when the wave has gone by,'" as Moore writes), she also found affirmation in the space left for "reverence for mystery" that their hermeneutical practices constructed. The believing critics' faith in the supernatural guidance that would be provided for devoutly minded biblical interpretation enabled them to pursue venues of higher criticism without anxiety regarding traditional biblical interpretations and to insist cheerfully on recognition of the semantic gaps that are inherent to all language. Indeed, it was in the intermediate spaces between signifier and signified where the dynamic meeting between believer and the divine took place and where the natural and supernatural intersected.

In Moore's Bible class notes, Kellogg alludes to this interstitial place with reference to several passages from Forsyth's books, particularly using the terms "the real" and "the actual" to indicate separate but related metaphysical realms. Moore records Kellogg's recounting of the Old Testament prophet Joshua's prayer for the sun to stand still when the Israelites were winning in battle (Joshua 10:12–15, an example that Moore also links to a corresponding page in Gordon's *Poets*): "The sun did stand still for Joshua—didn't ACTUALLY stand still but did really stand still—in light of God's eternally triumphant will. . . . The distinction between really and actually is a philosophical one but a valid one." Quoting another of Forsyth's books, *Positive Preaching and the Modern World,* Kellogg goes on to delineate: "The actual is the present hour. The real is the eternal pr. [power]" (Rosenbach VII:08:03; Forsyth, *Positive* 173). For Moore, both the terms ("the real" and "the actual") and the concept were felicitous. Here was a model of language and Scripture reading in which there were boundaries that the modern mind might respect, but also a type of spiritual interrelatedness in which the natural and supernatural could be held in tension without resorting either to materialism or to what would later be termed "fundamentalism."

She uses the phrase during the same years when other references to Kellogg's class appear directly in her work, titling her 1922 *Dial* review of Alfeo Faggi's sculpture exhibit "Is the Real Actual?" "The preoccupation today is with the actual," she begins the essay, "the fifty-fathom deep materialism of the hour" (*CPr* 73). In contrast with "the actual," however, is "spiritual imagination," a capacity "especially potent in interpreting subjects which are spiritual, seeming to derive feeling from the subject rather than to have to bring feeling to it as in the theme which is palpable and easily comprehensible." The difficulty in reviewing a work as spiritually genuine as Faggi's sculpture of Dante, she explains, is that "face to face with such sincere expressions, one suspects that in the vulgarity and peremptoriness of one's passions, either in praise or blame, one may be as St. Augustine says he was prior to his conversion, 'like a dog snapping at flies'" (74). In other words, Moore writes, modernizing the Calvinist dictum of reliance on supernatural revelation for perception of things unseen, "to grasp the nature of the phenomenon which Dante represents, is perhaps impossible to many of us since one cannot discern forces by which one is not oneself unconsciously animated," nor could Boccaccio, "as Symons says, comprehend a nature more metaphysical than his own." And yet, she insists, "a reverence for mystery is not a vague, invertebrate thing. The realm of the spirit is the only realm in which experience is able to corroborate the fact that the real can be also the actual. Such work as Mr. Faggi's is a refutation of the petulant patronage which for instance assigns Plato to adolescents—which remarks: 'How Plato hated a fact!'" (74). As Forsyth and Kellogg do before her in their Augustinian-informed Calvinism, in "Is the Real Actual?" Moore reverses the Enlightenment order of confirmation: only by having one's own spiritual "experience" may one also "corroborate the fact that the real can be also the actual"; that is, mathematical proofs, logical deduction, or natural theology can do little to prove the spiritual. In this sense for Moore, as she puts it here, to "experience" the spiritual is to experience fully the material (be it sculpture, curio, or the natural world) and to do so without negating either realm.

And of course it was in her poetry where Moore would truly develop and articulate her vision of art and language as liminal space where we might simultaneously encounter the physical and the numinous without collapsing the ontological boundaries of either. She deploys the concept of "the Real" and "the Actual" perhaps most famously in the 1919 version of "Poetry" where she lauds "literalists of the imagination" (language borrowed from Yeats) and "imaginary gardens with real toads in them" (her own verbiage). Yet even in her unpublished juvenilia, such as in "Kay Nielson's Little Green Patch in the Midst of the Forest," Moore is already working with similar inflections about what happens in the shared space between the material and the spiritual: the lines "When supernatural/Good elects to/Be more than a fiction in all/That's known as fact" could be yet another allusion to Kellogg's transmission of P. T. Forsyth's "real" and "actual" (Rosenbach I:02:46).

Very frequently Moore would situate her extended meditations on the overlap between "the Real" and "the Actual" in the natural world, a space she found an especially felicitous one from which to investigate the relationships between language, freedom, and identity. In addition to her love for the natural sciences, of course, Moore found in the believing critics a penchant for reviving some of the mechanics of Jonathan Edwards's natural typology, a system of signification whose metaphysics function with more utility in a literary universe of lived interpretation and experience than in the propositional universe of the previous generation's Princeton Scholasticism. Moore's notes show Kellogg discussing the way nature forms an intersection between the natural and supernatural realms in terms of the contrasting metaphysics of Judeo-Christian monotheism and Greek pantheism. On the one hand, "Greek art fills nature with life, nymphs, fauns, etc., but robs her of her own life," Moore transcribes, because "God [is] manifested only in nature [with] no transcendence at all"; on the other hand, "what gave the Psalmists their joy in nature was that there was a [transcendent] spirit in it." Kellogg, trained in Reformed theology, is in a sense explicating the same typological metaphysics Jonathan Edwards delineates in his notebooks, in which he describes the signifying difference-but-relation-between the natural and the supernatural and from which Edwards extrapolates his paradigm of being's consent to being, or being-in-relation. Moore keys her notes in this section of Kellogg's lecture to a page in Gordon's *Poets of the Old Testament,* on "God in Nature," writing in the margins, "not nature in itself but God in nature." Gordon's chapter "The Glory of God in Nature" (from which Moore borrows quotes for "Novices" and "When I Buy Pictures") strikes a particularly Edwardsean tone, describing nature as "daily upheld" by "Jaweh" and as "a shining mirror in which they [the ancient Hebrews] could trace the very features of the Divine" (149–50). Indeed, the topic of the relation between the physical world and spiritual correspondence remained one of interest to Moore, as her notes on a 1946 sermon comparing the "laws of God" which are "set forth by the stars in their courses" and "set forth in the moral law established by man" imply: "We cannot understand them; but we can and do live by them" (Rosenbach VII:09:11).

The natural objects in the poems Moore writes during the 1910s and 1920s, when she is most directly working with her books and notes from Kellogg's class, are keenly idiosyncratic and materially present in their kaleidoscopic renditions. Like Moore's view of the "realm of the spirit," the "defiant edifice" of barnacles in "The Fish" and the "unegoistic action of the glaciers" in "An Octopus" are forces with backbone; they are no "vague, invertebrate thing[s]." (See chapter 8 for a more complete discussion of materiality in Moore's early work.) In her animal poems of the 1930s and 1940s, however, Moore expands her focus to the relational dynamics within the liminal space where "experience is able to corroborate the fact that the real can be also the actual" (*CPr* 74). She does so by reifying her poetic subjects as seamlessly connected to broader ecological, ethical, and spiritual realms. In poems such as "The Jerboa," "The Plumet Basilisk," "The Frigate Pelican," "The Pangolin," and "His Shield," Moore's creatures never cease to represent embodiment even as she situates them in symbiotic relation to their natural environs on the one hand, and in discursive relation to the realms of art, language, and the supra-natural on the other. In these poems, the interconnectivity between the animals and what they metonymically signify suggests that setting the literal and the figural against each other is not merely a false dichotomy; in fact, reading two ends against the middle bifurcates the necessarily relational aspects of being itself, putting into conflict individual freedom and ethical responsibility when, as Moore repeatedly indicates, they need not be.

In her 1932 poem "The Jerboa," Moore contrasts the decadent and consumption-oriented societies of the Roman Empire and the Egyptian pharaohs with the "strange detail of the simplified creature," the desert-dwelling jerboa (*CP* 10–15). The poem's first fifteen stanzas, headed "Too Much," enumerate the various avaricious and perverted uses these rulers who "rob [nature] of her own life" (as Kellogg phrases it) make of the plants, animals, slaves, and "the poor" of the North African desert, while the poem's final twelve stanzas, beginning three stanzas before the second heading, "Abundance," detail the unassuming yet remarkable qualities of the "sand-brown jumping-rat," hopping "By fifths and sevenths/in leaps of two lengths," as do "the uneven notes/of the Bedouin flute." As John Slatin has pointed out, this metrical description of the jerboa's movement also delineates Moore's rhythmic pattern: the opening line of each stanza of the poem contains five syllables, and the final line contains seven. Consequently, although the poem opens with a description of the human conquerors, the jerboa's "invisible presence informs the poem from the outset" (206). Moore's underlying musical patterning is in keeping with the poem's overarching explorations of the dynamic play of "free" signifiers (these are seen in the movement of the "free-born" jerboa as opposed to the exhausted stasis of the slaveholding ruling classes).

Yet while the stanzaic pattern of the jerboa's leaps unifies the two sections, Moore's tone of ironic censure dominates the first half of the poem. The conquerors' domineering attitude toward those whom they subjugate is evidenced not only in their undignified use of animals as entertainment and sport but also in their merely imitative renditions of nature in what "passed/for art" and in their imperious treatment of their vanquished servants. The Romans' and Egyptians' rapacious orientation to their natural surroundings, Moore is insisting, is indicative of their broader failure to live in an ethical and aesthetic relation to being in general. The rulers knew "how to use slaves, and kept crocodiles and put/baboons on the necks of giraffes to pick/fruit"; and

> They had their men tie
> hippopotami
>   and bring out dappled dog-
>   cats to course antelopes, dikdik, and ibex;
>   or used small eagles. They looked on as theirs,
>   impalas and onigers.

In a water-deprived environment, moreover, the wealthy built elaborate gardens "combining planes, dates,/limes and pomegranates,/in avenues," complete with luxurious "square/pools of pink flowers, tame fish, and small frogs." They lack a basic respect for alterity—their motto is "the bee's food is your/food"—and even "those who tended flower-/beds and stables were like the king's cane in the/form of a hand." Ironically, however, in order to construct this artificial world of "fantasy/and a verisimilitude" that seems "right to those with, everywhere,//power over the poor," the pharaohs sacrifice their true freedom; they are compelled to rely on slave labor for the immense upkeep of "nothing but plenty."

Particularly revelatory of the Egyptians' loss of spontaneity and autonomy are their limited and controlling artistic conceptions of nature. In addition to their fondness for "small things," the elite prefer allegoric correspondence between the natural referent and the functional objects designed as containers for their cosmetic consumer goods. Their "toilet-boxes marked/with the contents" are semantically labeled in an attempt to direct and restrain the flow of possibly subversive signifiers contained in an object of art:

> Lords and ladies put goose-grease
> paint in round bone boxes—the pivoting
> lid incised with a duck-wing
>
> or reverted duck-
> head; kept in a buck
> or rhinoceros horn,
> the ground horn; and locust oil in stone locusts.

Furthermore, the Egyptians' insistence on literal representation of the supernatural—a realm that, like their natural world, they chiefly perceived according to their own image of themselves—has a recursive effect that is ultimately self- as well as other-limiting.

Thus, their servants

> . . . kept divine cows
> and bees; limestone brows,
> and gold-foil wings. They made
> basalt serpents and portraits of beetles; the
> king gave his name to them and he was named
> for them.

In giving "his name" to the gold and stone statues used for worship, the king effectively limits their possibilities of signification to himself; he is repaid for this egocentricity by being caught in a recursive and finally semantically deadening relation to his idols: as with a set of distorted and distorting mirrors in which it is no longer possible to distinguish between the original and the copy, so "he was named for them" and limited by their limitations.

In a reading notebook she kept during her time in Kellogg's Bible class, Moore makes a September 1914 entry from P. T. Forsyth's *Christ on Parnassus* concerning art and idolatry. Forsyth's preface reads: "In an age of culture the artist in various kinds means much. And, lest anything so fatal should take place as the substitution of an aesthetic for an ethical religion, or art be depraved by being idolised, it is well that we should know what art cannot do through those who duly own what it can" (ix). "It may be useful," Moore transcribes from the end of this passage into her notebook, "while some show how bad a master art may be, that others should indicate how good she can be as a servant" (Rosenbach VII:01:01). At the time of writing "The Jerboa," Moore had already alluded to the detrimental effect on human relations when self-regard is perverted into an idolatrous gaze in her 1923 poem "Marriage." In "The Jerboa," she meditates more extensively on "how bad a master art may be" when it is employed for similar ends. Explaining a comparable phenomenon, Jean-Luc Marion writes, "Because the idol allows the divine to occur only in man's measure, man can consign the idolatrous experience to art and thus keep it accessible" (15). The *modern* idol, Marion suggests, might be considered a "concept" that "consigns to a sign what at first the mind grasps with it" (16). By fixing a philosophical concept as a symbol with a closed interpretation, Marion asserts, the thinker effectively ends the chain of signification, and with it further possibilities of signifieds that may question or alter foregone conclusions. This done, the "*invisible,*" which Marion defines as that realm of unknown potentiality that always allows the possibility of exceeding itself, "finds itself, with an aim suspended by the fixed concept, disqualified and abandoned" (16). Likewise in Moore's poem, the pharaohs deny an ethical separation between their own identity and the separate identities of nature and the divine by their insistence upon conceiving the natural and supernatural worlds without any element of mysterious alterity, with every facet exposed to the gaze. Indeed, part of the effectiveness of Moore's choice to censure an extinct civilization relies on the reader's knowledge of that society's eventual decay and collapse; while the literal and semiotic line of the pharaohs is exhausted, the jerboa and its descendants live on.

The jerboa "that/lives without water," in fact, "has/happiness." Though Moore's illustration of the "simplified creature" emphasizes its diminutive size and its ability to do "without," the jerboa, whose "leaps should be set/to the flageolet," will not be contained by the second heading, and the description of the animal spills out three stanzas before the heading "Abundance." Of course, the jerboa's abundance consists not in the material "plenty" of the pharaohs but in a spiritual richness that it derives from living in a state of felicitous mutual interdependence with its environs. Moreover, in contrast with the Roman and Egyptian uses of art depicted in the first half of the poem, Moore's allusions to manmade objects in her description of the jerboa are few and associative rather than prescriptive and symbolic. In addition to the synesthetic comparison of the jerboa's leaps with "the uneven notes/of the Bedouin flute," we are told it moves "on little wheel castors" and has "a three-cornered smooth-working Chippendale/claw." Most often, the jerboa is compared to other animals, such as "the fawn-breasted/bower-bird" and the "chipmunk."

Concomitantly, the relationship between the jerboa and the African desert is one of co-signification rather than one-sided domination:

> Abroad seeking food, or at home
> in its burrow, the Sahara field-mouse
> has a shining silver house
>
> of sand. O rest and
> joy, the boundless sand,
> the stupendous sand-spout,
> no water, no palm-trees, no ivory bed,
> tiny cactus.

The jouissance of the speaker's apostrophe and thrice-repeated "sand" reflects the "boundless"-ness of the jerboa's signifying existence as it joyfully attests to the worth and significance of its environs, a state that is comparable to the spiritual state of the Psalmists, who, Kellogg asserted, found "their joy" in nature because of the transcendent "spirit in it." Moore's rat "can rest and then do/the opposite"; it does not need to strive to accomplish its part in the type-antitype relation, but merely exercises those qualities by which it is adapted to the sandy environment. Thus Moore engages five stanzas to delineate matter-of-factly the "sand-brown jumping-rat['s]" abilities to survive in the desert. Its "match-thin hind legs" and "the tail as a weight," for instance, enable it to jump long distances at great speeds, and "the fine hairs on the tail,/repeating the other pale//markings," serve as camouflage. Instead of attempting to divert and to fill an idolatrous gaze as do the grandiose pharaohs, this being-in-relation becomes a model for the workings of a self that has no need for the worship of others. Moore depicts an animal whose existence consists of gesturing beyond itself, finding and signifying its identity as it does so: "It/honors the sand by assuming its color"; in turn, whether the jerboa is "Abroad seeking food, or at home/in its burrow," it "has a shining silver house//of sand." Evoking the rat's survival strategies, the desert provides both shelter and sustenance for the animal. Hence the jerboa is a natural type whose qualities reveal the qualities of its unique habitat; concomitantly, the antitypic desert both gives rise to its "pale//markings" and fulfills those markings in the concealment that the sand provides.

Moore also aligns the "free-born" rat with three peoples who exemplify a human complement to the jerboa's spiritual freedom. In addition to the nomadic Bedouins, both the jerboa and "the blacks, that choice race with an elegance/ignored by one's ignorance," are "untouched" by the ostentatious greed of the rulers and conquerors of Africa. The third desert-dwelling race Moore associates with the jerboa are the Hebrews, who, after the time of Jacob, were slaves in Egypt for four hundred years:

> Part terrestrial,
> and part celestial,
>   Jacob saw, cudgel staff
>   in claw-hand—steps of air and air angels; his
>   friends were the stones.

The reference to Jacob is from Genesis 28, the chapter in which Jacob falls asleep on his journey through the desert, his head on a stone. In the narrative, Jacob dreams of a ladder on which angels are ascending and descending between earth and heaven. God speaks to him in the dream and tells him that his descendants will be as numerous as the grains of sand.[9] In response, Jacob erects a stone altar, exclaiming: "Surely the Lord is in this place; and I knew it not. . . . [T]his is none other but the house of God, and this is the gate of heaven" (Gen. 28:16–17). In the New Testament, Jacob is mentioned as a prefiguration of the spiritual Church.[10] Moreover, in John 2:51, Jacob's ladder becomes a type of Christ. Referring to himself as the fulfillment of Jacob's dream of a bridge between heaven and earth, Christ says to his disciples, "Verily, verily, I say unto you, Hereafter ye shall see heaven open, and the angels of God ascending and descending upon the Son of man."

The practice of reading the Old and New Testaments together in search of theological and narrative themes is evident in Moore's notes to Kellogg's lectures in places such as where he states, "The N.T. [is] Latent in the O.T.," and "The word of God is one in its testimony of Christ"; these were constructions that would have seemed familiar to Moore from the typological practices of Reverends Warner and Norcross. Indeed, like Calvin and their other Reformed predecessors, George Adam Smith and Alexander Gordon still read the Old and New Testaments as a single, unified story (albeit a more complex one) and continued to put the Testaments in conversation with each other. Smith explains that since they are intimately linked as part of a literary and spiritual whole,

> the Old Testament, one cannot too often remember, lies not *under*, but *behind* the New. It is not the quarry of the excavator or archaeologist—a mere foundation packed away out of sight beneath the more glorious structure that has been reared upon it. Far rather . . . is the Old Testament the "Hinterland" of the New: part of the same continent of truth, without whose ampler areas and wider watersheds the rivers which grew to their fulness in the new dispensation could never have gained one-tenth of their volume or their influence. (*Modern* 3–4)

Much of the emphasis of Gordon's book is concentrated on demonstrating how the Old Testament "anticipates" a "fuller conception" and "unveiling" of God in Christ as revealed in the original Hebrew (140–41). He asserts that the Old Testament "reach[es] forward to the New," is "fulfilled" in the New, and reaches "ripe development" in Christian mysticism (347).

In Moore's poem, the typological allusion to what "Jacob saw"—a figural ladder between heaven and earth—marks a moment of epiphanic insight connecting disparate elements into a significant and numinous whole, the earthy "Sahara field-mouse" in its "shining silver house// of sand" translated to the numinous and eternal. Jacob's response to the divine vision makes a profound contrast with the pharaoh's static "basalt serpents and portraits of beetles." Instead of Jacob's attempting to confine the numinous "steps of air and air angels" within a symbolic image and so to break off the signifying process, his "friends were the stones"; he is content to allow an un-"marked" stone to signify an ineffable experience. Instead of being an allegoric idol, the entire desert is a liminal, typological, and semiotic space—"part terrestrial,/ and part celestial"—for the Jacob/jerboa (aligned in their "claw-hand") of the poem. Like the Jacob of Genesis 28 who refuses to differentiate between what is secular and what is sacred ("This is none other but the house of God, and this is the gate of heaven," declares the biblical Jacob), Moore's Jacob and jerboa are at ease in these surroundings, having no need to construct protective boundaries between an insular self and a rapacious divine Other that might subsume them.

Thus, at the nexus of the "real" and the "actual" (in a sense, Moore's typological space), "The Jerboa" and other animals of her mid-career poems model the "boundless" spiritual, aesthetic, and discursive in-betweenness of what might be termed Moore's metonymic self. In a construction not unlike Jonathan Edwards's, Moore translates typology into a state of being in which identity itself consists in pointing away from self toward the other and may be chiefly perceived through its transitory, signifying attributes. Certainly, contemporary feminist scholars have already underscored connections between Moore's concerns with agency and subjectivity and her use of techniques such as Kadlec's "aesthetic of accident," emphasizing genetic and semiotic unpredictability. Considering the possibility of Moore's constructions of a gendered self, for instance, Cynthia Hogue notes Moore's "modernist poetics of multiple discourses" and "subject positions" which are "equivocally inhabiting, and exposing, a masculinist position," even as they posit feminist perspectives (*Scheming* 73–74). Sabine Sielke finds that Moore's construction of female subjectivity "emerges as an ambivalence, as a variable position of 'in-betweenness' and double-voicedness" (9). Cristanne Miller identifies Moore's strategy of refusing both self-assertive presence and self-negating absence as Moore's "abstractly personal" and "unempathetic 'I' " (*Questions* 36, 35).

What Miller, Hogue, Sielke, and others have established concerning Moore's constructions of multiple subjectivity, gender, and the lyric self, I would argue, may also be examined through the lens of Moore's Augustinian/Edwardsean philosophical underpinnings. The position of the metonymic self in Moore's poetry is that of continual signification, coming into being only as it dis-places "an other in the semiotic network in which it resides. . . . [It is] a disposition, a position *whose meaning consists in pointing beyond itself to an other*" (Daniel, *Philosophy* 134, emphasis added). Thus, in addition to constructing natural images that are ontological rather than merely allegorical, Moore, like Edwards, uses nature to suggest the inherently discursive and hence relational character of the universe itself. For Moore, existence itself may be conceived of as a type that is fulfilled as it points toward semiotically relational antitypes greater than itself. Moore chooses to foreground the symbiotic relationships between plants, animals, and environs that she learned about in her studies of the natural world as semiotic and contiguous relations in her poetry; by extension, she suggests to her audience what a human life lived as a more broadly spiritual, ethical, and metonymic self might look like.

"The Plumet Basilisk" (1932) is one of Moore's most dazzling poems to dramatize the contiguity of material existence. Hiding among the Costa Rican "feather capes // and hawk's-head moths and black-chinned / humming-birds," the plumet basilisk is "our Tower-of-London / jewel that the Spaniards failed to see" (*CP* 20–24). Like the Spanish conquistadors who miss the jewel under their noses, as readers we must train our eyes to follow this mythical yet actual lizard as it transforms throughout the poem from animal to legend to object of art and back again. We find the basilisk in its most literal, biologically defined state halfway through the poem, "where sapotans drop / their nuts out on the stream" and where it "feeds on leaves and berries and has / shade from palm-vines, ferns, and peperomias; or lies basking on a / horizontal branch // from which sour-grass and orchids sprout." While the basilisk is in symbiotic harmony with its environs, however, it is also a whirlwind of dynamic change. "He runs, he flies, he swims," we are told, and only when forcibly held still, "captured—stiff / and somewhat heavy, like fresh putty on the hand," is the basilisk "no longer // the slight lizard" whose metonymic, chameleon-like abilities connect and give meaning to the disparate ideas and images that make up the poem as a whole.

Thus, like the sea, which through the constant motion of "surrendering / finds its continuing" ("What Are Years?"), Moore's polysemous plumet basilisk appears and reappears throughout the poem, gliding steadily not through masks or disguises but through various significant and signifying relations. In one moment it moves with "wide water-bug strokes, / in jerks which *express* / a regal and excellent awkwardness"; in the next, it "*portrays* / mythology's wish / to be interchangeably man and fish—" (emphasis added). To "express" and to "portray," as Moore configures her type-antitype relationships, is no longer to be bound as a symbol in which a figure *stands for* a higher order of excellence or mythology. Instead, Moore's basilisk as an entity is glimpsed through such signifying attributes; it is a being-in-relation and subject-in-process which is fashioned by the artist as a moving position always in relation to other imaginative constructs—its discursive antitypes to which it points.

Moore's imagery and constant metonymic renaming of the basilisk throughout the poem underscore the importance of its function as a connector between dissimilar words, ideas, and states of being. It is "the amphibious falling dragon, the living fire-work" and "the ruler of Rivers, Lakes, and Seas, / invisible or visible." The basilisk even seems to become an image of incarnation, a spiritual being that temporarily dwells in, but is not confined by, a physical body. For instance, "inhabiting // fire eating into air," the lizard is momentarily "nested / in the phosphorescent alligator that copies each digression of / shape." Furthermore, the poem's multiple references to divinity, royalty, and the basilisk's ability to walk on water (for example, "If / beset, he lets go, smites the water, and runs on it—a thing / difficult for fingered feet") include among their many gestures of signification a Christic, typological reference. The phrase "smites the water, and runs on it" is in fact reminiscent of two biblical references: in addition to Christ walking on the Sea of Galilee, Moses is referred to in passages in the New Testament as a precursor, or type, of Christ; in the Old Testament, he "smote" the Nile river to turn it to blood (Exodus 7:20). Like the basilisk, Christ, the God/man, is a figure fully at home in and master of both material and spiritual contexts. Yet, because Moore's poetry resists not only symbolic functions but also the insistence on dividing sacred from secular, the basilisk's Christic allusions are neither more nor less important than the lizard's other suggested referents. (In fact, the basilisk is sometimes referred to as the Jesus lizard for its ability to run across the surface of water on its hind feet.)

Instead, the brilliance of Moore's contiguous juxtapositions of concrete imagery and abstract conceptions continually foregrounds the associative and contingent properties of language and metonymic being—which the poet reminds us are properties of music as well. In "The Plumet Basilisk" artifice and nature are combined, separated, and recombined in kaleidoscopic patterns that change at the dizzying speed of musical improvisation:

> As by a Chinese brush, eight green
> bands are painted on
>   the tail—as piano keys are barred
> by five black stripes across the white. This octave of faulty
>   decorum hides the extraordinary lizard
> till night-fall.

The stanza flows with smooth association from Chinese calligraphy to the basilisk's tail markings, from the piano to a suggested "octave of faulty / decorum" which actually camouflages the lizard in its natural surroundings. In keeping with this musical motif, the nighttime jungle becomes a symphonic "acoustic shell." Among the "squeak of bagpipes/and of bats. Hollow whistled monkey-notes disrupt/the castanets," and we discern the plumet basilisk merely by its feet, "traveling rapidly upward, as/spider-clawed fingers can twang the/bass strings of the harp."

Yet, despite the numinous "noiseless music that hangs about/the serpent when it stirs or springs," the poet reminds us, "No anonymous/nightingale sings in a swamp, fed on/sound from porcupine-quilled palm-trees/that rattle like the rain." "The Plumet Basilisk" is no Keatsean "Ode to a Nightingale." This music, which Moore suggests with her rhythmic cadences and internal, end, and off-rhymes, is evocative of something alien to all but intuitive understanding; the basilisk, though at home in this strange symphony, remains foreign to us. In Keats's poem, the nightingale "singest of summer in full-throated ease" and flies on "the viewless wings of Poesy"; it comes to symbolize romantically through its music the eternity of art and the tragedy of feminine "Beauty" that "cannot keep her lustrous eyes,/Or new Love pine at them beyond tomorrow." Moore's rugged lizard, by contrast, comes to signify a non-gendered beauty and a metonymic self that consists of humble signification beyond oneself. Thus we are left at the end of the poem with a curiously translucent presence that marks the imaginary place where the playful signifier has already been. The basilisk's "quicksilver ferocity" is "quenched in the rustle of his fall into the sheath/which is the shattering sudden splash that marks his temporary loss."

At the level of personal belief, the degree to which Moore's appropriation of the believing critics' hermeneutic as an interpretive model for thinking about art translated to her own ideas about the inspiration of the Bible is unknown. According to Moore's biographer Linda Leavell, in the late 1910s and 1920s, following their departure from Carlisle and her brother's parsonage, Moore and her mother attended church rarely. During their years in the Village, Sundays were the only days when Moore could sleep in and take a much-needed rest from her intensive labors as editor at *The Dial;* additionally, the two women did not care for the pastor at their local Presbyterian church.[11] The period was marked neither by the intense personal connectivity that Moore had had with her pastors Norcross and Kellogg and their families in Carlisle, nor by the later associations she forged with her Presbyterian church in Brooklyn beginning in the mid-1930s until the end of her life. Moore seems to have kept mum even with the members of her own family concerning her religious proclivities during this time, so much so that she once shocked her very devout mother by commenting on her naval chaplain brother's lack of faith (Leavell, *Holding*).

Yet one clue to answering the question whether Moore adopted Kellogg's stance to her own understanding of Scripture during the twenties and later is found in her positive 1927 *Dial* book review of *A New Standard Bible Dictionary*—a topical Bible study help published at the height of the fundamentalist-modernist controversy. The dictionary, in the words of its editors, attempts to "present the readers and students of the Bible the results of a reverent scholarship, committed to the accepted facts of criticism, open-minded to its unsettled problems, and thoroughly loyal to the basal truths of an evangelical Christianity" (*New Standard* x). In her review, Moore praises the editors for being "courageously definite in . . . [their] exposition of disputed questions" of manuscript scholarship. She finds their conclusions to be "in marked contrast with, yet not contradicting early literalism" (*CPr* 249). Which "disputed questions" Moore is specifically referring to might be guessed at from the ongoing controversies of the day. Concerning the relationship of the Old Testament to the New, for instance, the editors align themselves in their thinking with the adherents of the early Christian Church, writing:

> Their belief that God's purpose and plan of redemption culminated in Jesus Christ, we share heartily. But not always for their reasons and not always by their arguments. We too recognize in the OT history an essential preparation for the NT, but not an allegorical or obscure anticipation of its truths. . . . Instead of a mechanical uniformity between the two Testaments, we note a historical development of revelation which makes the connection between the two organic and vital. (*New Standard* 10)

Like Smith, Forsyth, and Kellogg, the editors find that revelation is "unmistakably present in the Bible," but "just what this Divine guidance secured in the delivery of the message the Biblical data do not explicitly indicate" (771–72).

To "contrast with, yet not contradict earlier literalism" is a fine phrase Moore uses in this 1927 review to encapsulate not only the believing critics' project but also her own characteristic equipoise between a modernist remaking of forms and a traditionalist "reverence for mystery," as she put it in 1922. Methodologies might be challenged and changed; dogmatism questioned; racism, sexism, and tyranny resisted; and, by all means, poetry "made new," as Pound phrased it. Nevertheless, as Moore so often reminds us in her writing, the poet also serves to make observations and affirmations of the profound and indefatigable truths that will be there "when the wave goes by," as she wrote in "In the Days of Prismatic Color." Moore's inheritance of the Reformed typological conventions (particularly as reconceived by the believing critics in terms of "the real" and "the actual") provided her a meta-poetic framework from which to affirm both the boundaries of and the connection between the physical and spiritual worlds and to recast poetic traditions locating the numinous in the natural. By aligning the discursively based "realm of the spirit" with an ethical "reverence for mystery," Moore creates a spiritually thing-infused poetry without reliance on the symbolic or on an essentialist assertion of the transcendent. When viewed as semiotic entities, Moore's animal subjects of the thirties and forties—her metonymic selves—function as "types" in the sense that the poet's language calls attention to this process of meaning in signification; her natural figures self-consciously open outward in a kind of endless deferral of final meaning even as they retain existence apart from contextual intent. They do not merely represent and so suggest a closure of the chain of signifiers, as would a symbol. Rather, finding their fulfillment in the play of their unendingly signifying "antitypes," these natural objects exist semiotically in the action of pointing toward another object or idea; as parts of a sign system, the one *is* the other, and in multiple ways that the poem never fully exhausts. For Moore, it is the combination of scientific observation and art that reveals this discursive and multiply perspectival condition of material and spiritual existence. Analysis of her natural figures as part of type-antitype relations highlights this aspect of Moore's poetic project as a whole, for the "spontaneity" and "gusto" Moore celebrates in her meditations on art and the imagination are also applicable to the joyfully idiosyncratic and signifying realm of nature itself.

8

"Integration Too Tough for Infraction"

Being, Ethics, and Aesthetics in Early and Late Moore

There is a marked movement in the scope and tenor of Moore's poetry over her long career—a movement from the sharply drawn forms and social protest of her early years before her editorship at *The Dial* through a concomitant emphasis on the connectivity of the metonymic self with its environs in her animal poems of the 1930s and early 1940s, and, finally, to the more abstract, theoretical, and sometimes even didactic "unparticularities" ("By Disposition of Angels") in the poetry of the final thirty years of her life.[1] Indeed, some critics, such as John Slatin, lament outright what he terms the "simplifying, moralizing tendency which mars so much of Moore's work after 1940" (14); others attribute the changes in Moore's work to the death of her mother in 1947 (and the resulting loss of her mother's criticism and collaboration), to Moore's desire to be read by a broader public (as Linda Leavell argues persuasively in *Holding On Upside Down*), or as Bonnie Costello comments of Moore's enormously popular World War II poems such as "In Distrust of Merits," to Moore's buckling under "too much pressure . . . of the news" (110).[2]

Despite the fact that her later poems become increasingly occasional and less consciously avant-garde, however, Moore never abandons the modernist values she helped to create. If the best of her final poems are simple, they are deceptively so, for they are built on the complex meta-poetic and metaphysical frameworks that she had so painstakingly developed in the earlier poetry. Moore's emphasis on the individuation of natural forms from their symbolic contexts in the first third of her career—and her later foregrounding of the association between "the Real" and "the Actual" as semiotic relations between signifiers and signifieds in the second (as discussed in chapter 7)—necessarily precede and underlie the fundamental epistemological assertion that is always present in her work but is highlighted in, and sometimes the subject of, the poems of her final years. This assertion is Moore's insistence on a specific tripartite category in which being, aesthetic rendition, and ethical action "attain integration too tough for infraction" ("Efforts of Affection").

As indicated in chapters 6 and 7, one of the sources of this epistemological interchange can be located in the deep and previously unexplored roots Moore had in American Reformed thought, both through her family and through her own hermeneutical training. As explored in chapter 2, for Jonathan Edwards—the Augustinian philosophical forebear of the American knowing/seeing/being tradition—the three-way connections between beauty, being as a kind of signifying "excellency," and virtue are inherent. As Edwards defines the term, "excellency" is a state of existence in which there is "the consent of being to being, or being's consent to entity"; existence itself, in other words, consists of a being's consensual relation and deferral to other things and beings around it, a kind of humility toward all creation (*WJE* 6:334). By the same token, for Edwards, a student of optics and physics as well as theology, the variety of the material world, rather than the refined and predictable finish of manmade objects, represents what is aesthetically pleasing. Beauty, according to Edwards, is determined by the mutually reinforcing signification between an object and that toward which it self-forgetfully gestures. Consequently, beauty is not merely a separate, aesthetic category but a term that may be applied to spiritual as well as visual relations. As the Edwards scholar Stephen Daniel remarks: "The beauty or excellence of a thing consists in its relations to others. Since the very existence of a thing consists in those relations, the ontological and aesthetic dimensions of the thing cannot ultimately be differentiated, without reducing its moral relations to mere accidents" (*Philosophy* 177).

While there is no evidence that Moore read Jonathan Edwards herself, she was well versed in the writings of Augustine and early Protestant reformers such as Calvin and Luther. (Even in 1955 she makes a note to herself to "reread Martin Luther" in a notebook she kept for Bible classes at her Brooklyn church) (Rosenbach VII:07:12). More salient to the point, her own notions of the relation between being, doing, and aesthetic creation were greatly informed by two pastors who were very fluent in Edwards's theology: the Reverend E. H. Kellogg (as discussed at length in chapter 7) and her grandfather, the Reverend John Riddle Warner, who attended a Reformed seminary in the mid-nineteenth century at the height of the Edwardsean influence on ministerial training.[3] Warner's book of sermons, published by Moore's mother after his death in 1895 and revered by Moore and her brother, bears a heavy imprint of Jonathan Edwards's thinking, particularly of his 1746 treatise *Religious Affections,* arguably the most far-reaching and influential theological text for the seminarians of Warner's generation. According to *Religious Affections,* the Christian life is lived not by strength of willpower but by a supernatural change in desires, and these "affections," or desires, are the impetus for the soul on its pilgrimage toward unification with God. The self, though divinely elected, is still able to make choices as to whether to enhance or impede its own progress through transformative regeneration by the proclivities with which it aligns itself. In short, the soul eventually resembles that which it "aims at," "signifies," or "habitually" (all Edwards's terms) desires most. In the Christian view of the concept, however, unification with God does not annihilate the self; rather, as Edwards asserts, difference is meant not to be obliterated but to be preserved, for "two beings can agree one with another in nothing else but relation; because otherwise the notion of their twoness (duality) is destroyed and they become one" (*WJE* 6:335).

One example of Reverend Warner's explaining this role of the affections in a Christian's life is in his sermon "Things in the World Which are Not Transient." The sermon exposits 2 Corinthians 4:18, in which the Apostle Paul uses metaphors of sight to remind his early readers to bear up under the beatings, imprisonments, and executions they were facing: "We do not look at the things which are seen, but at the things which are not seen. For the things which are seen are temporary, but the things which are not seen are eternal." As Warner interprets the passage:

> In God's infinite love He has so ordered the laws of our moral life that one cannot "look"—in the sense of this word in the text—at anything with habitual desire and favor without partaking of its moral qualities and characteristics. Consciously or unconsciously, we put on a resemblance. We shine in its light, or we darken in its blackness. If it be a morally hateful thing we look at, and we look without any abhorrence, or with secret stirrings of desire, we grow hateful as we gaze. If the thing be morally fair and we love it, while we look we grow fairer in the measure of our affection. Good or bad, hateful or lovable, seen and temporal, or spiritual and eternal, the soul grows by what it feeds on, and like to that which feeds it. (128)

While Warner's sermon rings judgmental and essentialist to our twenty-first-century ears—and while Moore certainly never expressed identical beliefs nor in such an evangelical framework—she did take away from her Presbyterian upbringing a lifelong and deep conviction that society, art, and the natural world, for good or ill, stood in consequential relation to one another. If Reverend Warner's enjoinment is read in the light of Edwards's metaphysic of "being's consent to being," the underlying philosophical precept here is not so much a fear of a moral contagion coming from outside the self as it is an acknowledgment of the moral, ontological, and even aesthetic interrelatedness of creation and an insistence that a life lived for its own self-interest and pleasure is a life made woefully inadequate to itself and others, both in the here and now and in the broader light of eternity.

Although they would state the proposition according to their own centuries, neither Edwards nor Reverend Warner nor Moore herself believed that it is possible to extract the self-as-a-relationally-moral-being in any meaningful way from its environs. Concomitantly, the trope of the "look" or "gaze," as contemporary theorists would deem it, indicates that not only is one in an ethical relationship with what one gazes at, but also one is morally complicit in the relation so formed because of the mutually transformative nature of that connection. In her many book reviews throughout her career, Moore shows herself to be keenly attuned to this principle of spiritual vision as relation when it is expressed in other writers' works. In 1942, for instance, she praises José Garcia Villa's first book of poetry for lines such as "'My human eyes' become 'God's lens/Through which I see—all of Love,'" stating that his poetry "truly constrains us to admit that transfiguration is not incompatible with intimacy and that what one seeks one shall find" (the final clause is from Luke 11:10) (*CPr* 371–72).

The possibilities of being-as-relation, however, are paradoxically dependent on firm ontological boundaries that resist dissolution even in the most intimate of connections. Correspondingly, the importance of individuating objects from both poetic conceit and the mirroring and possibly rapacious gaze of the beholder is one of the central issues of Moore's work in the 1910s and early 1920s, and this individuation is directly related to the poet's broader and lifelong concern with definitions of beauty itself. The plants and animals in Moore's early poetry are distinguished by the fact that they resist dissolution into a kind of post-Christian, Emersonian Transcendentalism.[4] For Moore (like Edwards), beauty that is aesthetically noteworthy is not the Greek form of idealized—and masculinized—beauty which is based on anthropomorphic images. Instead, Moore constructs rugged natural objects that challenge our mind's eye; this is the unpolished thingness of both the biology lab that Moore loved as a student at Bryn Mawr and her Reformed heritage of a monotheism that completely separates creature and Creator (be that creator human artist or divine). In her longest poem, "Marriage" (1923), Moore explicitly critiques the human tendency to use the gaze to obfuscate boundaries between self and Other, and in so doing, to reduce the Other to a function of ego reflection. When one "he" of the poem "experiences a solemn joy / in seeing that he has become an idol," he is narcissistically attached to the image of himself that he sees in his gaze at his beloved (*Becoming* 296).

Indeed, Moore ridicules the mutual self-adoration and construction of the Other in a subservient position to the self that both sexes may at times participate in:

> he loves himself so much,
> he can permit himself
> no rival in that love.
> She loves herself so much,
> she cannot see herself enough—
> a statuette of ivory on ivory,
> the logical last touch
> to an expansive splendor
> earned as wages for work done. (*Becoming* 303)

In these lines, the self-obsession of "he" is constructed as a voracious, self-reflexive, and receptive appetite that, actively, "can permit himself / no rival in that love" which is reflected back to him from his own gaze at the Other. The "she" of the pair, conversely, "cannot see herself enough." As Luce Irigaray has written, the unrecognized absence of woman in patriarchal representation results in a specular discourse in which, alienated from herself as occupying a derivative position of lack, she can neither see nor act. For the "she" in Moore's poem, this is the Pygmalion project in reverse: the "logical last touch" of her objectification as mirror for the male gaze and as symbol of beauty, "earned as wages for work done," is her transformation into an idolatrous "statuette of ivory on ivory," an illusionary Venus flytrap of signification from which she cannot escape. In the same fashion, Moore's refusal in her early poetry to present uncomplicated, stereotypic images of the natural world, particularly insofar as they relate to feminized versions of nature, serves to undermine the subsuming and mirroring action of the gaze. Indeed, true beauty, Moore tells us in the 1925 poem "The Monkey Puzzle," is that which "defies one." It defies the compartmentalization that comes from facile understanding, and it defies description in symbolic language that originates from the possessive masculine gaze.

Yet for Moore, the early emphasis on idiosyncratic and rugged resistances to absorption by the Other did not develop into a celebration of a stark and detached individualism. As explored in chapter 7, in her animal poetry of the 1930s and 1940s Moore instead chose to develop an equal and balancing aim toward metonymic and ethical relation, suggesting that in the space between "the [physically] Real" and "the [spiritually] Actual" lies a sense of interconnectivity that also relies on individual identity. While her poetry of the pre-*Dial* years recasts conceptual ideals of gender and the aesthetic by questioning discrete epistemological categories, post-*Dial* Moore extends this reach to conceive of a kind of metonymic self that is known through its signifying attributes, thus troubling the subject position and erasing boundaries between being and doing as well as between the enactment of a moral quality or virtue and its relation to art.

Specifically in Moore's late poetry, which I loosely date from the end of World War II until the publication of her last poem in 1970, the signifying possibilities of natural figures are increasingly inseparable from their aesthetic and moral or spiritual qualities. Indeed, it is in her late typological renderings of the natural world that Moore's associative links between ethics, ontology, and the creative role of the artist can often be seen most clearly. In these years, Moore highlights a hermeneutical principle that had always been present in her work: that ethical and aesthetic appraisals are a part of what constitutes subjectivity's relation to the signifying matrix. Thus choices and preferences are not in themselves arbitrary, for the judgments of a signifying metonymic self—a state of being-in-relation—put the self into a relationship with what it prefers. Hence, in "In Distrust of Merits," for example, "patience patience / patience, that is action or / beauty" juxtaposes a moral practice ("patience") with signifying "action," which in turn is conjoined with "beauty." Likewise, in "Efforts of Affection," a poem in which love is known metonymically through its effects, unity temporarily achieved through art is conflated with ethical soundness, and both are perceived through observable "efforts": "Thus wholeness— // wholesomeness? say efforts of affection— / attain integration too tough for infraction." Or, as Moore puts it more succinctly in "To a Steam Roller" (1915), "impersonal judgment in aesthetic / matters" is "a metaphysical impossibility."

In this chapter I demonstrate that while there are numerous differences in tone and style between the poetry Moore wrote early and late in her more than fifty years of productivity, the undergirding meta-poetic values in her work remain remarkably consistent. Although there is a movement over time from an early emphasis on the mysterious alterity of natural objects such as the monkey puzzle tree (and a concomitant refusal to blanket these objects with allegory or symbol) toward a heightened appreciation of the relational connectivity that her later poems applaud, Moore's subjects always retain an ontological otherness that affirms their materiality. The poet's insistence on the primacy of an individuated identity, on the "brilliance" of individual objects—along with the "co-ordination" between self and Other provided by "thorns"—remains unabated ("Roses Only"). With the gathering political strains that led to World War II, she finds affinities in this ethical vision in the work of a fellow Reformed thinker, Reinhold Niebuhr. Consequently, as the maturing Moore draws upon the philosophical roots of her Reformed heritage to develop a category of being in which she substitutes observable, metonymic attributes for tropes of essence and origin, she builds on a concomitant understanding that there remain semipermeable boundaries that protect against erasure of the self or object altogether.

In 1905, during her freshman year at Bryn Mawr College, Moore's English professors complained that her writing was "a network of quotations," but she excelled in the sciences and gained "a vast reputation in biology" (Leavell, *Holding* 67). Moore's interest in science, particularly optics and the life sciences, was indeed passionate and lifelong; Robin Schulze records that she read at least 150 books in the natural sciences just in the decade between 1910 and 1920 ("Textual Darwinism"). Later in life she was a frequent visitor to the several New York–area zoos, as well as to the American Museum of Natural History, and she corresponded with the museum's curator Dr. Raymond Ditmars in the course of thoroughly researching animals such as the jerboa and the plumet basilisk for her poems of the same names.[5] "Did laboratory studies affect my poetry?" Moore responded in 1963 to a question regarding her years at Bryn Mawr. "I am sure they did. I found the biology courses—minor, major and histology—exhilarating. . . . Precision, economy of statement, logic employed to ends that are disinterested, drawing and identifying, liberate—at least have some bearing on—the imagination, it seems to me" (Hall, "Art" 23).

As has often been observed by her critics, Moore's love of scientific economy and precision is particularly evident in her treatment of the natural world—and in her appraisals of normative cultural shorthand frequently used to render that world. Her 1915 "To Browning" offers a complex critique of the manner in which symbolic attribution obfuscates and devalues the significance of a natural object rather than clarifying it, particularly when that natural object—a rose—is one traditionally gendered female. After originally publishing the poem in Ezra Pound's journal *The Egoist,* Moore made several revisions to the piece throughout its publication history (including changing its title to "Injudicious Gardening" in 1924) and—as was not the case with many of her early poems—retained it in the *Complete Poems* in 1967 with significant changes to two lines of its second and final stanza. Moore's notes indicate that the poem was at least partially inspired by two entries in *Letters of Robert Browning and Elizabeth Barrett,* one that refers to infidelity as the meaning of yellow roses in "the dictionary of flowers," and the other that seems to imply a breech of fidelity by Browning himself: "I planted a full dozen more rose-trees, all white—to take away the yellow-rose reproach!" (*CP* 275). In the first stanza of the *Egoist* version, the speaker dismisses conventional, even superstitious wisdom that would taint our observations of these flowers:

> If yellow betokens infidelity,
> I am an infidel.
> I could not plant white roses on a hill
> Because books said buff petals boded ill,
> White promised well. (*Becoming* 174)

Here the speaker rebels against the kind of fidelity to reductive, romantic interpretation of the natural world that "books" by male authors demand of her; in defense of the yellow rose's resistance to symbolic erasure, she aligns her own identity with the rose itself, declaring herself to be an unbeliever rather than give the emotional and intellectual allegiance prescribed by authoritative texts. "If yellow betokens infidelity," she declares, "I am an infidel."[6]

In the second stanza, the speaker directly addresses another persona, ostensibly Browning himself:

> However—your particular possession—
> The sense of privacy
> In what you did, deflects from your estate
> Offending eyes and will not tolerate
> Effrontery.

Turning on the word "however," the second half of Moore's poem seems to be an indictment of Browning's unethical appropriation of the rose's conveniently symbolically tainted color—its vulnerability to poetic "possession" and concomitant loss of ontological significance—in order to cover a possible "infidelity" alluded to in the first stanza. His "particular possession," which is a guilty "sense of privacy/In what you did," causes him to refuse to "tolerate" a truth-telling "effrontery" that would expose his actions. Moore's line break and syntax make possible a double reading of the third line: the false use of the implied white roses "deflects" the ethical value "from your estate" as well as "deflects . . . /Offending eyes." Thus, the example of the speaker's refusal to obliterate the yellow roses in favor of white in the first stanza becomes the standard for ethical boundaries and truth-telling which is violated in the second. In this manner, the addressee of the second stanza is doubly indicted: refusing to plant yellow roses because of their meaning as "infidel" in the masculine lyric tradition and appropriating white roses to cloak oneself in their equally stereotyped suggestion of purity are part and parcel of the same misguided principle of symbolic erasure. Both actions show unquestioning acceptance of the superimposition of symbolic attribute over identity. In this sense the poem offers a troubling image of the manner in which women are frequently caught in a cultural double bind: women may be appropriated for their exchange value of silent purity when they follow their prescribed scripts and summarily dismissed as "infidels" when they speak up and stray from them.

Moore's changes to the poem from the time it was originally published in 1915 to its final form in the 1967 *Complete Poems* broaden the range of possible interpretations from a poetic address strictly to Robert Browning to a poem more generally about the yellow rose's resistance to symbolic appropriation. In addition to changing the name from "To Browning" to "Injudicious Gardening," Moore softens and abstracts the second stanza:

> However, your particular possession,
> the sense of privacy,
> indeed might deprecate
> offended ears, and need not tolerate
> effrontery. (*CP* 81)

By substituting a comma for a dash after "possession" and deleting the accusatory "In what you did," Moore makes the "your" in the first line much more ambiguous. Whereas in the earlier version "Offending eyes . . . will not tolerate / Effrontery," in the final version "offended ears" merely "need not tolerate" the aforementioned "effrontery." In this rendition, the speaker may be addressing the yellow rose itself; the rose's "particular possession," its "sense of privacy," might be a positive quality that indicates its uniqueness and inviolability. "Offended" and "effrontery" are no longer solely ironic references to Browning's prideful judgments of others but literal evaluations of those who would prefer the yellow rose to offer no resistance to their symbolic confiscations. Hence, while the yellow rose's insistence on difference "indeed might deprecate offended ears," by right of its own existence, it "need not" "tolerate / effrontery."

The rose as a symbolically gendered natural object is the center of another of Moore's early pieces, "Roses Only" (1917). The poem (published originally in Alfred Kreymborg's *Others: An Anthology of New Verse* and reprinted by Moore in the 1921 *Poems* and the 1924 *Observations* but not in later volumes) works to undermine the male-dominant lyric conventions that associate roses with feminine beauty, fragility, and subservience to the passage of time by offering a counter-symbolic significance of its own; the speaker tells the rose that not petals but "your thorns are the best part of you":

> You do not seem to realize that beauty is a liability
>   rather than
>   An asset—that in view of the fact that spirit
>   creates form—we are justified in supposing
>   That you must have brains. For you, a symbol
>   of the unit, stiff and sharp,
>   Conscious of surpassing—by dint of native superi-
>   ority and liking for everything
> Self dependent—anything an
>
> Ambitious civilization might produce: for you, un-
>   aided to attempt through sheer
>   Reserve, to confute presumptions resulting from
>   observation, is idle. You cannot make us
>   Think you a delightful happen-so. But rose, if
>   you are brilliant, it
>   Is not because your petals are the without-which-
>   nothing of pre-eminence. You would look—
>   minus
> Thorns—like a what-is-this, a mere

Peculiarity. They are not proof against a worm, the
elements, or mildew
But what about the predatory hand? What is
brilliance without co-ordination? Guarding the
Infinitesimal pieces of your mind, compelling audience to
The remark that it is better to be forgotten than to
be remembered too violently,
Your thorns are the best part of you. (*Becoming* 228–29)

In Moore's poem, the rose's significance comes not from the much-celebrated charm of its "petals" but from the thorns, which differentiate it from other flowers and actively arm it against "the predatory hand." Yet the addressee of the poem itself seems unaware of its potential for resistance. In her "educational advice" (as Rachel Blau DuPlessis phrases it) to a rose whose duplicitous attitude toward itself and its viewers resembles the feminine internalization of the male gaze, Moore observes, "You do not seem to realize that beauty is a liability rather than/An asset" (Genders 45). Moreover, the poem continues, "in view of the fact that spirit creates form—we are justified in supposing/That you must have brains"—despite what we may infer to be the rose's inclination to fool us into believing otherwise. Indeed, this rose is "Conscious of surpassing — by dint of native superiority and liking for everything/Self dependent—anything an//Ambitious civilization might produce." Consequently, for the rose to "attempt through sheer/Reserve" to deny what it knows to be its own "brilliance," and in so doing "to confute presumptions resulting from observation, is idle. You cannot make us/Think you a delightful happen-so." The bourgeois artifice of an "Ambitious civilization" that instructs women to use silence and "Reserve" strategically in order to "confute presumptions" and to apply themselves to becoming drawing room bric-a-brac, "a delightful happen-so," Moore states flatly, is "idle."

Moore's rose needs to be reminded that it possesses what the poets have forgotten: its thorns. Both recalling and dismissing the limiting, emblematic convention in which the rose attempts and fails to disguise itself, Moore offers a counter-narrative, deeming it "a symbol of the unit, stiff and sharp."[7] Overtly designating an object as a symbol or representative idea is a characteristic gesture Moore would make throughout her poetic career. Paradoxically, by foregrounding and thus calling attention to the artificiality of object as symbol, Moore lifts her natural objects out of their representational contexts, undermining the strictly symbolic function that would obliterate their materiality and close the open-ended chain of signification to which they belong. The ostrich, for instance, in "He 'Digesteth Harde Yron'" (1941) is at one moment in the poem deemed "a symbol of justice"; similarly, the "Rosemary" in the 1954 poem of the same name, "imitating the blue robe of Mary, / is not too legendary // to flower both as symbol and as pungency." In "Roses Only," Moore redirects the specter of a specifically gendered symbolism in order to expose the trope as an essentialist rather than a liberating term.

Consequently, in reading the rose's thorns, what Moore offers her reader is not a new set of feminist allegorical terms but rather a new way of defining both beauty and being. John M. Slatin has called attention to the poem's Emersonian (and hence Neoplatonic) influences, particularly in Moore's references to Emerson's 1842 lecture "The Transcendentalist" with her choice of terms such as the rose's "native superiority," its "liking for everything / self-dependent," and "the fact that spirit creates form." In the Emersonian sense, Slatin says, the "beauty of the rose is not imposed from without but is the external manifestation of the 'spirit' within" (62). At the same time, however, it is the jagged edge of the thorns' contact with material reality that balances and braces its spiritual "form" against its dissolution into a "what-is-this, a mere / peculiarity." Ontologically speaking, the rose exists in the liminal state of both "spirit" and substance, and the poem functions to reinforce both their distinction and their mutual dependence.

Thus, instead of becoming a new trope that *stands* for and replaces the rose, its thorns are metonymic attributes—"the best part of you"—that enforce the rose's physical and spiritual boundaries, as well as being the source of its mental "brilliance." While they are not "proof against" the ravages of time ("a worm, the elements, or mildew") which will eventually destroy physical beauty, they do ward off the "predatory hand" of the too ardent observer. Moreover, "Guarding the / Infinitesimal pieces of your mind," these thorns, and the unusual prosody of the poem itself, also deflect our own subsuming tendencies as readers, "compelling audience to / The remark that it is better to be forgotten than to be remembered too violently." In addition to its awkward line lengths, line breaks, and diction, "Roses Only" displays six dashes and six hyphens, visually highlighting its "stiff and sharp" conviction. As Cristanne Miller has observed: "For the poem to be 'brilliant,' it, too, must be more than merely 'beautiful.' In fact, it must be prickly, must warn its reader against a too aggressive appropriation of its meaning" (*Questions* 113). For Moore, then, the natural object ethically conceived and aesthetically depicted resists deployment on *solely* the symbolic register, a distinction that Emerson finally does not make. Instead, Moore erects clearly defined and fiercely defended boundaries between the me and the not-me, between spirit and substance, and between reader, interpretations, and text. While the thorns' characteristics may variously remind us of other objects, ideas, or values, they nevertheless retain ontological distinction.

Similarly, in "The Monkey Puzzle" (first published in 1925 in *The Dial*), Moore depicts, through multiple perspectives, a very ancient species of evergreen whose "porcupine-quilled, complicated starkness" offers a visual complement to resistance, "proportion," and "beauty." According to Moore's notes in the 1925 second edition of *Observations*, the monkey puzzle tree (*Araucaria imbricata*), so named because its limbs are difficult for monkeys to ascend, is native to Chile; *imbricata* or *imbricatus* refers to its sharp leaves, which are "crooked like a gutter, or roof, tile; or laid one under another like tiles" (96). In photographs of the tree taken by Moore during her 1922 visit to Bremerton, Washington, it is possible to see how, in addition to its having spiky leaves, the monkey puzzle's branches grow in a pattern of four upwardly curved limbs on each ring, its concentric circular silhouette still preserving the typical conifer's triangular shape (Willis, "Monkey"). Moore's poem reads:

> A kind of monkey or pine-lemur
> not of interest to the monkey,
> in a kind of Flaubert's Carthage, it defies one—
> this "Paduan cat with lizard," this "tiger in a bamboo thicket."
> "An interwoven somewhat," it will not come out.
> Ignore the Foo dog and it is forthwith more than a dog,
> its tail superimposed upon itself in a complacent half spiral,
> this pine-tree—this pine-tiger, is a tiger, not a dog.
> It knows that if a nomad may have dignity,
> Gibraltar has had more—
> that "it is better to be lonely than unhappy."
> A conifer contrived in imitation of the glyptic work of jade and
> hard-stone cutters,
> a true curio in this bypath of curio-collecting,
> it is worth its weight in gold, but no one takes it
> from these woods in which society's not knowing is colossal,
> the lion's ferocious chrysanthemum head seeming kind by
> comparison.
> This porcupine-quilled, complicated starkness—
> this is beauty—"a certain proportion in the skeleton which
> gives the best results."

> One is at a loss, however, to know why it should be here,
> in this morose part of the earth—
> to account for its origin at all;
> but we prove, we do not explain our birth. (*CP* 80)

In a 1924 essay for The Dial titled "Sir Francis Bacon," Moore suggests that Bacon's line "There is no excellent beauty that hath not strangeness in the proportion" is reminiscent of Burke's comment in "On the Sublime and the Beautiful" that "beauty is striking as deformity is striking—in its novelty" (CPr 98).[8] "The Monkey Puzzle" depicts a strange natural beauty that "defies one"; both poem and tree are highly resistant to interpretation and categorization. Indeed, as Cristanne Miller has noted, "Moore's statements about art, as well as the unconventionalities of her forms, reflect her preference for a 'beauty' that is wild, prickly, and ethical rather than iconic, aesthetic, elite, and for a speaker who is idiosyncratic and emotional without being personal, representative, or transcendent" (Questions 115). The multiplicity of perspectives given of the tree and the difficulty the speaker has in naming and thus conceptualizing its appearance is indicative of its "prickly" physical and spiritual nature, as well as signaling the speaker's ethical refusal to cap her difficult subject matter with a "personal, representative, or transcendent" metaphor on top.

The poem is replete with images and references that are suggestive of determined, inviolate immobility. The tree is "in a kind of Flaubert's Carthage, it defies one" (the reference is to Flaubert's novel about besieged Carthage, *Salammbô*) and is aligned with "Gibraltar." It is suggestive of the claws and teeth of the feline, such as a "Paduan cat with lizard" and a "tiger in a bamboo thicket," and it makes "the lion's ferocious chrysanthemum head" appear "kind by comparison." The tree "knows" that "it is better to be lonely than unhappy," and though "it is worth its weight in gold," and "a true curio," it wards off human appropriation: "no one takes it/from these woods in which society's not knowing is colossal." Moreover, the monkey puzzle even opposes the speaker's tongue-tied attempts to name and so explain it; Moore employs the demonstrative pronoun "this" five times in the poem, "it" seven times, and the modifier "not" four times, as well as using frequent appositive phrases (e.g., "this pine-tree—this pine-tiger, is a tiger, not a dog"). In the shortest and least convoluted sentence of the free verse poem, Moore deems the tree "'An interwoven somewhat,' it will not come out." The abstraction of this assertion is important, for it underscores the multiple referentiality of the poem as a whole. *What* "will not come out"? The "tiger in a bamboo thicket"; the visual, "interwoven" patterning of the "Foo dog" and its "tail superimposed upon itself in a complacent half spiral"; the stubbornly resistant soldiers in their fortresses at Carthage and Gibraltar; the knot of the poem's quadruply repeated "not"; or the math problem, the "Puzzle" that is closure to the meaning of the poem itself?

Whatever the monkey puzzle's indefinable form may finally indicate, the tree's "porcupine-quilled, complicated starkness," like the thorns that protect from the "predatory hand" in "Roses Only," ensures its continued existence as an object viewed from a respectful distance. "This is beauty—" Moore declares, "a certain proportion in the skeleton which gives the best results." Its exterior defensiveness and its habitat in "woods in which society's not knowing is colossal" are dually the source of its "beauty," or attractiveness, to the speaker's eye and the off-putting of the same. The monkey puzzle as Moore renders it is an aesthetic, intellectual, and spiritual tease; it woos and repels, keeping us fascinated, but at that distance which its proportionate boundaries require. Thus its "proportion," like Edwards's "proportionate" relations between types and antitypes, holds it ontologically separate from, yet meaningfully engaged with, poet, reader, and natural world.

By the same token, the last four lines of the poem remind us of the tree's final inaccessibility to our assumptions of knowing and categorical knowledge: "One is at a loss, however, to know why it should be here, / in this morose part of the earth— / to account for its origin at all; / but we prove, we do not explain our birth." Although the artist may pronounce with some certainty that "this is beauty," "one" (poet as well as reader) is still "at a loss" to "explain" the why and the how of this tree's existence (or any existence). Art, history, and individual experience may each offer shifting perspectives of the monkey puzzle, but the tree, and, by extension, nature itself, may not be summed up from any one perspective. Instead, being "proves" its existence through resistance, through presenting prickly boundaries by which we must infer worth rather than grasp the object itself. (Indeed, in her subtle monetary allusions throughout the poem, such as "a true curio," "worth its weight in gold," to be at a "loss," and to attempt to "account for," Moore effectively undermines the acquisitive logic of the conqueror.)

In her closing pronouncement that "we prove, we do not explain our birth," Moore metonymically substitutes effect for cause, and observable attributes and qualities for essences and "origins" in her definition of being. To "prove" birth certainly functions within the poem's overall extended metaphor of offering mathematical proofs or possible answers to a "Puzzle," or might even be read with moral connotations (such as in "to prove oneself"). Yet the word also serves in two archaic senses: that of undergoing or experiencing (as in Christopher Marlowe's poem "The Passionate Shepherd to His Love," "Come live with me and be my Love, / And we will all the pleasures prove") and to be found or shown to be (such as in "she was proved to be innocent"). In this final sense, the poem's last line might be read as "we can only indicate, or signify toward, our existence; life must be evinced through an ontology of signification rather than an ontology of essence." While the shift in pronouns in the poem from "it" to "one" to "we" seems to indicate a move to a more personal subjectivity on the part of the poet, it is a subjectivity that does not attempt to "know" the natural world through intellectual mastery and explanation but that acknowledges the limits of language, art, and absolute perception.

Moore's use of the term "proportion" in "The Monkey Puzzle" foreshadows her growing aesthetic interest in constructing her natural forms in such as way as to balance their beautiful singularity with inherent connectedness to their material and spiritual matrixes. Making a sharp distinction between creature and Creator is foundational to Reformed, monotheistic thought. As previously discussed, for Jonathan Edwards, the term "proportion" summed up one of the key aspects of natural typology: the inherent connections between a type in nature and the spiritual realm it gestures toward in no way undermine the essential goodness or "excellency" of the materiality of nature itself. Instead, the spiritual and the physical exist in a "proportionate" relation. As with two dancers in a box formation, there is just the right amount of resistance and give, of distinction and mutuality, to keep alterity and connection in balance. In this sense, "proportion" is a metaphor for the underlying structural tension that holds the universe, and each created "being," in place and in "relation" to all other beings, producing a state of what Edwards termed "complex beauty" (*WJE* 6:333). A similar state of equipoise is frequently the subject of Moore's later work. For example, in two poems celebrating the Brooklyn Bridge, "In Lieu of the Lyre" (1965) and "Granite and Steel" (1966), Moore finds aesthetic and moral import in structural laws that, as in the case of the Brooklyn Bridge, hold elements together while holding them apart. With "In Lieu of the Lyre," Moore highlights what to the civil engineer may be of greater import than the metaphysical "waterfall, pilgrim and hat-brim" of a "verbal pilgrim": "you might have preferred," she quips, "a valuable axiom such as / 'a force at rest is at rest because balanced by some other force,'/or 'catenary and triangle together hold the span in place'" (*CP* 206). In "Granite and Steel," she addresses the bridge directly: "'O catenary curve' from tower to pier,/implacable enemy of the mind's deformity,/of man's uncompunctious greed."[9] Here, Moore celebrates the bridge as a visual embodiment of opposing yet conjoined forces: that ethical self-restraint which keeps one group of humanity from aggressively dominating and possessing another and that particularly American "affirming inter-acting harmony!" which ideally shares its "Liberty" with all (*CP* 205).

By the same token, also nascent in Moore's early work but pronounced in the poetry of the final thirty years of her life is the threefold convergence of a kind of metonymic being with moral and ethical doing and with notions of beauty or "style." Moore's meditation in "To a Snail" includes ontological as well as aesthetic claims. According to the poem, style is neither decorative nor a by-product of content, neither "the acquisition of any one thing/that is able to adorn" nor "the incidental quality that occurs/as a concomitant of something well said." Rather, since it would kill the humble snail attached to its shell, to pry style apart from message would destroy both. What "we value in style," the poem concludes, is "the principle that is hid:/in the absence of feet, 'a method of conclusions';/'a knowledge of principles,'/in the curious phenomenon of your occipital horn" (*CP* 85). Moore's snail embodies a type of style—that is, a type of aesthetic being-as-relation—that is "hid" and observable through its "absence," pointing away from itself, as does the snail's "occipital horn." In this sense, with its *aesthetic*, metrical "absence of feet," its *virtuous* "contractility" and "modesty" and *signifying* "principle that is hid," the snail illustrates an epistemological "knowledge of principles" that unites aesthetics and ethics with an ontological state of being-in-relation.

Moore considers similar rules of aesthetics in an essay written twenty-five years later, "Humility, Concentration, and Gusto." Framing her discussion in the contexts of war, freedom, and the art of the pen as a way to "persuade the enemy to change his mind," Moore reiterates the principle she had set forth in "To a Snail" that humility and style are interrelated, asking rhetorically, "It is true, is it not, that 'style does not depend on decoration but on simplicity and proportion?'" (*CPr* 420). (She does not allude to her 1924 poem directly but seems to be reminded of her original metaphor as she quotes four stanzas from William Cowper's "The Snail," whose "house" and "master" are one.) As Moore asserts, humility not only "armor[s]" one against the humbling consequences of false pretense but is also intellectually liberating (420). Recalling, in the 1920 "Picking and Choosing," an anecdote the Reverend E. H. Kellogg of Carlisle Second Presbyterian once told about himself, she writes that although "Caesar's *Commentaries* . . . now seem to me masterpieces . . . . [through anxiety and lack of humility] I was originally like the Hill School boy to whom I referred in one of my pieces of verse, who translated *summa diligentia* (with all speed): Caesar crossed the Alps on the top of a diligence" (*CPr* 420). In other words, for Moore, humility lifts the veil on the literal sign to reveal idiomatic or poetic potentialities beneath. In turn, she continues, the poet with the moral virtue of humility is liberated from the need for self-protection or autocratic control over the object of representation; she may then exercise the aesthetic discipline of "concentration" (or "compression," as she terms it in "To a Snail." Finally, "humility is an indispensable ally, enabling concentration to heighten gusto," that part of the sign whose potentiality is never exhausted in the process of signification. Gusto itself "thrives on freedom," yet, paradoxically, "freedom in art, as in life, is the result of a discipline imposed by ourselves," Moore states, thus returning potentiality to the realm of the aesthetic and the ethical (426).

Moore's ultimate refusal to delineate between the aesthetic and moral spheres and being itself as ethical relation to the other is illuminated by her affinity during the last three and a half decades of her life with Reinhold Niebuhr, an American philosopher, theologian, and activist, whom Linda Leavell credits at least in part for Moore's resurgent interest in religion after she moved to Brooklyn in the 1930s (*Holding*). Niebuhr, who began his career as a Lutheran pastor at a small church in Detroit, rose to prominence as a vocal supporter of social and racial justice in that city and as a religious leader with pacifist leanings during the First World War. He joined the faculty at Union Theological Seminary in 1928, and for his next thirty-two years there he was a prolific author of not only academic books and essays but also myriads of articles, reviews, and opinion pieces that regularly appeared in popular magazines and newspapers such as *The Nation*, *The Spectator*, and the *New York Herald Tribune*. Niebuhr's political positions moved dialectically during the long course of his career, but he always remained an unapologetic critic of both conservative and liberal theologians: he was too Augustinian in his view of human nature and the arc of history to accept the "sunny liberalism" of many of his academic contemporaries at Union, but at the same time too receptive of higher criticism to accept the older Biblicism of the traditionalists.[10] During the Second World War, Niebuhr was asked to become an adviser to the State Department's Policy and Planning staff; afterwards he frequently worked abroad as an advocate for international democracy, and in 1964 Lyndon Johnson awarded him the Presidential Medal of Freedom.

Moore began reading Niebuhr by at least 1937, when Elizabeth Bishop recommended him to Moore after hearing him speak at Vassar and when Moore herself heard him speak at Lafayette Avenue Presbyterian (Leavell, *Holding*). A year later she admiringly compares Bishop and Niebuhr in a letter to Bishop: "You and Dr. Niebuhr are two abashing peaks in present experience for me. Never have I heard an abler man nor seen a more insidiously innocent and artless artifice of innuendo than in your prison meditations" (*Letters* 390). After reading Niebuhr's article "Germans and Nazis" in a 1939 issue of *The Spectator*, Moore approvingly summarizes for her brother Warner what is a typical Niebuhr argument concerning the shared guilt of the participants of even a "just" war. "He reminds us that intolerance is at work in us all, *in all* countries—," she writes," that we ourselves 'persecute' Jews & Negroes & submit to wrongful tyranny. Or at least feel 'superior' in sundry ways" (*Letters* 395). Her admiration for the theologian, whom she listed late in life as one of a "few men of Socratic wisdom among us," was genuine and profound, such that in 1946 she would even gently venture to Ezra Pound that one of Niebuhr's sermons she had recently heard might be of benefit to him (*CPr* 648; *Letters* 461).

By the 1950s, Moore occasionally socialized with Niebuhr and his wife, Ursula, who were both admirers of the arts and who also counted among their mutual friends with Moore the poets W. H. Auden and T. S. Eliot. Moore's correspondence with the couple from 1952 to 1962 shows that the relationship was one of reciprocal support and intellectual admiration. She congratulates Niebuhr on the 1952 publication of *The Irony of American History*, for instance, for having written a book that contains "certain axioms rivaling scriptures. . . . 'Nothing however virtuous can be accomplished alone' and 'even the best human actions involve some guilt'; a point that strikes me more forcibly perhaps than any other—that virtue is never unmixed."[11] Niebuhr, in turn, replied gratefully to her for her support, responding to her 1955 letter concerning *The Self and Dramas of History*, "Your encouraging words are quite a tonic, particularly when I am not at all sure about the book."[12] When Moore gave the couple a copy of her translation of *The Fables of La Fontaine* in 1954, he wrote Moore to tell her it was a "wonderful work of art" and "a great artistic achievement," concluding that he and Ursula had "spoken of you frequently and rejoice in all your creative work."[13] That same year he invited Moore to speak to his students at Union Theological Seminary. It is not surprising that Moore and Niebuhr would have been fast friends: both spent their earliest years in late nineteenth-century Missouri parsonages (Niebuhr's father was a Lutheran minister), and Niebuhr attended Yale only a few years after Moore's brother Warner. Both shared a deep concern for social justice and held the Hebrew prophets of the Old Testament as exemplars of speaking lyrical truth to power. And in the years between the First and Second World Wars, both had modulated their earlier pacifist responses to armed conflict to pragmatic concerns about using force to justly resist oppression, about the dangers of excessive nationalism, and about the need for local and national communities in which love and justice both protect individuals and call them into accountable relations with their neighbors.[14]

But two of the deepest consanguinities between poet and theologian were their beliefs about the efficacy of symbolic language to convey spiritual truths and their categorical alignment of being, poetry, and ethics, an epistemological construction both based on their hermeneutic approaches to the sign systems of the Bible. Moore, as discussed in chapter 7, navigated a middle road through the early twentieth-century fundamentalist-modernist controversies of the Presbyterian Church with her poetic deployment of the concept of "the Real" and "the Actual," separate but overlapping material and spiritual verities, which she studied in the writings of believing critics such as P. T. Forsyth and George Adam Smith in the Reverend E. H. Kellogg's Bible class. The hermeneutics of the believing critics provided a way to incorporate the latest findings of historical criticism while also preserving what they believed to be the figural intent of the biblical texts. As Moore transcribed Kellogg's cautionary admonition in 1914: "We should be on our guard against slavish and hard literalism—we do not subject other literature to it and should not the Bible. What is imaginary in things of faith? All parts of heaven and earth work together" (Rosenbach VII:08:03).

Niebuhr, only five years younger than Moore, had likewise been raised in traditional Reformed circles, and he attended a Lutheran college and a Lutheran seminary before earning degrees at Yale Divinity School in 1915. He developed what he eventually termed a "mythical method" of biblical interpretation and what some scholars have named a "hermeneutic ontology" (McCann 28). For Niebuhr, deeming parts of the Bible "myth" meant not that they are untrue but that they are an attempt at linguistic expression of "eternally valid truths" based on "existential encounters between God and man" ("Reply" 437). "I do not know how it is possible to believe in anything pertaining to God and eternity 'literally,'" he wrote in 1956, "but I do not equate 'symbolically' with 'subjectively'" (446). He often compared the role of the poet with that of the theologian or the prophet, explaining that both worked in the powerful realm of the symbolic to bring the numinous to bear on corporal experience. As he wrote in his journal as a young pastor: "Religion is poetry. The truth in the poetry is vivified by adequate poetic symbols and is therefore more convincing than the poor prose with which the average preacher must attempt to grasp the ineffable" (*Leaves* 50). For Niebuhr, the "ineffable" and the unknown ought always to be acknowledged in theology and biblical interpretation. Far from affirming familiar assumptions about the nature of truth, being, and ethical relation, however, the truly mysterious is awe-filled and troubling, intersected as it is by the presence of the radically Other. As he defines the concept in one of his final essays, "mystery in short is the shadowy realm of twilight where both coherence and incoherence are known or intimated, as well as the threshold of glory which gives light but does not reveal its nature" ("Faith" 5). Thus "the human story," he concludes, "is too grand and awful to be told without reverence for the mystery and majesty that transcend all human knowledge" (13). It was this concept of mystery as both disturbing and sustaining that Moore resonated with in her readings of Niebuhr and referred to in a letter to Elizabeth Bishop: "Dr. Niebuhr says Christianity is too much on the defensive, that it is more mysterious, more comprehensive, more lastingly deep and dependable than unsuccessfully simpler substitutes which objectors to it offer" (*Letters* 391).

Yet to allow such a pervasive sense of mystery to be at work at the core of an interpretation of a biblical text required a faith in the final ends of a God-given existential freedom and a willingness to let go of an absolutist authoritative claim over that text (which is not to say that any or all readings would be considered valid; Moore and Niebuhr both asserted the importance of submitting individual interpretations to the balancing interpretations of the local and historical church body). With their "reverence for [hermeneutic] mystery" and their Augustinian-influenced concepts of selfhood, Moore and Niebuhr shared a notion that ontology and ethics were inherently connected. On the one hand, the self has a potential for unlimited transcendence and freedom beyond the confines of an essentialist selfhood; as Niebuhr observes, while "the Hellenic component of our culture generated our sciences and philosophies[,] . . . [w]hen we deal with aspects of reality which exhibit a freedom above and beyond structures, we must resort to the Hebraic dramatic and historical way of apprehending reality. Both the divine and the human self belong to this category" ("Reply" 433). On the other hand, the entirety of the self is also intertwined with and implicated in its ethical and moral choices; the self may not be partitioned, for example, between virtuous reason and base desire. Hence, Niebuhr writes, echoing Jonathan Edwards's *Freedom of the Will* as well as Augustine, "the fundamental biblical, and I think true, proposition about man's evil is that its root is in the self and not in the mind or in the body. When Augustine places it in the self's will, he insists also that the self expresses itself in its will" (447).[15]

Metonymically expressed through its attributes and relations, the self in Niebuhr's philosophy is one aspect of a broader material and spiritual reality in which "things and events are in a vast web of relationships and are known through their relations" (*Christian Realism* 175). He develops this idea most completely in *The Self and the Dramas of History* (1955), observing: "While the self is a unique center of life, it is indeterminately 'open' to other selves. There are no geographic or temporal limits for the self's dialogue with others" (33). At the same time, however, the genuine self "recognizes the other as the limit of its expansiveness. It is the 'other'; and the otherness includes a final mystery that even the most imaginative love cannot penetrate. It is an independent and unique life which, ultimately considered, cannot be fitted into any, even common, purpose or project. There must therefore be an element of reservation and reverence for the other in even the most mutual relations" (32). Thus the self most fully comes into being in dialogical relation to its community and to a God who is a part of but also outside of this human community.[16]

Moore, who, like Niebuhr, conceived of selfhood as a kind of being-in-relation, found spiritual and intellectual confirmation in *The Self and the Dramas of History,* and wrote to him shortly after the book was published to say she found "exhilaratingly impeccable the statement: 'The self does not realize itself most fully when self-realization is its conscious aim.'"[17] She would repeat the statement a year later in "Idiosyncrasy and Technique," a lecture she presented at the University of California at Berkeley and then published in 1958. Here, as she had in the 1949 "Humility, Concentration, and Gusto," Moore elucidates the concurrence between the ontological, the ethical, and the aesthetic as they cohere within the artist's creative process. This time she subtly redirects the heretofore masculine-coded notion of "genius"—poetic or otherwise—away from romantic and egocentric essentialism and toward a paradigm of metonymical attributes. With a doubly removed displacement of the father of ego psychology ("Mr. Burnett drew attention to the biography of Dr. Freud by Ernest Jones"), she points to "what is said there of genius as being *not a quality but qualitative*—a combination of attributes which differs with the person" (*CPr* 515, emphasis added). Three of these signifying attributes, she continues, are "honesty," an ethically connotative characteristic that might be correlated with naturalness and humility; "a sense of the really significant," which is a quality of other-centered perception reminiscent of the significance through outwards signification she alluded to as "gusto" in her earlier essay; and the aesthetically focused "power of concentration" (515).

Moore also returns here, albeit obliquely, to the ethical trope of vision and the gaze. Perhaps mindful of Niebuhr's "self" that "does not realize itself most fully when self-realization is its conscious aim," she quotes in full "Blessed Is the Man," a poem she composed for an address to students at Columbia and had published recently in the *Ladies' Home Journal* (*CPr* 509). Moore explains that she wrote the poem "about denigration as treason," as an expression of her unhappiness at the "too much sarcasm" expressed by "our smart press" at "any touch of unfeigned gusto" (513, 511). The final stanza reads: "Blessed is the man whose faith is different / from possessiveness—of a kind not framed by "things which do appear"— / who will not visualize defeat, too intent to cower; / whose illumined eye has seen the shaft that gilds the sultan's tower" (513). For Moore, the antidote to "the mildew of disrespect"—the penchant to "denigrate, depreciate, denunciate," as she phrases it in the poem—is vision, seeing "of a kind not framed by 'things which do appear'" (*CPr* 512). Her reference to Hebrews 11:3 and to the "illumined eye" that "has seen the shaft that gilds the sultan's tower" (a phrase she attributes to the title of a book, *The Citadel of Learning*) harkens back to the Reformed teachings of her grandfather Warner and his sermon "Things in the World Which Are Not Transient," in which he contrasts the nonpossessive gaze of the one who is focused on eternal realities with the more grasping vision of one focused on the material "things which are seen" (2 Cor. 4:18).

In her late poems about the "things which do appear" in the material and natural world, Moore's signifying and ethical reconstruction of the gaze enacts this paradigm for understanding the relationship of observer to the observed—a perceptual category in which the ending or continuing of signification becomes a function of ethical intent. As she did in her earliest poetry, Moore continues to configure the discourse between the natural world and the self with permanent boundaries of reticence that prohibit the eclipse of nature and, by extension, the other, by the individual ego. As her friend Niebuhr had concurred, this indeterminacy and alterity of the other is that which must precede and underlie the equal and confirming ecstatic excess of any momentary union with nature; it is embodied in the blessed "man whose faith is different/from possessiveness." Yet, while her earliest poems about such natural objects stress both their aesthetic, "porcupine-quilled, complicated starkness" and their metonymic contiguity with their environs, the figures in her later poems depict a broader and serene equipoise that, assuming both individual existence and inherent connection with others, goes on to emphasize the hermeneutic "mystery" of this relation between the physical and the spiritual, and the ethical stance that is content to let it remain so.

In "By Disposition of Angels" (1948), for instance, Moore posits a hermeneutic of awe for reading the Book of Nature, a method that may still make gentle claims for "eternally valid truths" based on "existential encounters between God and man," as Niebuhr phrased it, but without insisting on intellectual mastery of those entities:

> Messengers much like ourselves? Explain it.
> Steadfastness the darkness makes explicit?
> Something heard most clearly when not near it?
>   Above particularities,
> these unparticularities praise cannot violate.
>   One has seen, in such steadiness never deflected,
>   how by darkness a star is perfected.
>
> Star that does not ask me if I see it?
> Fir that would not wish me to uproot it?
> Speech that does not ask me if I hear it?
>   Mysteries expound mysteries.
> Steadier than steady, star dazzling me, live and elate,
>   no need to say, how like some we have known; too like her,
>   too like him, and a-quiver forever. (*CP* 142)

In a metaphysics similar here to Emily Dickinson's, Moore introduces nature as a speaking Silence, a series of communicating yet finally ungraspable "unparticularities" that the romantic poet's "praise cannot violate." Moore's first biographer, Charles Molesworth, makes mention of a September 19, 1948, letter to Elizabeth Bishop in which Moore tells Bishop that the poem "was based on a passage in the New Testament, Acts 7:53, 'We have received the law by disposition of angels and have not kept it'" (Molesworth 333). The context of the verse, coming as it does at the end of Stephen's fury-producing jeremiad to the ruling Jewish council in Jerusalem and immediately before they order his martyrdom, would seem to support Molesworth's understanding of the poem as one that "meditates on the theme of virtue revealed by adversity," the ethical importance of prophetic truth-telling despite persecution (333). Another clue about the sources of Moore's inspiration for this poem also relates to suffering and faith. In the conclusion of her 1944 essay "Feeling and Precision," she recollects how the Catholic philosopher Jacques Maritain, "when lecturing on scholasticism and immortality, spoke of those suffering in concentration camps, 'unseen by any star, unheard by any ear,' and the almost terrifying solicitude with which he spoke made one know that belief is stronger even than the struggle to survive" (CPr 402).

Furthermore, the juxtaposition of the angels of the poem's title and the thrice-mentioned star also indicate that the poem is a meditation on the major biblical concurrence of both angels and a star, the Proclamation—the angelic heralding of Christ's birth, an event that had been preceded by the appearance of a "star in the east" (Matt. 2:2).[18] The angels and the star are liminal figures in both poem and biblical narratives, signs that dually signify beyond themselves and seem to mark the boundaries between heaven and earth, the material and the spiritual; they are thus fit to be emissaries or "messengers" between the visible and the invisible. Indeed, the angels of the title are "messengers" both by their inherent "disposition," or that defining quality of metonymic being that signifies, or communicates, beyond itself, and by their power of "disposition" to order, arrange, and proclaim their revelatory declaration.

But what is their message? Moore's poem proceeds by a series of six oxymoronic rhetorical queries—queries by whose very articulate inarticulateness is expressed a mixture of awe and doubt, and yet belief sturdy enough to frame the questions at all. This is the *via negativa*, what Saint John of the Cross termed "the dark night of the soul," in which the spiritual seeker proceeds by the loss of the ability to rely on logical reasoning and the senses and finds paradoxical illumination through the experience of negation and darkness.[19] The speaker begins with the question and responsorial challenge of line one—"Messengers much like ourselves? Explain it"—which jointly connects the poem to its title and to the meditation that follows; then the speaker progresses not with explanation but with two further questions that posit binary oppositions.[20] The "steadfastness" of the star that "darkness" contrarily "makes explicit" and the "something"—the incomprehensible speech of the angels, perhaps, or the communicating signification of the star itself—that is "heard most clearly" only when one is "not near it" serve to lift the speaker's musings out of the realm of the known and the symbolic and into unknowing. Such a state is reminiscent of the semiotic chora Kristeva once defined as that which "precedes evidence, verisimilitude, spatiality, and temporality" (26)—or the inchoate space of Niebuhr's "mystery." Highlighting language as language, Moore withholds the expected symbolic and romantic payoff the questions seem to imply in favor of an undefined state in which solutions must remain intuitive rather than verbally expressed.

Although the speaker can neither "Explain" nor make "explicit" this "steadfastness" which is categorically "Above particularities," nevertheless, she asserts, "one has *seen,* in such steadiness never deflected,/how by darkness a star is perfected." As a pinpoint of light stands out most visibly when it is surrounded by a dark field, optical, intellectual, and spiritual "darkness" serves to reveal the star that may be known metonymically only by its quality of unending "steadiness never deflected." In celebrating slippery "unparticularities," Moore redirects the viewer's eye away from a fixed, natural symbol. Instead, advancing through the poem by negation and the concomitant refusal to close meaning and signification, she presents us with a photographic negative. Our inverse gaze at the star must infer the invisible behind it, just as the ethical gaze of love sees unbidden the invisible beneath the visible. This star, "by darkness . . . perfected," is thus made visible by a glimpse into the star's discursive trace, its potential for signification.

The three questions opening the second stanza all serve to frame the natural, external world as a place with a separate ontological existence needing neither interpretation nor interference from humanity: "Star that does not ask me if I see it?/Fir that would not wish me to uproot it?/Speech that does not ask me if I hear it?" The star, the fir (a wry reference to a Christmas tree that the poem's connotations of Nativity evokes), and "Speech" (again, possibly the speech of the angels or a more general speaking and signifying nature itself) recollect natural types of the Edwardsean typology and the natural objects of Moore's early poetry. Retaining their own identity as beings-in-relation, an identity that constitutes the metonymic gesture beyond themselves, they signify an ethical and aesthetic "steadiness" beyond the human which cannot be separated, epistemologically speaking, from their ontological, metonymic existence. The speaker finishes her questions with an affirmation that seems in direct reply to the demand to "Explain it" in the first stanza: only further "Mysteries," she assents, "expound mysteries."

It is not until the final three lines of the poem that Moore gestures toward the tradition of romantic, lyrical interpretation of nature: "Steadier than steady, star dazzling me, live and elate, / no need to say, how like some we have known; too like her, / too like him, and a-quiver forever." Cristanne Miller classifies this among what she terms Moore's late love poems, poems that "do not idealize a beloved" but rather constitute a critique of the genre by "disrupting the traditional power differential between active speaker/lover and silent, subservient, passive beloved" (*Questions* 195). Miller further notes how the dual references to "her" and "him" direct the poem toward "'some' rather than a single one loved person" (198). Certainly, as a love poem locating the beloved's beauty "above particularities," "By Disposition of Angels" is a far cry from a conventional romantic lyric such as Byron's "She Walks in Beauty." Byron's poem, which marches forward in masculine-rhymed *ababab* iambic tetrameter, praises Lady Wilmot Horton's appearance as "like the night / of cloudless climes and starry skies," and the evening sky is merely a vehicle symbolizing how "all that's best of dark and bright / Meet in her aspect and her eyes." Moore's two stanzas cohere with each other in less obvious ways. In addition to their characteristically matching syllabic meter (10, 10, 10, 8, 14, 13, 10), the unusual rhyme scheme of the seven-lined stanzas (*aaabcdd* and *aaabcee*) is vaguely reminiscent of a Shakespearean sonnet with its closing couplets, an allusion that is heightened by their typographical indentation on the page.

In Moore's poem, however, unlike in the proposition-solution form of the sonnet, it is the last four lines of each stanza that set out to reply to the questions posed in the first three lines; and these first three lines stress the importance of their queries by their strongly trochaic—not iambic—pentameter. At the same time, the polysyllabic and unstressed, or feminine, rhymes of the final four lines of each stanza ("particularities" / "mysteries"; "violate" / "elate"; "deflected" / "perfected"; "too like her" / "forever") prevent the poem from having the strong sense of closure or finality that a lyric such as Byron's would. Finally, perhaps most revealing of Moore's strategic prosody here are the primarily stressed words in the paired sixth lines of the two stanzas, "seen" and "say." Moore's rhythmic emphasis here highlights the idea that while "one has *seen*" the awe-inspiring beauty of the heavens in the first stanza, still there is "no need to *say*," or capture in words, completely and finally, "how like" the star is to "some we have known" in the second stanza. Instead, the poet is content merely to trace the contours of signifying, yet mysterious and only partially decipherable, natural and spiritual worlds.

The "star dazzling me," which the speaker describes as "live and elate," is multi-referential and indeterminate; whether the apostrophe is ultimately directed to "her," "him," "some we have known," or to a Christic antitype figure, it is the poet's final refusal to capture such a beloved in fixed symbolism that indicates an ethical, nonproprietary stance toward both nature and the Other.[21]

In other poems from the final third of her career, Moore ponders the antitheses of "humility," "concentration," and "gusto"—rapacious individuality, a denial of the boundaries of the other, and a concomitant refusal to continue signification ethically, aesthetically, and semiotically beyond the self. Unlike the denizens of the plant and animal kingdoms, humans may harbor the assumption that the individual self might have ontological meaning and existence outside its part in the signifying matrix, apart from relation to the broader community of humanity or nation. Thus Moore wonders in the 1960 "Tell Me, Tell Me"

> where might there be a refuge for me
> from egocentricity
> and its propensity to bisect,
> mis-state, misunderstand
> and obliterate continuity? (*CP* 231)

"Egocentricity," with its deadening stasis and self-referentiality, prefers to "obliterate continuity" rather than defer beyond itself to the chain of signification. In "its propensity to bisect, / mis-state, misunderstand," egocentricity becomes a willed impasse, substituting a monotonous sameness and sterile, mimetic reproduction in place of "gusto" and "idiosyncrasy." The artist's steadfast determination to give way, to give place to the other—ethically and semiotically—seems to offer the only "refuge" from such "verbal ferocity": "Even so; 'deference'; / yes, deference may be my defense" (CP 232).

Of course, even in 1921 Moore insists that it is the poet's task to resist the temptation to objectify the other, and at the same time

> to convince snake-charming controversialists
> that one keeps on knowing
> "that the Negro is not brutal,
> that the Jew is not greedy,
> that the Oriental is not immoral,
> that the German is not a Hun."
> ("The Labors of Hercules," *CP* 53)

The "snake-charming controversialists'" use of binary pairs (black/white, Jew/Gentile, good/bad, and so on) is based on an epistemological assumption in which there is discontinuity between the self and the other and which allows them the luxury of negative projection. For Moore, this is a category of non-"knowing," of "snobbishness" that "is a stupidity," for it effectively undercuts the ontological, ethical, and aesthetic connections between self, other, and community. As Cristanne Miller argues: "Prejudice, xenophobia, selfishness, materialism, greed, cynical distrust of others—these for Moore are the enemies of an ethical (for her, democratic or 'free') community of individuals against which wars, internal and international, should be fought. For her, such abstractions—and their contrasting qualities: love, trust, tolerance, willingness to compromise, skill at some activity or art, generosity—constitute selfhood more important than aspects of physical being" (Questions 165). For Moore, the attempt to define and distinguish the self not only as over and against the other, but also as a unit whose supreme importance is conceived of only insofar as it is apart from that other, necessarily leads to crime, wars, and the troubling detachment of self from community that is a part of modern angst.

In this sense, Fredric Jameson's critique of Edvard Munch's *The Scream,* a painting that he believes to be "a canonical expression of the great modernist thematics of alienation, anomie, solitude, social fragmentation, and isolation" (11), might serve as a visual comparison with Moore's censoring of "egocentricity" and "stupidity." According to Jameson, *The Scream*'s voiced yet voiceless gesture of horror and unalloyed despair

> shows us that expression requires the category of the individual monad, but it also shows us the heavy price to be paid for that precondition, dramatizing the unhappy paradox that when you constitute your individual subjectivity as a self-sufficient field and a closed realm, you thereby shut yourself off from everything else and condemn yourself to the mindless solitude of the monad, buried alive and condemned to a prison cell without egress. (15)

Certainly Moore would agree with Jameson that the egocentric and ontologically essentialist "I," constructed as "a self-sufficient field and a closed realm," when left to itself quickly reverts to the state of the Miltonic "Myself am Hell." In its refusal of the in-between, liminal state of signification beyond self-referentiality—again, choosing to embody "the propensity" to "obliterate continuity" instead of "deference," as Moore phrases it in "Tell Me, Tell Me"—individual subjectivity, be it modern or romantic, becomes imprisoned within its own solipsism. This is an ontology that is nonconductive, to borrow another of Moore's illustrations; it lacks that "creative power" that is metonymically evinced "by its capacity to conquer one's detachment" ("The Labors of Hercules," *CP* 53).

Where Moore's later vision differs in emphasis from the despairing zeitgeist Jameson detects in the modernist painters he explores in *Postmodernism, or, The Cultural Logic of Late Capitalism* is in her more hopeful assertions that through art and observation, love and faith, it *is* possible for humanity to participate in meaningful discourse beyond what Jameson terms "the individual monad." The artist's close observation and multi-perspectival renderings of natural typology—the signifying and significant "animals' power of adaptation to environment," as she reminds us in her 1955 essay "What There Is to See at the Zoo" (*CPr* 473)—reveals that we too might learn that "deference" may be our "defense" ("His Shield"). In "The Icosasphere" (1950), for instance, Moore sets nature alongside both human cupidity and human creativity, offering the hope that "integration" between self and the other, between the aesthetic and the ethical, and between the natural and the spiritual is indeed possible.

Moore's notes for "The Icosasphere" tell us that the poem is based on three sources: a comment beginning "In Buckinghamshire hedgerows" attributed to her friend Edward McKnight Kauffer, an illustrator and graphic artist; a 1949 *New York Times* article detailing a $30 million "snuff fortune" of an heirless widow and the concomitant crimes committed in the attempts by pretenders to claim the money; and a 1950 *New York Times* piece titled "Economy in the Use of Steel" detailing "a steel globe of a design invented by J. O. Jackson" (*CP* 281–82). The poem's three, highly irregular six-line stanzas contiguously link first an image of birds' nests "in parabolic concentric curves," then a listing of crimes committed by those "avid for someone's fortune," and finally a meditation on the "icosasphere" and the Egyptian engineering achievement of erecting a "seventy-eight-foot solid / granite vertically" (*CP* 143).

In the poem's opening stanza, the birds who make their nests "In Buckinghamshire hedgerows" of "merged green density" labor to "'weave little bits of string and moths and feathers and thistledown, / in parabolic concentric curves' and, / working for concavity, leave spherical feats of rare efficiency." Their modest construction materials, their symbiotic relation to their environment, as well as their focused engineering prowess and "rare efficiency," indicate that they are creatures who are in harmonious unity with their purposes and their surroundings; what they are "working for"—"concavity"—they achieve. "Whereas," Moore continues, "through lack of integration," twenty-one people who are "avid for someone's fortune" are variously involved in murders, suicides, and "perjury." "But then," she adds, in the tongue-in-cheek language of an advertising brochure, "there is the icosasphere / in which at last we have steel-cutting at its summit of economy." The icosasphere, shaped like an "icosahedron" and made of "twenty triangles conjoined," is able to "wrap one // ball or double-rounded shell / with almost no waste."

Moore ends the poem, however, not so much on a final note of praise for the achievement, but with a subtle reminder of the limits of human understanding. Just as we cannot fully comprehend how birds perform the simple chore of making their nests, neither are we capable of outstripping what the ancient Egyptians constructed without the benefit of modern technology:

> Would the engineers making one,
> or Mr. J. O. Jackson tell us
> how the Egyptians could have set up seventy-eight-foot solid
> granite vertically?
> We should like to know how that was done.

Enacting that "integration" by which the poem's imagery turns in the first stanza, "The Icosasphere" is constructed with multiple rhyming patterns. The endings of lines two and five in each stanza rhyme on unaccented syllables ("density" / "efficiency"; "perjury" / "economy"; "geometrically" / "vertically"), while the third and sixth lines rhyme chiefly on accented endings, with the exception of the thematically important and slant-rhymed "integration" ("thistledown" / "integration"; "run" / "one"; "one" / "done"). Moore also includes internal rhyme, such as stanza one's "concavity" and "efficiency" in line five and "weave" and "leave" between lines three and five. Furthermore, even the pattern of the poem's left-hand indentation offers a visual counterpart to that "concavity" of the first stanza. The "parabolic, concentric curves" of the birds' nests and the rounded icosasphere thus dramatize what Moore envisioned to be a categorical unity between a natural order of being which signifies larger ideals by the very act of its existence, the ethical realm of human choice between such positive signification and self-referential greed, and the aesthetic representation of this "economy" and "integration" through poetry, engineering, and architecture. In this sense, Moore's meta-poetic is finally a redemptive one: if we are able to refuse the "avid" greed for taking what does not belong to us, we are capable, like the birds, of channeling our energies into making our own "icosasphere."

"If it is unpermissible, in fact fatal / to be personal and undesirable // to be literal—detrimental as well / if the eye is not innocent—," Moore ponders in the opening stanzas of her 1963 "To a Giraffe," "does it mean that // one can live only on top leaves that are small / reachable only by a beast that is tall?" (*CP* 215). In "To a Giraffe," Moore returns to a familiar meditation in which she juxtaposes the natural world with the manmade one of artifice and uses the contrast to make a statement about poetry: as in her 1919 "Poetry," she implies here that a natural reticence which embodies rather than equivocates says more by saying less. The "irresistible," "exceptional" giraffe serenely knows what it is about, unlike the "emotionally-tied-in-knots animal," "plagued by the psychological." Yet in poking fun at the human condition, Moore never becomes misanthropic. Like the giraffe, whose feet are on the ground but who is able to see over the trees, she implies, we too are capable of living simultaneously in two worlds (as are the famous amphibians of her earlier poems, such as her "real toads" and the plumet basilisk).

Having weathered the fundamentalist-modernist controversies from within the Presbyterian Church, Moore found intellectual and imaginative liberation in the "interacting" "verities" (to borrow terms from the title of a 1947 poem) of the believing critics, who asserted that equally real though disparate realms might indeed be linked in meaningful ways through the work of poetry, biblical or otherwise. For these theologians and scholars, as well as for Moore, the space of language and literary interpretation is the place of transubstantiation, where "the initial great truths" are illuminated in the experience of the reader. In her later years Moore's thoughts concerning the role and authority of the Bible still sound remarkably similar to those of the Progressive Era believing critics, as exemplified by her pastor E. H. Kellogg. Concerning the relationship between science and faith, for instance, she strikes the same tone in 1950 as she did in her 1922 essay praising a "reverence for mystery" (and echoes her grandfather Warner's and friend Niebuhr's sermons, in substance if not in form): "Experience is almost certain to accept the fact that mystery is not just a nut which diligence can crack. Mystical belief which is not unthinking belief, seems to find that science does not discredit the supernatural but reinforces it. That is to say, we see that reverence for science and reverence for the soul can interact" (*CPr* 677).

For Moore and other Presbyterians of her ilk, the Bible in the twentieth century remained a trustworthy authority that was open to testing and open to questions. Its authority was supported by personal experience, but experience that needed to be checked by reason and by spiritual community. As Moore remarks to the *Partisan Review*, "Convictions . . . are the result of experience—corroborated by the thinking of others—and the moral law (which is self-demonstrating, most of us admit)" (*CPr* 677). These "others" include not only the personal testimony of the present church community but also the historical and universal church. Hence, in the tribute she wrote for her Brooklyn pastor Alvin Magary's retirement, Moore would tell the congregation that they had been "reminded by Dr. Magary that the heroes of the Bible are, indeed, 'saints without halos'" (654). The Bible, Moore continues, is a book of "remembrance—of God's mercy accorded men through no merit of their own, a memorial of escape from bondage, not because they were few but because the Lord loved them" (654). As a record of the heroic experiences of people who knew God, the Bible is tested and testable, a belief that Magary would allude to frequently, as in his 1930 sermon "The Secret Things": "So we come back to the word of Moses, to the word of Jesus, to the word of all them that in the face of a thousand mysteries are yet wise enough to believe and trust" (4).

In 1980, eight years after Moore's funeral there, the Lafayette Avenue Presbyterian Church in Brooklyn held a celebration of Moore's life in a morning service titled "The Faith of Marianne Moore." The Reverend Dr. George Litch Knight, Moore's last pastor, said of Moore: "Her theological insights were uncanny; an involvement with WORDS gave her a very special concern for meaning in terms of the Christian Faith" (Willis, "MM"). Like the best of poets, Moore fashioned her lifework around keen observation, strenuous, disciplined craftsmanship, and deep meditation on language. Hers is a poetic universe that, while acknowledging the darkness in human behavior that she had observed in two world wars and in racism and injustice in her own nation, remains ultimately hopeful that even in partialness there remains beauty and truth that art can affirm. As she writes in "To a Giraffe":

> After all
> consolations of the metaphysical
> can be profound. In Homer, existence
>
> is flawed; transcendence, conditional;
> "the journey from sin to redemption, perpetual." (*CP* 215)

Notes

1. Jonathan Edwards: A Reconsideration

1. The broad contours of the academy's first resuscitation of Edwards's image, a story of literary revivification by now well known, continue to cast a long shadow on our attitudes toward Edwards-as-writer today. Briefly, after the divine's reputation had fallen into near obscurity by the end of the nineteenth century, scholars at the start of the twentieth understood a need to find a literary connection between the colonial era, the various mid-eighteenth-century American intellectual engagements with the European Enlightenment, and the consequent rise of literary romanticism. To fill this spot, a number of scholars resurrected a divided Jonathan Edwards to serve as either the sire of a grand American literary and philosophical lineage or, conversely, as the whipping boy for America's intellectual failings. See, for instance, the work of H. R. Niebuhr, Perry Miller, Vernon L. Parrington, and Van Wyck Brooks.

2. Miller's interpretation of Edwards as modernist and his typology as a precursor to a Neoplatonic, Emersonian "Correspondence" had far-reaching effects on several generations of scholars and may be traced in such influential works as Alan Heimert's *Religion and the American Mind* (1966), Ursula Brumm's *American Thought and Religious Typology* (1970), and Mason Lowance's *Language of Canaan* (1980).

3. Bercovitch's work, along with a number of other highly influential studies published in the 1970s and early 1980s, also traces the development of Puritan typology into a nationalistic and prophetic reading of key leaders and events in early New England. See especially the edited collection *Typology and Early American Literature,* as well as "Typology in Puritan New England," and "Horologicals to Chronometricals." It is worthwhile to note that contemporary scholars of early American religious history are reexamining these claims. For instance, the editors of *Cotton Mather and Biblia Americana* write, "Significantly, we have so far not discovered one single instance in which Mather's 'Biblia' uses typology other than in a traditional Christo-centric form" (Smolinski and Stievermann 10).

4. The Jonathan Edwards Center at Yale University provides free digital access to the entirety of Edwards's *Works.* (While the published series stops at twenty-six volumes, the total online and searchable volumes numbered seventy-three at the time of this writing.) The website's vast and growing Edwards resources include the interdisciplinary

digital journal *Jonathan Edwards Studies,* a multimedia library, and ongoing digital sermon editing and encyclopedia projects. See http://edwards.yale.edu.

5. *WJE* 26 includes two previously unpublished notebooks, a "Catalogue" with 720 entries listing books Edwards hoped to acquire and an "Account Book" listing books he had lent to fellow clergy and parishioners. Thomas H. Johnson's 1931 "Jonathan Edwards' Background Reading" focused only on Edwards's "Catalogue."

6. The richness of Edwards's typological vision is borne out over the breadth of his writings. He overtly theorizes about natural typology in several major notebooks and a plethora of sermons. These notebooks include the following: "Miscellanies," begun in 1722, when Edwards was nineteen, and continued until the end of his life, is contained in nine manuscript volumes and is the largest collection of his theological, biblical, and philosophical commentaries; "The Mind," begun in 1723, details Edwards's lifelong metaphysical concerns; "Images of Divine Things," begun in 1728 or 1729, was specifically set aside for observations about natural typology; and "Types," begun in the mid-1740s, contains important reflections on his system of natural typology. In addition, Edwards works out the implications of this natural typology in quite a few sermons, constantly striving to demonstrate to his congregations both the accessibility and the dynamism of God's voice in the world around them. Even Edwards's final treatises, such as *Dissertation I. Concerning the End for which God Created the World* (1755), exhibit the influence of Edwards's early and lasting typological metaphysics.

7. Despite the intensely paternal mores of eighteenth-century society, as Edwards's biographer George Marsden notes, "Jonathan was growing up in a home that was, practically speaking, a world of women" (18). Marsden describes Edwards's mother, Esther, as a woman "of impressive intelligence, learning, and theological acumen," who, "after her husband died, remained an avid reader and teacher. Until she was in her nineties, women of East Windsor regularly came to afternoon sessions in the old parlor–school room for readings of the Bible and theological writers punctuated by her acute commentary" (19). From the little information that survives concerning his family, it appears that Edwards's sisters thrived in the family's highly intellectual environment; they learned Latin along with him, and all but one were sent to a finishing school in Boston.

8. Edwards also lived much of his life under constant threat of warfare with the French Canadians and their Native American allies. As Marsden phrases it, during his formative years New England was "at the vortex of conflict among three civilizations—the British Protestant, the French Catholic, and the Indian. Each was fiercely struggling to control North America" (3). A maternal aunt and cousins were killed a year after his birth in the French and Indian raid on Deerfield; his uncle John Williams (author of the pious 1707 best-seller *The Redeemed Captive, Returning to Zion*) and cousins subsequently spent several years as captives in Canada. During his childhood, his father, Timothy, briefly took part in Queen Anne's War as a chaplain with the colonial forces; intermittent hostilities continued throughout his life, culminating in the 1755–1764 French and Indian War.

9. An account of his early conversion experiences, the "Narrative" was written when Edwards was thirty-six and, as a pastor, had guided anxious congregations through the conversion process for more than fifteen years. Stressing the beauty and graciousness of God rather than His severity, the "Narrative" is generally more joyous and hopeful in tone than the standard Puritan conversion narrative and demonstrates how the Book of Nature is a key primer in Edwards's spiritual growth. In fact, before the mature Ed-

wards worked out his simplified morphology of conversion in *A Faithful Narrative* and elsewhere, he had some concern as to the normalcy of his spiritual experience because it differed from the multiple stages that had been set out by Puritan clergy such as Thomas Hooker. As Edwards worried in his "Diary" on December 18, 1722, "I cannot speak so fully to my experience of that preparatory work, of which divines speak," and "I do not remember that I experienced regeneration, exactly in those steps, in which divines say it is generally wrought" (*WJE* 16:759).

10. "Not that the saints are made partakers of the essence of God, and so are 'Godded' with God, and 'Christed' with Christ, according to the abominable and blasphemous language and notions of some heretics," Edwards hastens to add, "but, to use the Scripture phrase, they are made partakers of God's fullness . . . , that is, of God's spiritual beauty and happiness" (*WJE* 2:203).

11. Miller first explored the link between Edwards and Emerson in his essay "From Edwards to Emerson" (1940). And while Miller was not the earliest scholar to assert this connection, his argument was by far the most influential. Scholars who had previously suggested such an alignment include Mrs. John T. Sargent, editor of *Sketches and Reminiscences* (1880), and Alexander V. G. Allen, in his *Jonathan Edwards* (1889). See also Miller, "Jonathan Edwards on the Sense of the Heart," and "The Rhetoric of Sensation" in *Errand into the Wilderness.*

12. As Stephen J. Stein observes, "Edwards never waffled on the primacy of Scripture as the principal source of divine revelation, nor on the usefulness of biblical typology as an interpretive device" ("Spirit" 125). Edwards's own writings show that he is always aware he is charting a narrow course, or a "medium," as he puts it, "between those that cry down all types, and those that are for turning all into nothing but allegory and not having it to be true history; and also the way of the rabbis that find so many mysteries in letters" (*WJE* 11:151). Throughout his notebooks "Images of Divine Things" and "Types," he urges a freedom of interpretation of natural types, for "by the Scripture it is plain that innumerable other things are types that are not interpreted in Scripture (all the ordinances of the Law are all shadows of good things to come)" (152). As long as the explications of their *spiritual meaning* fall within the bounds of scriptural doctrine, the individual natural image need not be one that is explicitly referred to in the Bible. Indeed, although a great many of the types Edwards describes *are* traditionally biblical (e.g., the dove as a type of the Holy Spirit or the sun as a type of Christ), he has confidence in the ability of the divinely led believer always to remember that, as he writes in "Images" no. 156, "the Book of Scripture is the interpreter of the book of nature two ways: viz. by declaring to us those spiritual mysteries that are indeed signified or typified in the constitution of the natural world; and secondly, in actually making application of the signs and types in the book of nature as representations of those spiritual mysteries in many instances" (106). Consequently, as he writes in "Images" no. 70, "wherever we are and whatever we are about, we may see divine things excellently represented and held forth, and it will abundantly tend to confirm the Scriptures, for there is an excellent agreement between these things and the Holy Scriptures" (74).

13. See Schafer's extensive explanation of his dating system in his introduction to *WJE* 13; see also Wallace Anderson's discussions of the dating controversy as it relates to Miller in *WJE* 6:24–27 and 11:17–18.

14. As Thomas Schafer, the editor of *WJE* 13, asserts, "Although other Puritan pastors in colonial New England kept theological notebooks or intellectual diaries, none

surpasses that of Edwards in length, breadth of content, or depth of thought" (1). In addition to the notebooks mentioned in note 6, others include "Notes on Scriptures," "Notes on the Apocalypse," various sermon notebooks, and "Miscellaneous Observations on the Holy Scriptures" (also referred to as the Blank Bible), which Edwards used to keep a running commentary on blank pages interleaved between the pages of the Old and New Testaments.

15. *The Theology of Jonathan Edwards* is the most comprehensive overview to date of the entirety of Edwards's studies. The book, a tremendous scholarly reference written so as to be accessible to nonspecialists, offers essays in three major sections: Edwards's social, historical, and cultural contexts; his theology and metaphysics; and his intellectual and spiritual legacies.

16. In his *Institutes,* Calvin appreciates the natural beauty of the world and instructs the regenerate not to "decline to take a pious delight in the clear and manifest works of God" in "this most beautiful theater"; they should "contemplate the immense treasures of wisdom and goodness exhibited in the creatures, as in so many mirrors [of God]" (1.14.20–21).

17. On typology in Edwards and Calvin, see also Butler, "God's Visible Glory"; Jones, "Edwards, Dickinson, and the Sacramentality of Nature"; Knight, "Learning the Language of God"; and Lane, *Ravished by Beauty.*

18. In the second half of the eighteenth century in Germany, Frei continues, interpretation of biblical narrative first came to involve permanent fragmentation of the various textual elements in such a way as to no longer embody meaning holistically; rather "the explicative meaning of the narrative texts came to be their ostensive or ideal reference. Their applicative meaning or religious meaningfulness was either a truth of revelation embodied in an indispensable historical event or a universal spiritual truth known independently of the texts but exemplified by them, or, finally, a compromise between the two positions amounting to the claim that while the historical fact is indispensable to revelation, the meaningfulness of revelation depends on its being set in some broader religious or moral context" (124).

19. See particularly Lewalski, *Protestant Poetics,* and Miner, *Literary Uses of Typology,* on seventeenth-century ways of reading and reflecting on nature, as well as comment on Reformation theology in relation to typology. Also, on Edwards's use of the English Puritan writers, see especially the introductions by John E. Smith in *WJE* 2; Wallace Anderson in *WJE* 11; and Peter J. Thuesen in *WJE* 26; as well as Thuesen, "Jonathan Edwards and the Transatlantic World of Books"; and Sweeney, "The Biblical World of Jonathan Edwards."

20. Dyrness reports that Richard Baxter regarded *The Bruised Reede and Smoaking Flax* (1630) by the Puritan Richard Sibbe as key to his own awakening; Edwards cites *The Bruised Reed* as yet another source in the Johannine/Augustinian tradition in his own *Religious Affections.*

21. On recent work concerning Edwards's hermeneutical methods and use of commentators, see also Brown, "The Bible"; Stein, "Cotton Mather and Jonathan Edwards" and "Edwards as Biblical Exegete"; and Noll, "Jonathan Edwards' Use of the Bible."

22. "Edwards was particularly stimulated by the Queries that Newton added at the end of the *Optics,*" Wallace Anderson, the editor of Edwards's *Scientific and Philosophical Writings,* observes. Edwards's notes indicate that he was especially interested in Newton's suggestion that "many phenomena cannot be explained by mere mechanical col-

lisions among particles of matter, but must arise from attractive and repulsive forces by which the particles act upon each other without surface contact" (*WJE* 6:23).

23. Also on Locke, Edwards, and the new sense, see especially Cherry, *The Theology of Jonathan Edwards;* Erdt, *Jonathan Edwards;* Fiering, *Jonathan Edwards's Moral Thought;* Kuklick, *Churchmen and Philosophers;* McClymond, *Encounters with God;* and Chamberlain's introduction to *WJE* 18.

24. There is an extensive literature concerning Miller and his critics. For bibliographic reviews of these often complex debates, see especially Weber's introduction to the 1981 edition of Miller's *Jonathan Edwards* and "The Figure of Jonathan Edwards." Some of the most pertinent critiques of Miller's position on Locke, Edwards, and the new sense include Cherry, *The Theology of Jonathan Edwards* and *Nature and the Religious Imagination;* Kuklick; McClymond; and Chamberlain. Scholars who have dealt specifically with the problems of Miller's assessment of Edwards's natural typology include Diana Butler in "God's Visible Glory"; Janice Knight in "Learning the Language of God"; and Stephen H. Daniel in *Philosophy.*

25. McClymond and McDermott's *Theology* offers a comprehensive overview of Edwards's literary and theological legacies in American culture. For notable recent essays examining Edwards's influence, see also Noll, "Edwards's Theology after Edwards"; Gura, "Edwards and American Literature"; Lesser, "Edwards in 'American Culture'"; Kimnach, "The Literary Life of Jonathan Edwards"; Svetlikova, "Alternative Viewpoint"; and Crisp and Sweeney, *After Jonathan Edwards.*

2. Beauty and the Eye of the Beholder

1. Delivered and subsequently published at the request of the Presbyterian Synod of New York, "True Grace" was originally preached to his Northampton congregation in 1746.

2. See especially Edwards's *Religious Affections, Treatise on Grace,* and the 1733 sermon "Divine and Supernatural Light" for some of his most thorough and frequently cited treatments of this "sense of divine beauty" as a primary indicator of conversion.

3. For overviews of Edwards's Biblicism, see Stein's excellent introductions to the Yale *WJE* editions of *Notes on Scripture* (15) and *The Blank Bible* (24); Brown's *Jonathan Edwards and the Bible* and "The Bible"; McClymond and McDermott's *Theology of Jonathan Edwards;* and Nichols's *Jonathan Edwards's Bible.*

4. For discussions of Edwards and the Cambridge Platonists, see Fiering, *Jonathan Edwards's Moral Thought* and "Rationalist Foundations"; Anderson's introduction to *WJE* 11; Daniel, *Philosophy of Jonathan Edwards;* and Lee, *Philosophical Theology.*

5. There has been a lively debate among Edwards scholars concerning which of these terms is most central to his philosophy. Roland Delattre believes the keystone of Edwards's thought to be "beauty and sensibility" (*Beauty and Sensibility*), Norman Fiering asserts it is the moral philosophy of "excellency" (*Moral Thought*), Sang Hyun Lee focuses on his "dispositional ontology" (*Philosophical Theology*), Stephen Daniel argues for semiotics, and Michael J. McClymond makes the case for "theocentrism." More recently, McClymond and McDermott offer the elegant model of a symphony orchestra composed of various instrumental parts (such as "Trinitarian communication" and "creaturely participation" playing in harmony) (4–5).

6. In his overview of the philosophical roots of "consent," Fiering paraphrases this

idea as "consent of heart" and finds "its connotation . . . includes both intellectual union (as in the old term in logic, 'consentaneity') and affection, without the suggestion of condescension that clings to benevolence" (*Moral Thought* 325). "The word 'excellency,'" he also notes, "was widely used in both secular and theological writing before Edwards, but one does not find it often with quite Edwards's emphasis" (73n60).

7. The *Oxford English Dictionary* lists four pertinent definitions of "signify," all of which antedate Edwards's usage of the word: "to be a sign or symbol of" (ca. 1275); "to mean, denote" (ca. 1300); "to indicate that (something) is going to take place; to presage, portend; to prefigure" (ca. 1384); and "to make known, indicate, announce, declare" (ca. 1325).

8. For Edwards on language, see also, for example, *Concerning the End* (*WJE* 8:527); *Freedom of the Will* (*WJE* 1:376); *Religious Affections* (*WJE* 2:97); "The Mind" nos. 18, 23, and 35 (*WJE* 6); and "Miscellanies" nos. 83 (*WJE* 13) and 1066 (*WJE* 20).

9. Daniel offers convincing evidence that Edwards's ontological and epistemological thought should be reread in the light of the Renaissance logic of Peter Ramus and the ontology of early Stoicism. Daniel finds that Edwards's discourse theory "allows him to reveal a unity among things that other thinkers of his era cannot discern" (3).

10. As Delattre argues, Edwards's concept of beauty is "primarily objective, structural, relational, and creative or formative, rather than primarily subjective, emotional, relativist, and created or well-formed" ("Beauty and Theology" 140). Such beauty gestures toward its connections with the other, and its model is "the beautifying rather than the beautified" (Delattre, *Beauty,* 25). By the same token, "deformity rather than ugliness is the opposite of beauty" because it "refers to the object and to *objective relations,* while ugliness refers to the subject and to *subjective responses*" (22, emphasis added). Edwards's final major work concerning the beauty of the natural world in conjunction with the spiritual is the 1755 treatise *Nature of True Virtue* (*WJE* 8). For thorough discussions on this text and differences between primary and secondary beauty in Edwards's philosophy, see books by Delattre and by Fiering, and Ramsey's introduction to *WJE* 8.

11. In "Miscellanies" no. 238 Edwards illustrates this idea by appealing to the functioning of the human mind as it reflects on the idea of emotions. To have an idea of love is to "so frame things in our imagination that we have for a moment a love to that thing or to something we make represent it, or we excite for a moment that love which we have and suppose it in another place. . . . [A]nd so certainly it is, in all our spiritual ideas. They are the very same things repeated, perhaps very faintly and obscurely, and very quick and momentaneously, and with many new references, suppositions and translations. But if the idea be perfect, it is only the same thing absolutely all over again" (*WJE* 13:353–54).

12. See, for instance, "The Mind" nos. 3, 9, 13, 27, 34, and 61 (*WJE* 6).

13. Edwards probably developed his idealism in part as a critique of Hobbes's materialism. In brief, Edwards's idealism differs from Kant's in that reality is based in God's mind rather than man's. It differs from Bishop Berkeley's subjective idealism in the sense that Edwards stressed that in the world, humanity experiences God's ideas directly rather than weakened reflections of God's ideas. Substantive treatments of Edwards's idealism may be found in Smith, "Jonathan Edwards and 'The Way of Ideas'"; Kuklick, *Churchmen and Philosophers;* Anderson's introductions to both *WJE* 6 and 11; Hall, "Did Berkeley Influence Edwards?"; McClymond, *Encounters with God;* and Zakai, *Philosophy of Nature.*

14. On Edwards's definitions of love, see also "Miscellanies" no. 530 and *The Nature of True Virtue* (*WJE* 8).

15. The passage reads in full: "Both the moral and natural *qualities* of those things in us, that are the conditions of both these covenants, are more or less in the inward principle and exercises, or the transitive and overt acts, according as the *being* of those things lies more or less in them. The being of obedience lay more in the overt practical act of obedience. . . . So the being of a closing with and adhering to Christ lies more in the transitive practical acts of a principle of unition and adherence" (Misc. 819, *WJE* 18:531).

16. In his explanation of what he terms Edwards's dispositional ontology, Lee cites Edwards's "Miscellanies" no. 241: "[The soul's] essence consists of powers and habits." Lee elucidates: "When there is a habit or disposition, it functions like a prescriptive law that certain events will, not only may, occur whenever certain circumstances prevail. Habits or dispositions, in short, are ontologically real and causally active law-like powers" ("Edwards" 18).

17. See especially Brown's groundbreaking work in *Jonathan Edwards and the Bible* on Edwards's engagement with Deists and eighteenth-century debates on epistemology.

18. On Edwards's role in defending orthodox Trinitarian Christianity against the Trinitarian Controversy, see Minkema's introduction to *WJE* 14:42–45.

19. Like Augustine, Edwards defined the first, second, and third Persons as "God, and the idea of God, and the love of God" ("Miscellanies" no. 308, *WJE* 13:393). Christ is God's perfect idea of Himself; as the Word of God He is "a transcript of the divine perfections" ("Miscellanies" 94, 259). In turn, the Holy Spirit is "the act of God between the Father and the Son infinitely loving and delighting in each other" (260). The mutually signifying Trinitarian relation is "God's infinite consent to being in general" (*WJE* 6:364). On Edwards and the Trinity, see especially *WJE* 21, *Writings on the Trinity;* and Pauw, *The Supreme Harmony of All.*

3. Immersed in the Reformed Hermeneutic

1. The references to Jonathan Edwards and Jesus follow a poem she titles "The Bumble Bee's Religion," in which she mischievously contrasts "Industry and Morals / and every righteous thing" with "the divine Perdition / Of Idleness and Spring" (L712). Gilbert would have been around six years old at the time of the letter, which makes one think the joke was intended as much for the rest of Dickinson family as it was for the little boy. Still, Dickinson seems to have very much wished for her two nephews to inherit a faith that emphasized the love and mercy of God, rather than to struggle with the frightening aspects of the God of the Reformed tradition as she had. See also her letter to her nephew Edward that contains her oft-quoted "The Bible is an antique Volume –" in which she concludes, "Orpheus' Sermon captivated – / It did not condemn –" (L753). She also writes of the importance of gaining faith in childhood in a letter to her cousins in 1881 concerning the death of George Eliot: "The gift of belief which her greatness denied her, I trust she receives in the childhood of the kingdom of heaven. As childhood is earth's confiding time, perhaps having no childhood, she lost her way to the early trust, and no later came" (L710).

2. She describes an 1873 revival to her cousins the Norcross sisters: "There is that which is called an 'awakening' in the church, and I know of no choicer ecstasy than to see Mrs. [Sweetser] roll out in crape every morning, I suppose to intimidate antichrist; at least it would have that effect on me" (L389). In an 1880 letter to Elizabeth Holland, Dickinson writes, "The Snow is so white and sudden it seems almost like a Change of Heart – though I don't mean a 'Conversion' – I mean a Revolution" (L678).

3. See Miller, *Reading in Time;* and Barrett, *To Fight Aloud Is Very Brave.* For an excellent overview of recent trends in Dickinson scholarship, see Zapedowska, "Critical History II"; as well as "Further Reading," a compilation on Dickinson by subject area, in Richards, *Emily Dickinson in Context,* 353–68.

4. My argument is less concerned with taking a biographical stand on the moving target of Dickinson's personal belief than on asserting the manner in which Reformed hermeneutics were central to her typological imagination. Linda Freedman shares a similar stance concerning Dickinson's work and the influence of theology in her book *Emily Dickinson and the Religious Imagination* and, more recently, in "Touching the Wounds."

5. Jane Donahue Eberwein points out that Colton's colloquial tones of direct address, his ability to "balance carefully contrived complex sentences with lists, fragments, questions, apostrophes, and reversals," and his "versatility in exploring fresh approaches to familiar texts" would surely have impacted Dickinson's own rhetoric ("Ministerial" 10, 11).

6. See Eberwein, "Outgrowing Genesis," for a detailed analysis of the poet's wide exposure to nineteenth-century developments in science and religion.

7. See Conforti, *Jonathan Edwards.*

8. In "The Preparation of a Poet," Rowena Revis Jones thoroughly documents the religious nature of Dickinson's studies at home, Amherst Academy, and Mount Holyoke. Jones demonstrates how a preponderance of Dickinson's textbooks, such as Isaac Watts's *Improvement of the Mind,* are "based upon a careful consideration of natural and revealed revelation" and "encourage the full development of human reason, but limits its capacity to arrive at knowledge without divine aid" (305).

9. In particular, in *Trying to Think with Emily Dickinson,* Deppman examines Dickinson's fascination with the inner workings of thought processes. He traces the presence of both Scottish and German philosophies in her schooling and environment, dueling influences that he frequently delineates under the broader categories of Locke and Kant. He asserts that Dickinson's great strength is her ultimate refusal to be subsumed by either of those philosophical categories, deeming her "too skeptical and analytical for the Transcendentalists, too speculative and exhilarated for the mental philosophers" (108). A similar description might be made of Jonathan Edwards.

10. Dickinson's relationship with Charles Wadsworth, whom she referred to as "My Shepherd from 'Little Girl'hood'" (L766), has been explored at length in St. Armand, *Emily Dickinson and Her Culture;* and Lease, *Emily Dickinson's Readings of Men and Books.* See also the biographies by Sewall and Habegger.

11. Although Dickinson undoubtedly read a great many of Wadsworth's sermons, the only sermon we can specifically identify by her own reference is "God's Culture," which she offers to send her friend Elizabeth Holland in an 1877 letter (L487). Thomas Johnson, the editor of her letters, identifies the sermon as having been preached and published in November 1876; if so, Wadsworth was re-preaching a condensed version of an 1860 sermon by the same name that anticipated the Civil War.

12. The biographies by Sewall, Habegger, and Lundin provide the most exhaustive and detailed examinations of Dickinson's religious heritage to date. See also Jones, "The Preparation of a Poet" and "A Taste for 'Poison'"; Eberwein, *Strategies of Limitation,* "'Graphicier for Grace,'" and "'Is Immortality True?'"; Miller, *A Poet's Grammar;* New, *The Regenerate Lyric* and *The Line's Eye;* Oberhaus, *Emily Dickinson's Fascicles;* Doriani, *Emily Dickinson, Daughter of Prophecy;* McIntosh, *Nimble Believing;* and Freedman, *Em-*

ily Dickinson and the Religious Imagination. Siegfried's "Bibliographic Essay" is the most comprehensive literature review of studies of Dickinson and religion prior to 1980.

13. Capps provides a chapter on Dickinson's use of the King James Version, as well as appendices that identify and number her allusions to individual books of the Bible.

14. From the Dickinson Family Library copy, Emily Dickinson Room, EDR 8, Houghton Library, Harvard University; available online. On Dickinson's Bible, see especially Seelbinder, "The Bible."

4. Reading with "Compound Vision"

1. Sewall reports that Dickinson "was known among her friends for her detailed knowledge of the flora around Amherst" (345).

2. See especially essays by Hubbard and by Noble.

3. Several twentieth-century Dickinson critics dismissed the possibility of Dickinson as a typological writer, a stance that I would assert is based on an oversimplification of Edwards's typologies (often derived from a reliance on Perry Miller's faulty readings of Edwards), a narrow conception of Dickinson's spiritual vision, or both. As I show in this chapter, Dickinson's revisionary use of types does not rid her cosmology of uncertainty and awe, nor does her fascination with the transcendent preclude her idiosyncratic celebration of immanence and indeterminacy.

4. I have borrowed the term "immanent transcendentality" from Edwards scholar Stephen H. Daniel's brilliant *Philosophy of Jonathan Edwards* (43).

5. Although there are no full-length studies of Dickinson and typology, a number of scholars have addressed Dickinson's treatment of typology within the framework of their own broader arguments. The most substantial of these are Eberwein, *Strategies of Limitation;* Gelpi, *The Mind of the Poet;* Hagenbüchle "Emily Dickinson's Poetic Covenant," "Sign and Process," and "Precision and Indeterminacy"; Keller, *The Only Kangaroo among the Beauty;* Loeffelholz, *Boundaries of Feminist Theory;* Porter, *The Modern Idiom;* Weisbuch, *Emily Dickinson's Poetry;* and Freedman, *Religious Imagination.*

6. Eberwein reads this poem as one that underscores a fundamental sense of alienation Dickinson perceived between herself and nature. Taking issue with interpretations that the poem contains positive allusion to the Catholic or Anglican liturgy, she notes the poem's "heretical quality": "Christ is the antitype to whom all typological emblems should point in Puritan thinking, and Christ's presence should itself be the reality of the sacrament for Catholics. Yet this ritual typifies nothing but the emotion of finite creatures, thereby draining communion of its spiritual power" ("Calvinist Sacramental Tradition" 76–77).

7. Franklin lists the variants as follows: "typic, hearty, bonnie, breathless, spacious, tropic, warbling (*written twice*), ardent, friendly, magic, pungent, winning, mellow." "Warbling" was Dickinson's choice in the other two extant copies of the poem. Moreover, the first and second of the three manuscript variants contains the fourth and fifth lines "Subjects – Bethlehem – / Genesis – Bethlehem's ancestor"; Dickinson changed the fifth line in the final version to "Eden – the ancient Homestead." I would assert that both the original lines and the change indicate the poet's knowledge of the typological relationship frequently constructed between God's warning to the serpent in Eden about its eventual defeat (see Genesis 3:15) and Christ as the fulfillment of that promise in the New Testament.

8. Dickinson's iconoclastic stance toward representations of God should be distinguished from an outright rejection of any transcendent deity. As Eberwein remarks in *Strategies of Limitation,* "The God whom Dickinson loved . . . is better represented by the name 'Awe' or by his own 'I AM THAT I AM' (Exodus 3:14) than by any personal attributes. She felt free to quarrel with the jealous, angry, cruel figment of other people's imaginations because that figure was not the divinity she never stopped worshipping" (245). In *Emily Dickinson and the Life of Language* Budick goes further, seeing Dickinson's poetry as a polemic eschewing "the excesses of symbolic literalness that are often expressed by the Puritans and the Transcendentalists" (137). As Budick explains, "Both groups seemed convinced of the infallibility of their judgments, and therefore they dramatized their beliefs—reified them—in their fragmenting symbols" (140–41).

9. Dickinson had no qualms about mocking doctrines, however. For instance, in a poem sent to her nephew Edward, Dickinson confronts the double bind of the Reformed belief in original sin: If sin is imputed to humans before their birth, how is it that sin must be repented for since it has not been undertaken by one's own volition? Thus Dickinson addresses God in a facetious sinner's prayer: "'Heavenly Father' – take to thee / The supreme iniquity / Fashioned by *thy* candid Hand" (F1500, emphasis added). Referencing the Genesis account of God making humankind from the dust of the earth, Dickinson concludes with sarcastic obeisance that although "'We are Dust' – / We apologize to thee / For thine own Duplicity –."

10. Three seminal studies examining these nineteenth-century hermeneutical controversies and their lasting effects on both American seminaries and American literature are Gura, *The Wisdom of Words;* and Turner, *Without God, without Creed* and *Language, Religion, Knowledge.*

11. Hagenbüchle ("Precision," "Sign and Process"), Kher (*Landscape of Absence*), Miller (*Poet's Grammar*), and Sielke (*Fashioning the Female Subject*) have explored at length the non-mimetic, indeterminate, and polysemantic features of Dickinson's language. Hagenbüchle describes Dickinson's poetry in terms of its "metonymically constructed metaphors," ambiguity, *absence présente,* negation, process, and indirection ("Precision" 40), while Kher focuses on Dickinson's existentialist attempts to construct meaning by confronting absence. Miller analyzes the surface and deep structures of Dickinson's language and finds in her syntax, semantics, diction, and grammar evidence that the poet's chief strategy of "disruption" "more closely resembles theories of what feminist writing, or a woman's writing, an *écriture feminine,* would be than it resembles the actual work of other—even women—writers" (161). Building on Miller's findings and Kristevan semiotic theory, Sielke asserts that Dickinson's poems "destablilize syntactic linearity, semantic coherence, and referentiality," thus rendering the subject position "troubled, divided and scattered rather than unified" (28).

12. Revelation 4:4: "And round about the throne were four and twenty seats: and upon the seats I saw four and twenty elders sitting, clothed in white raiment; and they had on their heads crowns of gold."

13. John 3:3 states, "Jesus answered and said unto him, Verily, verily, I say unto thee, Except a man be born again, he cannot see the kingdom of God." Dickinson refers to this dialogue (John 3:1–21) quite frequently in her poems and letters; see, for example, letters L552, 614, and 899 and poems F90, F361, and F1218.

14. On Dickinson's "typology of death," see Weisbuch's excellent two-part discussion in *Emily Dickinson's Poetry.* See also Hagenbüchle's identification of what he terms

Dickinson's "transcend," a mode of representation that he distinguishes from allegorical emblem, romantic symbol, or type. In Hagenbüchle's analysis, the transcend functions in Dickinson's poetry as does the Symbolist sign, in as much as it is "metonymically related to what is meant and only refers to it without being part of it" ("Precision" 41). In this important distinction, the transcend comes into play when immortality rather than death is the aim of Dickinson's poem. In the case of a poem such as "From cocoon forth a butterfly," Dickinson's butterfly, "Extinguished – in the Sea –" of immortality rather than death, lacks the ontological, teleological, and mutually completing properties of the typology discussed thus far. For further discussion of death as antitype, see also Hagenbüchle, "Precision and Indeterminacy" 41–53 and "Sign and Process" 143–50.

15. In "The Infinite in Person," Megan Craig argues that both Levinas and Dickinson "describe the infinite varieties of space we find ourselves subject to and the essential ambiguity of space definitive of the human condition. To be human is to be capable of feeling displaced, to be opened or knocked out of phase. For Dickinson this means that the 'self' is a precarious achievement, prone to disappearance. For Levinas this means the 'subject,' never stable, issues out of a core of vulnerability" (209).

16. "Dont you know you are happiest while I withhold and not confer – dont you know that 'No' is the wildest word we consign to Language?" is Dickinson's famous rejoinder in this vein to Otis Lord in 1878 (L562).

17. I would contrast such a moment, of course, with poems such as "I heard a fly buzz when I died" (F591) and "I felt a funeral in my brain" (F340), in which Dickinson reflects on the horrifying possibility that in fact there might be *no* eternal, invisible realm beyond death.

18. On the atoning, or connective, work between the immanent and transcendent realms that Christian theology asserts Christ's death and resurrection performed, see, for example, Colossians 1:19–20: "For it pleased the Father that in him [Christ] should all fulness dwell; And, having made peace through the blood of his cross, by him to reconcile all things unto himself; by him, I say, whether they be things in earth, or things in heaven."

19. Divine knowledge is rendered as "Light" throughout the Old and New Testaments; Dickinson's treatment in this poem of "Light – enabling," or giving rise to, further "Light" particularly recalls Psalm 36:9: "For with thee is the fountain of life: in thy light shall we see light." As examined in chapter 1, Augustine's formulation *crede ut intelligas*, "Believe that you may understand," and his notion of divine illumination as the original source of knowledge, are the classical explications of such passages.

20. Weisbuch and Hagenbüchle ("Emily Dickinson's Poetic Covenant") have clearly established Dickinson's propensity for inferential thought. Hagenbüchle goes so far as to assert, "With the possible exception of Hopkins, Dickinson's oeuvre presents a higher degree of semantic implication than that of any other nineteenth-century writer" (33).

21. The passage itself is Paul's amplification of Christ's words concerning himself in John 12:23–24: "And Jesus answered them, saying, The hour is come, that the Son of man should be glorified. Verily, verily, I say unto you, Except a corn of wheat fall into the ground and die, it abideth alone: but if it die, it bringeth forth much fruit."

22. In a number of places in her poems and letters, Dickinson uses the word "pod" to represent the yet-to-be resurrected body. In the 1863 Christocentric poem "He gave away his life," for instance, she describes Christ's resurrection as the moment when he "Broke – perfect – from the Pod –" (F530). In an 1881 letter to the Norcross sisters,

Dickinson humorously uses the word "pod" in a similar fashion alluding to the Gospel of John: "Vinnie is picking a few seeds – for if a pod 'die, shall he not live again'" (L711).

23. Dickinson's use of "move" here is suggestive of the need for the stone to be rolled away from Christ's tomb after his resurrection; as she puts it in "A pang is more conspicuous in spring," "Why, Resurrection had to wait/Till they had moved a stone –" (F1545 B).

5. "Myself – the Term between"

1. For Marion, "every pretension to absolute knowledge" of the Other amounts to self-reflexive idolatry (23).

2. In this poem Dickinson conflates several moments in Moses's life: in Exodus 3 God speaks from the burning bush, and in Exodus 33 and 34 He tells Moses, "No man shall see me and live"; but in these later chapters Moses is also allowed a glimpse of God's glory and a relational intimacy that is expressed in colloquial terms as "face-to-face." Dickinson's frequent references to Exodus and Deuteronomy are not accidental. In Protestant thinking, these books are two of the most highly typological in the Bible. Moses himself becomes a type of Christ, leading the chosen people out of Egypt (sin) into the Promised Land (heaven).

3. "Creation stopped – for me" may be an oblique allusion to the miracle in Joshua 10 in which "the sun stood still in the midst of heaven, and hasted not to go down about a whole day" while the Israelites destroyed their enemies in battle.

4. In Levinas, also, the Other is made manifest through the metaphorical/metaphysical encounter with a mysterious "face" and "speech"; both are Old Testament terms that Dickinson uses in her descriptions of encounters with an unnameable Other in nature. See Craig for a more specific discussion of Levinas's and Dickinson's use of these terms.

5. Johnson identifies the remark (L459A) as one of several messages to Higginson composed in the spring of 1876; it was either sent by itself or, as its folds suggest, enclosed in the letter that Johnson prints above it (L459).

6. In an 1883 letter consoling Elizabeth Holland on the death of her sister, Dickinson again makes use of the 2 Corinthians passage, commending to her "the open Air – That is nearest Heaven –," and asserting, "The first Abode 'not made with Hands' entices to the second –" (L797). Here, creation itself, rather than the body, is the house "not made with Hands" (a connection she also makes explicit in the poem "Eden is that old fashioned house" and elsewhere). And although the natural world can be consolatory because it is "nearest Heaven," she is also reminding her friend that nature works to "entice" one, to pull signification forward beyond the individual self, rather than to fulfill the mortal life.

7. The word "paradise" is of Persian and then Greek origin, referring to the parks used by Persian nobility; the term was used by the translators of the Septuagint to refer to the Garden of Eden. In the King James Version the word is used only three times, all New Testament references to heaven itself: Luke 23:43, 2 Corinthians 12:4, and Revelation 2:7.

8. On Mary Moody Emerson and her religious influence on her nephew, see particularly Barcus, "Emerson, Calvinism, and Aunt Mary Moody Emerson"; and Williams, "The Wilderness Rapture of Mary Moody Emerson."

9. On Emerson and "the double consciousness," see especially Davidson, "This Consciousness"; and Milder, "From Emerson to Edwards."

10. We can also presume that Emerson read Jonathan Edwards's *Religious Affections,* not only because of the volume's ubiquity but also because it was a book in Emerson's personal library.

11. On the similarities and differences between Emerson's and Dickinson's broader typological outlooks, see especially Wolosky, *Poetry and Public Discourse;* and Freedman, *Emily Dickinson and the Religious Imagination.*

12. Sharon Cameron, for instance, explores the manner in which the poet constructs the relation between language, presence, and loss; she draws on the notions of otherness and *différance* in Lacan, Derrida, and other philosophers to show that for Dickinson, alterity itself can be "what the self recognizes as other *within* itself in the form of an unconscious to which it can attest but not know; it is what the self rediscovers as other outside of its boundaries, a rediscovery predicated on images so archaic and primitive that they have been forgotten the way a beginning is forgotten" (186). In *Emily Dickinson: A Poet's Grammar,* Cristanne Miller finds important correlations between Dickinson's belief in the power of the written word, her structural, grammatical, and stylistic "disruptions," and the way her poetic anticipates the chief qualities of an *écriture féminine* that is later delineated in the works of feminist theorists such as Margaret Homans, Rachel Blau Du Plessis, Luce Irigary, and Julia Kristeva. Cynthia Hogue in *Scheming Women* and Sabine Sielke in *Fashioning the Female Subject* both offer comparative studies of Dickinson's female subjectivity by placing her work alongside the poetry of Adrienne Rich and Marianne Moore. Hogue locates in Dickinson "a resonant tolerance for internal alterity, which she terms *Ecstasy,*" and asserts that in response to the sublime, Dickinson constructs the subject position as a divided self that "does not, or cannot, 'put itself back together again' at the expense of a violence to an externalized feminine other, for in these instances, the violence accompanying specularity and unified subjectivity has no object but the feminine subject herself" (33, 56). Sielke, by contrast, ultimately concludes that "Dickinson's broken discourse serves to project an imaginary space in which the split that creates the subject is healed; in which self and other reintegrate in the endless embrace of an unmediated gaze of identity" (222). See also Dickie, *Lyric Contingencies;* Loeffelholz, *Dickinson and the Boundaries of Feminist Theory;* and Juhasz, "Adventures in the World of the Symbolic."

6. Rightly Dividing the Word of Truth

1. As for Moore's opinion of her literary predecessor, her only published comments on Dickinson's work are in her favorable 1933 review of the *Letters of Emily Dickinson,* edited by Mabel Loomis Todd. In "The Plucked String," however, Cynthia Hogue has examined Moore's private notes and reading diaries to find further evidence that "Moore developed a remarkable appreciation of Dickinson" (90). In "Marianne Moore's Emily Dickinson," Linda Leavell examines Moore's biographical circumstances before and after she wrote the review and comes to similar conclusions. Since these two exceptional articles thoroughly explore most of what we know of Moore's direct relationship with Dickinson, I have not re-covered that ground here.

2. Both Andrew J. Kappel and Jeredith Merrin have argued at length for the broadly religious influence of Puritan and Renaissance writers on Moore's poetry. Merrin's study *An Enabling Humility* offers valuable insights into Moore's concentrated reading of seventeenth-century prose writers such as Thomas Browne and Edward Topsell.

She finds numerous affinities between Moore's strategies and the emblematic or symbolic manner in which these late Renaissance authors interpret the visible Book of Nature as a primer of the invisible world; she reiterates how Moore employs strange and fanciful animals to signify spiritual truths, yet also to demonstrate the separation of the natural world from the human. Likewise, Kappel examines Moore's Presbyterian penchant for moral reasoning and her affection for metaphysical poets such as Henry Vaughan and George Herbert and Puritan authors such as John Bunyan and Richard Baxter ("Notes" and "World"). In a similar vein, in *The Savage's Romance,* John Slatin notes Moore's view of nature as it relates to her Puritan forebears, commenting that Moore, "a devout Presbyterian and a theological descendant of Winthrop and Wilson and Edwards, may be said to share their attitudes toward the natural world at least to the extent that for her, as for them, nature is never simply *there.* It is always a highly symbolic realm in which the workings of God are made manifest and the order of things is made clear. That order is always moral; and in Moore, as in the Puritan writers, it is most often the special, the complicating case which reveals that order most fully" (172).

3. Moore's papers contain an 1883 pamphlet by McCosh with her grandfather's name written on the cover: *Certitude, Providence and Prayer.* The pamphlet is held in the Moore archives at The Rosenbach of the Free Library of Philadelphia (XIVd:14:6).

4. Among Moore's unpublished juvenilia, written sometime between 1909 and 1916 in Carlisle, is a poem titled "Inheritance," a retelling of the Genesis 3 narrative of the fall of Adam and Eve and the "Inheritance" of the sin nature by their descendants, the human race. It is noteworthy in this discussion as further evidence of Moore's familiarity with conventional typological applications of Old Testament texts, as in this appropriation of Genesis 3:15 as a foretelling of the Messiah: "'Her seed,' God said/'Shall bruise your head'" (Rosenbach I:02:37).

5. All references to Moore's study with Kellogg are from the notebook she dedicated to the class (Rosenbach VII:08:03). Romans 5:14 refers to Adam as "a figure [or type] of him that was to come"; see also 1 Corinthians 15:45–49 on Christ as the "second" man. Hebrews 9, which contrasts the Old and New Covenants, reads in part: "But Christ being come an high priest of good things to come, by a greater and more perfect tabernacle, not made with hands, that is to say, not of this building; Neither by the blood of goats and calves, but by his own blood he entered in once into the holy place, having obtained eternal redemption for us" (11–12). All biblical references in this chapter are to the King James Version.

6. The "heart" is referred to throughout both the Old and New Testaments as the seat of the mind, will, and emotions of an individual. For example, Ezekiel 36:26 records God's promise to Israel, "A new heart also will I give you, and a new spirit will I put within you: and I will take away the stony heart out of your flesh and I will give you an heart of flesh." The writers of the New Testament use the word in a similar fashion; see, for instance, Luke's description of God "purifying their hearts by faith" (Acts 15:9).

7. The Jonathan Edwards scholar Sang Hyun Lee explains this process, citing Edwards's Misc. 241: "'[Since the soul's] essence consists of powers and habits,' when there is a habit or disposition, it functions like a prescriptive law that certain events will, not only may, occur whenever certain circumstances prevail. Habits or dispositions, in short, are ontologically real and causally active law-like powers" ("Edwards" 18).

7. "Part Terrestrial, and Part Celestial"

1. Scholars have variously denoted Moore's use of animals as fable (Ross, "Fables of the Golden Age"; and New, *Line's Eye*), as allegory (Jarrell, "Her Shield"; and Molesworth, *Marianne Moore: A Literary Life*), as Protestant emblem (Merrin, *An Enabling Humility;* and Kappell, "Notes on the Presbyterian Poetry of Marianne Moore" and "The World Is an Orphan's Home"), and as masks for the concealing, or the working out, of the poetic self (e.g., Eliot, "Introduction to *Selected Poems*"; Ostriker, *Stealing the Language;* DuPlessis, "No Moore of the Same"; and Heuving, *Omissions Are Not Accidents*).

2. On Moore's interest in science and its influence on her poetry, see also Steinman, *Made in America;* Leavell, *Marianne Moore and the Visual Arts;* and Schulze, "Textual Darwinism" and *The Degenerate Muse.* For eco-critical perspectives on Moore's work, see Weinstein, "Marianne Moore's Ecopoetic Architectonics"; and Hutchison, "The Eco-Poetics of Marianne Moore's 'The Sycamore.'"

3. All references to Moore's notes from Kellogg's class are from her religion notebook at The Rosenbach of the Free Library of Philadelphia (VII:08:03).

4. Moore's notes from Kellogg's Bible class refer to two other Bible helps (but they are not cited in her poetry): Arthur S. Peake's apologetic *Christianity, Its Nature and Truth* (1903); and James Stalker's 1891 classic Christian handbook, *The Life of Jesus Christ.* Peake (1865–1929), whose scholarship Gordon mentions several times concerning Job and Ecclesiastes in his *Poets of the Old Testament,* was an Old Testament Bible commentator, editor, and believing critic who was a professor of biblical exegesis at the University of Manchester. *Christianity, Its Nature and Truth* is an orthodox defense of the necessity of religion in a scientific age, of the argument from design, and of the historicity of Jesus and trustworthiness of the Gospel accounts of His supernatural birth, miracles, resurrection, and divinity. The Reverend James Stalker (1848–1927) was a pastor in the Free Church of Scotland and a professor of church history. Taking up eight pages in Moore's notebook, his *The Life of Jesus Christ* was a mainstay of orthodox Bible classes and was translated into numerous languages. Like Peake's book, *The Life* portrays Jesus as the fulfillment of Messianic prophecy and affirms His physical death, resurrection, and ascension, declaring Him "One whom the race could not from its own resources have produced—the perfect *Type,* the Man of men" (151, emphasis added).

5. George Adam Smith believed that his own Old Testament translations were restoring to the Church a moderate style of exegesis not unlike Calvin's own after years in which Princeton Scholasticism had, as the pabulum states, favored a strand of biblical interpretation more Calvinist than Calvin himself. "The soundest exegete of his time was John Calvin," he writes in *Modern Criticism and the Preaching of the Old Testament* (1901), "[and] considering his means and opportunities, we may call him the greatest expositor of all time" (240).

6. The last two lines of the poem have been attributed to comments by her brother Warner and by her mother.

7. As the Apostle Paul writes, the notion of the Messiah dying a humiliating death on a Roman implement of torture was "to the Jews a stumbling block and to the Greeks foolishness" (1 Cor. 1:23).

8. In the contexts of the early church, the embrace of a divine truth that could be both universal and intensely personal, thus superseding established religious authorities and the Roman emperor himself, radicalized followers to the point of accepting death rather than renunciation.

9. In general, Moore's biblical allusions in her poetry are not so much direct quotation as amalgams of biblical cadences, sensibilities, narratives, and images. Some of her late letters, by contrast, demonstrate an almost nineteenth-century propensity to cite extensively from the Bible without using quotation marks—an irony for a poet known for her liberal use of quotation. See, for example, Moore's 1954 letter to Edward McKnight Kauffer in *Letters*.

10. Jacob is renamed "Israel" by God in Genesis 32:32. As Israel, he comes to represent the entire nation that descends from him; in the New Testament, he is named by Paul as a type of the Christian spiritual descendants of Israel as well. See, for example, Romans 9:6–13 and Galatians 6:16.

11. Personal communication with Linda Leavell, March 8, 2013.

8. "Integration Too Tough for Infraction"

1. Margaret Holley's description of the broad contours of Moore's career is helpful here. She finds a "movement from subjective judgment to objective embodiment to shared advocacy" that is "part of a broad development in Moore's work from isolation, confrontation, and satire toward community, representation, and sympathy. The marked evolution in her poems from compression to expansion and, significantly, back to compression is accompanied by clear shifts from substantive to attributive metaphors and from observation as sight to observation as insight" (x).

2. Generally, scholars who have taken a position favoring one period of Moore's career over others have expressed a preference for the years between 1917 and either directly before or directly after World War II (e.g., Hugh Kenner, John Slatin, Jeanne Heuving, and Margaret Holley). Robin Schulze, analyzing Moore's lifelong revision of her poems, refuses to privilege specific versions, noting that the poet "adapted them in response to her changing social, cultural, and textual circumstances—a habit concurrent with a Darwinian vision of text that clearly occupied Moore during the period of the late teens and early twenties" ("Textual Darwinism" 299). Concomitantly, I argue that Moore's later poems, composed as they were during vastly differing national, cultural, and familial circumstances than those of her earlier oeuvre, are neither better nor worse than the more critically favored works; instead, they represent a kind of final "integration" that Moore's earlier verse points toward.

3. Although Moore was only six when her grandfather died (and by all accounts, he was remembered with fond affection by Moore and her brother Warner), she did close the distance between them somewhat when, more than thirty years later, she and her mother began attending the Presbyterian church in Brooklyn that was founded by one of her grandfather's role models, the Reverend Dr. Theodore Ledyard Cuyler. Cuyler was a well-known revivalist of the same generation as Charles Finney, Dwight L. Moody, and Charles Spurgeon. Under his leadership the Lafayette Avenue Church became the largest Presbyterian church in the United States at that time. Offering a rare public glimpse into her grandfather's religious affiliations, Moore wrote in an essay on Brooklyn for *Vogue* in 1960 that Cuyler's many books had "so excited his interest" that her grandfather "added them to his library in Missouri and when urged by his congregation to take a vacation, said he needed none, merely wished to visit Brooklyn sometime and hear Dr. Cuyler preach in the Lafayette Avenue Church" (*CPr* 541).

4. Joanne Feit Diehl has posited that in response to the Emersonian and Whitma-

nian sublime, which she has defined in part as a psychological "identification with the superior power" associated with fear and defeat, Moore creates a "poetics of deflection" and "rhetorical effacement" that refuses the traditionally gendered male romantic subject position. As Diehl explains, among other strategies, Moore uses a "heteroglossia of textual voices that itself functions to displace authorial point of view" and surface features that "draw us into the play between tropes and away from the relationship between feeling and language" to construct an "engendered redefinition of the American Sublime" (49, 60).

5. Moore's July 19, 1932, letter to her brother Warner, written during her work on "The Plumet Basilisk," provides an account of the sort of factual information Moore would accumulate in the process of composing one of her animal poems (see *Letters* 267–73).

6. Mary Chapman's research on modern print culture and the women's suffrage movement reveals another layer of political criticism in Moore's poem. Chapman documents ways both Moore and her mother participated in the movement and believes Moore was highly aware of the suffragists' use of yellow flowers to signify their cause to other sympathizers. Consequently, in "To Browning," Moore's yellow roses "articulate a commitment to a particular [suffragist] politic while veiling that commitment from 'offending eyes.' 'To Browning' celebrates the hermeneutic privacy that symbolic language permits" (144).

7. For a detailed reading of this poem in the light of Moore's interest in Darwin and Liberty Hyde Bailey, see Schulze, *Degenerate Muse.*

8. Moore's essay was composed between the time of her visit to Bremerton in 1922 and the publication of "The Monkey Puzzle" in *The Dial* in January 1925. In addition, "Sir Francis Bacon" begins with a citation of Lafcadio Hearn, who is also one of only two references listed in the notes to "The Monkey Puzzle": the quote "a certain proportion in the skeleton which gives the best results" Moore attributes to Hearn's *Talks to Writers* (*CP* 275).

9. In her notes to "Granite and Steel," Moore defines a catenary curve as "the curve formed by a rope or cable hanging freely between two fixed points of support" and quotes the civil engineer John Roebling as saying, "Engineering problems of the greatest strength, greatest economy, greatest safety . . . are all solved by the same curve" (*CP* 294). The engineering principle is most simply based on Newton's third law, which states that for every action force, there is an equal and opposite reaction force. Interestingly, Moore and Jonathan Edwards share a similar interest in Newton and the science of optics. Bonnie Costello mentions Moore's "detailed reading notes on Isaac Newton, especially from Brewster's *Life of Newton*" (265).

10. The influence of Augustine's thought on Niebuhr concerning human nature as fallen and humanity's concomitant need for illuminated revelation from outside the self—along with the rising horrors of the Second World War—especially helped precipitate his move away from Marxism and socialism in the early 1940s. In his intellectual autobiography, Niebuhr writes of being "surprised to note in retrospect how late I was in studying the thought of Augustine carefully," that is, not until after becoming chair of Christian ethics at Union Theological Seminary in 1928. "The matter is surprising because the thought of this theologian was to answer so many of my unanswered questions and to emancipate me finally from the notion that Christian faith was in some way identical with the moral idealism of the past century" ("Faith" 9).

11. Marianne Moore to Reinhold Niebuhr, May 20, 1952 (Rosenbach V:45:15).

12. Reinhold Niebuhr to Marianne Moore, April 11, 1955 (Rosenbach V:45:15).

13. Reinhold Niebuhr to Marianne Moore, May 26, 1954 (Rosenbach V:45:15).

14. For a deeper assessment of Moore's and Niebuhr's ethical responses to the Second World War, see my article "Certain Axioms Rivaling Scriptures."

15. When Niebuhr makes this assertion, he does so in reply to a broader concern about "a preconception that anyone who is critical of 'reason' must be an obscurantist who trusts 'blind faith' in place of reason. My criticisms against rationalism have been on two points: that it regards reason as the source of virtue and by inference places the source of evil in the sub-rational vitalities of the self. This error, derived originally from classical interpretations, is at the basis of many Christian and non-Christian heresies in the interpretation of man" ("Reply" 447).

16. Niebuhr's thinking here bears the imprint of Martin Buber and Søren Kierkegaard, influences he gladly acknowledged.

17. Marianne Moore to Reinhold Niebuhr, April 8, 1955 (Rosenbach V:45:15).

18. The use of the star is also reminiscent of the poet's more explicit reference to the Nativity in her poem of four years earlier, "In Distrust of Merits," in which she jointly aligns the Jewish and Christian symbols: "star of David, star of Bethlehem." Bethlehem, as the home of King David, is frequently referred to in Old and New Testament texts as "the city of David" (2 Sam. 5:9; Luke 2:4, 11; John 7:42). In her 1944 review of *Behold the Jew* in *The New Republic,* she explicitly connects those two stars again as part of a broader argument against anti-Semitism, quoting, "We cannot have love in our hearts for the one star and hatred in our hearts for the other star" (*CPr* 403).

19. In his best-known work, *The Dark Night of the Soul,* the sixteenth-century contemplative Saint John of the Cross describes how "through the dark night pride becomes humility, greed becomes simplicity, wrath becomes contentment, luxury becomes peace, gluttony becomes moderation, envy becomes joy, and sloth becomes strength." In her 1933 review of Eliot's *Sweeney Agonistes,* Moore notes the results of such a kenosis, or spiritual emptying: "'The Soul cannot be possessed of the divine union until it has divested itself of the love of created beings,' St. John of the Cross says; as all saints have said" (*CPr* 298).

20. The first question is also an indirect reference to Revelation 22:8–9, in which the Apostle John, overwhelmed by the vision of heaven he has been given, "fell down to worship before the feet of the angel which shewed me these things." The angel refuses John's worship, saying, "See thou do it not: for I am thy fellow servant, and of thy brethren the prophets, and of them which keep the sayings of this book: worship God."

21. Steeped in biblical literature as Moore was, it is not too much of a stretch to imagine that one of many referents she could have considered here might be Christ Himself. Such an allusion would be an amalgamation of many oft-quoted verses, such as those having to do with Christ pictured as a star ("I Jesus have sent mine angel to testify unto you these things in the churches. I am the root and the offspring of David, and the bright and morning star") (Rev. 22:16); with Christ as a light that is not overcome by darkness ("And the light shineth in the darkness; and the darkness comprehended it not") (John 1:5); and with Christ as a "steadfast" (a word Moore uses in line two of the poem) hope that is not negated by the darkness of death ("Which hope we have as an anchor of the soul, both sure and stedfast, and which entereth into that within the veil") (Heb. 6:19).

Works Cited

The following volumes of *The Works of Jonathan Edwards,* 26 vols. (New Haven: Yale UP, 1957–2008), are cited as *WJE* followed by the volume and page numbers:

Vol. 1. *Freedom of the Will.* Ed. Paul Ramsey. 1957.
Vol. 2. *Religious Affections.* Ed. John E. Smith. 1959.
Vol. 6. *Scientific and Philosophical Writings.* Ed. Wallace E. Anderson. 1980.
Vol. 8. *Ethical Writings.* Ed. Paul Ramsey. 1989.
Vol. 9. *A History of the Work of Redemption.* Ed. John F. Wilson. 1989.
Vol. 11. *Typological Writings.* Ed. Wallace E. Anderson, Mason I. Lowance, and David Watters. 1993.
Vol. 13. *The "Miscellanies," a–500.* Ed. Thomas A. Schafer. 1994.
Vol. 14. *Sermons and Discourses, 1723–1729.* Ed. Kenneth P. Minkema. 1997.
Vol. 15. *Notes on Scripture.* Ed. Stephen J. Stein. 1998.
Vol. 16. *Letters and Personal Writings.* Ed. George S. Claghorn. 1998.
Vol. 18. *The "Miscellanies," 501–832.* Ed. Ava Chamberlin. 2000.
Vol. 19. *Sermons and Discourses, 1734–1738.* Ed. M. X. Lesser. 2001.
Vol. 21. *Writings on the Trinity, Grace, and Faith.* Ed. Sang Hyun Lee. 2003.
Vol. 22. *Sermons and Discourses, 1739–1742.* Ed. Harry S. Stout and Nathan O. Hatch. 2003.
Vol. 24. *The Blank Bible.* Ed. Stephen J. Stein. 2006.
Vol. 25. *Sermons and Discourses, 1743–1758.* Ed. Wilson H. Kimnach. 2006.
Vol. 26. *Catalogues of Books.* Ed. Peter J. Thuesen. 2008.

The following abbreviations refer to the writings of Emily Dickinson:

F *The Poems of Emily Dickinson.* Ed. R. W. Franklin. 3 vols. Cambridge: Havard UP, 1998. Citation by poem number.
L *The Letters of Emily Dickinson.* Ed. Thomas H. Johnson. Cambridge: Harvard UP, 1986. Citation by letter number.

The following abbreviations refer to the writings of Marianne Moore:

Becoming	*Becoming Marianne Moore: The Early Poems, 1907–1924.* Ed. Robin Schulze. Berkeley: U of California P, 1998.
Letters	*The Selected Letters of Marianne Moore.* Ed. Bonnie Costello, Celeste Goodridge, and Cristanne Miller. New York: Alfred A. Knopf, 1997.
CPr	*The Complete Prose of Marianne Moore.* Ed. Patricia C. Willis. New York: Viking, 1986.
CP	*Complete Poems.* New York: Penguin Books, 1981.
Rosenbach	*The Marianne Moore Collection.* The Rosenbach of the Free Library of Philadelphia.

Alexander V. G. *Jonathan Edwards.* Boston: Houghton, 1889.

Anderson, Wallace E. Editor's Introduction. *WJE* 6:1–144.

———. Editor's Introduction to "Images of Divine Things" and "Types." *WJE* 11:3–49.

Auerbach, Erich. *Scenes from the Drama of European Literature.* Minneapolis: U of Minnesota P, 1984.

Barcus, Nancy. "Emerson, Calvinism, and Aunt Mary Moody Emerson: An Irrepressible Defender of New England Orthodoxy." *Christian Scholar's Review* 7.2 (1977): 146–52.

Barrett, Faith. *To Fight Aloud Is Very Brave: American Poetry and the Civil War.* Amherst: U of Massachusetts P, 2012.

Baxter, Richard. *The Saints Everlasting Rest.* New York: American Tract Society, 1840.

Bercovitch, Sacvan. "Typology in Puritan New England: The Williams-Cotton Controversy Reassessed." *American Quarterly* 19.2 (1967): 166–91.

———. "Horologicals to Chronometricals: The Rhetoric of the Jeremiad." *Literary Monographs.* Ed. Eric Rothstein. Madison: U of Wisconsin P, 1970. 3:1–126.

———, ed. *Typology and Early American Literature.* Amherst: U of Massachusetts P, 1972.

———. *The Puritan Origins of the American Self.* New Haven: Yale UP, 1975.

———. *The American Jeremiad.* Madison: U of Wisconsin P, 1978.

Brooks, Van Wyck. *America's Coming-of-Age.* Garden City: Doubleday, 1958.

Brown, Robert E. *Jonathan Edwards and the Bible.* Bloomington: Indiana UP, 2002.

———. "The Bible." *The Princeton Companion to Jonathan Edwards.* Ed. Sang Hyun Lee. Princeton: Princeton UP, 2005. 87–102.

Brumm, Ursula. *American Thought and Religious Typology.* New Brunswick: Rutgers UP, 1970.

Budick, E. Miller. *Emily Dickinson and the Life of Language: A Study in Symbolic Poetics.* Baton Rouge: Louisiana State UP, 1985.

Bushnell, Horace. *Sermons for the New Life.* 2nd ed. New York: Scribner, 1858.

Butler, Diana. "God's Visible Glory: The Beauty of Nature in the Thought of John Calvin and Jonathan Edwards." *Westminster Theological Journal* 52.1 (1990):13–26.

Calvin, John. *The Epistles of Paul the Apostle to the Romans and to the Thessalonians.* Ed. David W. Torrance and Thomas F. Torrance. Grand Rapids: Wm. B. Eerdmans, 1961. Vol. 8 of *Calvin's Commentaries.* 10 vols.

———. *Institutes of the Christian Religion.* Trans. Henry Beveridge. Vol. 1 of 2. Grand Rapids: Eerdmans, 1962.

Cameron, Sharon. *Lyric Time: Dickinson and the Limits of Genre.* Baltimore: Johns Hopkins UP, 1979.

Capps, Jack L. *Emily Dickinson's Reading, 1836–1866.* Cambridge: Harvard UP, 1966.

Chamberlain, Ava. Editor's Introduction. *WJE* 18:1–48.

Chapman, Mary. *Making Noise, Making News: Suffrage Print Culture and U.S. Modernism.* New York: Oxford UP, 2014.

Cherry, Conrad. *The Theology of Jonathan Edwards.* Garden City: Anchor Books, 1966.

———. *Nature and the Religious Imagination: From Edwards to Bushnell.* Philadelphia: Fortress Press, 1980.

Clark, Michael P. "The Eschatology of Signs in Cotton Mather's 'Biblia Americana' and Jonathan Edwards's Case for the Legibility of Providence." Smolinski and Stievermann 413–38.

Conforti, Joseph A. *Jonathan Edwards, Religious Tradition, and American Culture.* Chapel Hill: U of North Carolina P, 1995.

Costello, Bonnie. *Marianne Moore: Imaginary Possessions.* Cambridge: Harvard UP, 1981.

Craig, Megan. "The Infinite in Person: Levinas and Dickinson." Deppman, Noble, and Stonum 207–26.

Crisp, Oliver D., and Douglas A. Sweeney, eds. *After Jonathan Edwards: The Course of the New England Theology.* Oxford: Oxford UP, 2012.

Crocco, Stephen D. "Jonathan Edwards and Princeton." *Jonathan Edwards as Contemporary: Essays in Honor of Sang Hyun Lee.* Ed. Don Schweitzer. New York: Peter Lang, 2010. 223–38.

Daniel, Stephen H. *The Philosophy of Jonathan Edwards: A Study in Divine Semiotics.* Bloomington: Indiana UP, 1994.

———. "Edwards as Philosopher." *The Cambridge Companion to Jonathan Edwards.* Ed. Stephen J. Stein. Cambridge: Cambridge UP, 2007. 162–80.

Davidson, Frank. "'This Consciousness': Emerson and Dickinson." *Emerson Society Quarterly* 44 (1966): 2–7.

Delattre, Roland A. *Beauty and Sensibility in the Thought of Jonathan Edwards: An Essay in Aesthetics and Theological Ethics.* New Haven: Yale UP, 1968.

———. "Beauty and Theology: A Reappraisal of Jonathan Edwards." *Critical Essays on Jonathan Edwards.* Ed. William J. Scheick. Boston: G. K. Hall and Co., 1980. 136–50.

Deppman, Jed. *Trying to Think with Emily Dickinson.* Amherst: U of Massachusetts P, 2008.

Deppman, Jed, Marianne Noble, and Gary Lee Stonum, eds. *Emily Dickinson and Philosophy.* Cambridge: Cambridge UP, 2013.

Dickie, Margaret. *Lyric Contingencies: Emily Dickinson and Wallace Stevens.* Philadelphia: U of Pennsylvania P, 1991.

Diehl, Joanne Feit. *Women Poets and the American Sublime.* Bloomington: Indiana UP, 1990.

Doriani, Beth Maclay. *Emily Dickinson, Daughter of Prophecy.* Amherst: U of Massachusetts P, 1996.

Dorrien, Gary. *The Making of American Liberal Theology: Idealism, Realism, and Modernity, 1900–1950.* Louisville: Westminster John Knox Press, 2003.

DuPlessis, Rachel Blau. "No Moore of the Same: The Feminist Poetics of Marianne Moore." *William Carlos Williams Review* 14.1 (1988): 6–32.

———. *Genders, Races, and Religious Cultures in Modern American Poetry, 1908–1934.* Cambridge: Cambridge UP, 2001.

Dyrness, William. *Reformed Theology and Visual Culture: The Protestant Imagination from Calvin to Edwards.* Cambridge: Cambridge UP, 2004.

Eberwein, Jane Donahue. *Dickinson: Strategies of Limitation.* Amherst: U of Massachusetts P, 1985.

———. "Emily Dickinson and the Calvinist Sacramental Tradition." *Emerson Studies Quarterly* 33.2 (1987): 67–81.

———. "Emily Dickinson and Edwards Amasa Park: 'The Loveliest Sermon.'" *American Transcendental Quarterly* 1.4 (1987): 311–22.

———. "'Graphicer for Grace': Emily Dickinson's Calvinist Language." *Studies in Puritan American Spirituality* 1 (1990): 170–201.

———. "Ministerial Interviews and Fathers in Faith." *Emily Dickinson Journal* 9.2 (2000): 6–15.

———. "'Is Immortality True?' Salvaging Faith in an Age of Upheavals." *A Historical Guide to Emily Dickinson.* Ed. Vivian R. Pollack. Oxford: Oxford UP, 2004. 67–102.

———. "Outgrowing Genesis? Dickinson, Darwin, and the Higher Criticism." Deppman, Noble, and Stonum 47–67.

Eliot, T. S. "Introduction to *Selected Poems.*" Tomlinson 60–65.

Emerson, Ralph Waldo. *Essays and Lectures.* Ed. Joel Porte. New York: Library of America, 1983.

———. *The Complete Sermons of Ralph Waldo Emerson.* Ed. Wesley T. Mott. Columbia: U of Missouri P, 1992. Vol. 4.

Erdt, Terrence. *Jonathan Edwards: Art and the Sense of the Heart.* Amherst: U of Massachusetts P, 1980.

Fiering, Norman. *Jonathan Edwards's Moral Thought and Its British Context.* Chapel Hill: U of North Carolina P, 1981.

———. "The Rationalist Foundations of Jonathan Edwards's Metaphysics." Hatch and Stout 73–101.

Forsyth, Peter Taylor. *Positive Preaching and the Modern World.* New York: A. C. Armstrong and Sons, 1907.

———. *Christ on Parnassus: Lectures on Art, Ethic, and Theology.* New York: Hodder and Stoughton, 1911.

Freedman, Linda. "Touching the Wounds: Dickinson and Christology." Deppman, Noble, and Stonum 68–84.

———. *Emily Dickinson and the Religious Imagination.* Cambridge: Cambridge UP, 2011.

Frei, Hans. *The Eclipse of Biblical Narrative: A Study in Eighteenth and Nineteenth Century Hermeneutics.* New Haven: Yale UP, 1974.

Gelpi, Albert J. *Emily Dickinson: The Mind of the Poet.* Cambridge: Harvard UP, 1965.

Gordon, Alexander R. *The Poets of the Old Testament.* New York: Hodder and Stoughton, 1919.

Gura, Phillip F. *The Wisdom of Words: Language, Theology, and Literature in the New England Renaissance.* Middletown: Wesleyan UP, 1981.

———. "Edwards and American Literature." *The Cambridge Companion to Jonathan Edwards.* Ed. Stephen J. Stein. Cambridge: Cambridge UP, 2007. 262–79.

Gutjahr, Paul C. *An American Bible: A History of the Good Book in the United States, 1777–1880.* Stanford: Stanford UP, 1999.

Habegger, Alfred. *My Wars Are Laid Away in Books: The Life of Emily Dickinson.* New York: Modern Library, 2001.

Hagenbüchle, Roland. "Precision and Indeterminacy in the Poetry of Emily Dickinson." *Emerson Studies Quarterly* 20.2 (1974): 33–56.

———. "Sign and Process: The Concept of Language in Emerson and Dickinson." *Emerson Studies Quarterly* 25.3 (1979): 137–55.

———. "Emily Dickinson's Poetic Covenant." *Emily Dickinson Journal* 2.2 (1993): 14–39.

Hall, Donald. "The Art of Poetry: Marianne Moore, An Interview with Donald Hall." Tomlinson 20–45.

Hall, Richard A. S. "Did Berkeley Influence Edwards? Their Common Critique of the Moral Sense Theory." *Jonathan Edwards's Writings: Text, Context, Interpretation.* Ed. Stephen J. Stein. Bloomington: Indiana UP, 1996. 100–121.

Hart, D. G. "Poems, Propositions, and Dogma: The Controversy over Religious Language and the Demise of Theology in American Learning." *Church History* 57.3 (1988): 310–21.

Hatch, Nathan O., and Harry S. Stout, eds. *Jonathan Edwards and the American Experience.* New York: Oxford UP, 1988.

Heimert, Alan. *Religion and the American Mind from the Great Awakening to the Revolution.* Cambridge: Harvard UP, 1966.

Heuving, Jeanne. *Omissions Are Not Accidents: Gender in the Art of Marianne Moore.* Detroit: Wayne State UP, 1992.

Higginson, Thomas Wentworth. *Outdoor Studies and Poems.* Cambridge: Riverside, 1900.

Hitchcock, Edward. *Religious Lectures on Peculiar Phenomena in the Four Seasons.* Boston: Crosby, Nichols, Lee and Co., 1861.

Hogue, Cynthia. *Scheming Women: Poetry, Privilege, and the Poetics of Subjectivity.* Albany: State U of New York P, 1995.

———. "'The Plucked String': Emily Dickinson, Marianne Moore and the Poetics of Select Defects." *Emily Dickinson Journal* 7:1 (1998). 89–109.

Holifield, E. Brooks. *Theology in America: Christian Thought from the Age of the Puritans to the Civil War.* New Haven: Yale UP, 2003.

Holley, Margaret. *The Poetry of Marianne Moore: A Study in Voice and Value.* Cambridge: Cambridge UP, 1987.

Homans, Margaret. *Women Writers and Poetic Identity: Dorothy Wordsworth, Emily Brontë, and Emily Dickinson.* Princeton: Princeton UP, 1980.

Hubbard, Melanie. "Dickinson, Hume, and the Common Sense Legacy." Deppman, Noble, and Stonum 30–46.

Hutchison, Sharla. "The Eco-Poetics of Marianne Moore's 'The Sycamore.'" *Interdisciplinary Studies in Literature and the Environment* 18.4 (Autumn 2011). *OxfordJournals.org.* 29 June 2014.

Irigaray, Luce. *This Sex Which Is Not One.* Trans. Catherine Porter and Caroline Burke. Ithaca: Cornell UP, 1985.

Jameson, Fredric. *Postmodernism, or, The Cultural Logic of Late Capitalism.* Durham: Duke UP, 1991.

Jarrell, Randall. "Her Shield." Tomlinson 114–24.

Jenks, William. *Supplement to the Comprehensive Commentary.* Brattleboro: Brattleboro Typographic Company, 1838.

John of the Cross. *The Dark Night of the Soul.* Ed. E. Allison Peers. New York: Paulist Press, 1959.

Johnson, Thomas H. "Jonathan Edwards' Background of Reading." *Publications of the Colonial Society of Massachusetts* 28 (1931): 193–222.

Jones, Rowena Revis. "The Preparation of a Poet: Puritan Directions in Emily Dickinson's Education." *Studies in the American Renaissance* (1982): 285–324.

———. "Edwards, Dickinson, and the Sacramentality of Nature." *Studies in Puritan American Spirituality* 1 (1990): 225–53.

———. "A Taste for 'Poison': Dickinson's Departure from Orthodoxy." *Emily Dickinson Journal* 2.1 (1993): 47–64.

Juhasz, Suzanne. "Adventures in the World of the Symbolic: Emily Dickinson and Metaphor." *Feminist Measures: Soundings in Poetry and Theory.* Ed. Lynn Keller and Cristanne Miller. Ann Arbor: U of Michigan P, 1994. 139–62.

Kadlec, David. *Mosaic Modernism: Anarchism, Pragmatism, Culture.* Baltimore: Johns Hopkins UP, 2000.

Kappel, Andrew J. "Notes on the Presbyterian Poetry of Marianne Moore."

Marianne Moore: Woman and Poet. Ed. Patricia C. Willis. Orono: National Poetry Foundation, 1990. 37–51.

———. "The World Is an Orphan's Home: Marianne Moore on God and Family." *Reform and Counterreform: Dialectics of the World in Western Christianity since Luther.* Ed. John C. Hawley. New York: Mouton de Gruyter, 1994. 173–92.

Keller, Karl. *The Only Kangaroo among the Beauty: Emily Dickinson and America.* Baltimore: Johns Hopkins UP, 1979.

Kellogg, Edwin Henry. *Anniversary Sermon Delivered in the Second Presbyterian Church of Carlisle, Pennsylvania, on the Occasion of Its One-Hundredth Anniversary.* January 8, 1933.

Kenner, Hugh. *A Homemade World: The American Modernist Writers.* New York: Alfred A. Knopf, 1974.

Kher, Inder Nath. *The Landscape of Absence: Emily Dickinson's Poetry.* New Haven: Yale UP, 1974.

Kimnach, Wilson. "The Literary Life of Jonathan Edwards." *Understanding Jonathan Edwards: An Introduction to America's Theologian.* Ed. Gerald R. McDermott. Oxford: Oxford UP, 2009. 133–44.

Knight, Janice. "Learning the Language of God: Jonathan Edwards and the Typology of Nature." *William and Mary Quarterly* 48.4 (1991): 531–51.

———. *Orthodoxies in Massachusetts: Rereading American Puritanism.* Cambridge: Harvard UP, 1994.

Knutson, Andrea. *American Spaces of Conversion: The Conductive Imaginaries of Edwards, Emerson, and James.* Oxford: Oxford UP, 2011.

Korshin, Paul J. *Typologies in England, 1650–1820.* Princeton: Princeton UP, 1982.

Kristeva, Julia. *Revolution in Poetic Language.* Trans. Margaret Waller. New York: Columbia UP, 1984.

Kuklick, Bruce. *Churchmen and Philosophers: From Jonathan Edwards to John Dewey.* New Haven: Yale UP, 1985.

Lane, Belden C. "Calvinist Spirituality." *The New Westminster Dictionary of Christian Spirituality.* Ed. Philip Sheldrake. Louisville: Westminster John Knox Press, 2005. 162–64.

———. *Ravished by Beauty: The Surprising Legacy of Reformed Spirituality.* Oxford: Oxford UP, 2011.

Laurence, David. "Jonathan Edwards as a Figure in Literary History." Hatch and Stout 226–45.

Leader, Jennifer. "'Certain Axioms Rivaling Scriptures': Marianne Moore, Reinhold Niebuhr, and the Ethics of Engagement." *Twentieth Century Literature* 51.3 (2005): 316–40.

Lease, Benjamin. *Emily Dickinson's Readings of Men and Books: Sacred Soundings.* New York: St. Martin's, 1990.

Leavell, Linda. *Marianne Moore and the Visual Arts: Prismatic Color.* Baton Rouge: Louisiana State UP, 1995.

———. "Marianne Moore's Emily Dickinson." *Emily Dickinson Journal* 12.2 (2003): 1–20.

———. *Holding On Upside Down: The Life and Work of Marianne Moore.* New York: Farrar, Straus and Giroux, 2013.

Lee, Sang Hyun. "Edwards on God and Nature: Resources for Contemporary Theology." *Edwards in Our Time: Jonathan Edwards and the Shaping of American Religion.* Ed. Sang Hyun Lee and Allen C. Guelzo. Grand Rapids: William B. Eerdmans, 1999. 15–44.

———. *The Philosophical Theology of Jonathan Edwards.* 2nd ed. Princeton: Princeton UP, 2000.

———. Editor's Introduction. *WJE* 21:1–108.

Lesser, M. X. Editor's Introduction. *WJE* 19:3–36.

———. "Edwards in 'American Culture.'" *The Cambridge Companion to Jonathan Edwards.* Ed. Stephen J. Stein. Cambridge: Cambridge UP, 2007. 280–99.

Levinas, Emmanuel. *Totality and Infinity.* Trans. Alphonso Lingis. Pittsburgh: Duquesne UP, 1969.

———. *Basic Philosophical Writings.* Bloomington: Indiana UP, 1996.

———. *Entre Nous.* Trans. Michael B. Smith and Barbara Harshav. New York: Columbia UP, 1998.

———. *Is It Righteous to Be? Interviews with Emmanuel Levinas.* Ed. Jill Robbins. Stanford: Stanford UP, 2001.

Lewalski, Barbara Kiefer. *Protestant Poetics and the Seventeenth-Century Religious Lyric.* Princeton: Princeton UP, 1979.

Loeffelholz, Mary. *Dickinson and the Boundaries of Feminist Theory.* Urbana: U of Illinois P, 1991.

Longfield, Bradley J. *The Presbyterian Controversy: Fundamentalists, Modernists, and Moderates.* New York: Oxford UP, 1991.

Lowance, Mason. *The Language of Canaan: Metaphor and Symbol in New England from the Puritans to the Transcendentalists.* Cambridge: Harvard UP, 1980.

Lundin, Roger. *Emily Dickinson and the Art of Belief.* Grand Rapids: William B. Eerdmans, 1998.

Magary, Alvin. "The Secret Things." *Lafayette Record: The Organ of the Lafayette Avenue Presbyterian Church* 23.4 (1930): 1–4.

Marion, Jean-Luc. *God without Being: Hors Texte.* Trans. Thomas A. Carlson. Chicago: U of Chicago P, 1991.

Marsden, George M. *Jonathan Edwards: A Life.* New Haven: Yale UP, 2003.

Mather, Samuel. *The Figures or Types of the Old Testament.* New York: Johnson Reprint Corp., 1969.

Matthiessen, F. O. *American Renaissance: Art and Expression in the Age of Emerson and Whitman.* New York: Oxford UP, 1941.

McCann, Dennis P. "Hermeneutics and Ethics: The Example of Reinhold Niebuhr." *Journal of Religious Ethics* 8.1 (1980): 27–53.

McClymond, Michael J. *Encounters with God: An Approach to the Theology of Jonathan Edwards.* New York: Oxford UP, 1998.

McClymond, Michael J., and Gerald R. McDermott. *The Theology of Jonathan Edwards.* Oxford: Oxford UP, 2012.

McIntosh, James. *Nimble Believing: Dickinson and the Unknown.* Ann Arbor: U of Michigan P, 2000.

Merrin, Jeredith. *An Enabling Humility: Marianne Moore, Elizabeth Bishop, and the Uses of Tradition.* New Brunswick: Rutgers UP, 1990.

Milder, David. "From Emerson to Edwards." *New England Quarterly* 80.1 (2007): 96–133.

Miller, Cristanne. *Emily Dickinson: A Poet's Grammar.* Cambridge: Harvard UP, 1987.

———. *Marianne Moore: Questions of Authority.* Cambridge: Harvard UP, 1995.

———. "Marianne Moore and a Poetry of Hebrew (Protestant) Prophecy." *Sources: Revue d'Études Anglophones* 12 (Spring 2002): 9–47.

———. *Reading in Time: Emily Dickinson in the Nineteenth Century.* Amherst: U of Massachusetts P, 2012.

Miller, Perry. "From Edwards to Emerson." *New England Quarterly* 13 (1940): 589–617.

———. Editor's Introduction. *Images or Shadows of Divine Things,* by Jonathan Edwards. New Haven: Yale UP, 1948.

———. "Jonathan Edwards on the Sense of the Heart." *Harvard Theological Review* 41 (1948): 123–45.

———. *Errand into the Wilderness.* Cambridge: Harvard UP, 1964.

Miner, Earl, ed. *Literary Uses of Typology: From the Late Middle Ages to the Present.* Princeton: Princeton UP, 1977.

Minkema, Kenneth P. Introduction to "God's All Sufficiency for the Supply of Our Wants." *WJE* 14:471–73.

Molesworth, Charles. *Marianne Moore: A Literary Life.* New York: Atheneum, 1990.

Moore, Marianne. *Observations.* 2nd ed. New York: Dial, 1925.

Mullin, Robert Bruce. *The Puritan as Yankee: A Life of Horace Bushnell.* Grand Rapids: William B. Eerdmans, 2002.

New, Elisa. *The Regenerate Lyric: Theology and Innovation in American Poetry.* Cambridge: Cambridge UP, 1993.

———. *The Line's Eye: Poetic Experience, American Sight.* Cambridge: Harvard UP, 1998.

A New Standard Bible Dictionary. Ed. Melancthon W. Jacobus, Edward E. Nourse, and Andrew C. Zenos. New York: Funk and Wagnalls, 1926.

Nichols, Stephen R. C. *Jonathan Edwards's Bible: The Relationship of the Old and New Testaments.* Eugene, Ore.: Wipf and Stock Publishers, 2013.

Niebuhr, H. R. *The Kingdom of God in America.* Chicago: Willett, Clark and Co., 1937.

Niebuhr, Reinhold. *Christian Realism and Political Problems.* New York: Charles Scribner's Sons, 1953.

———. *The Self and the Dramas of History.* New York: Charles Scriber's Sons, 1955.

———. "Reply to Interpretation and Criticism." *Reinhold Niebuhr: His Religious, Social, and Political Thought.* Ed. Charles W. Kegley and Robert W. Bretall. New York: Macmillan, 1956. 431–51.

———. *Leaves from the Notebook of a Tamed Cynic.* New York: Meridian Books, 1965.

———. "Faith as the Sense of Meaning in Human Existence." *Faith and Politics: A Commentary on Religious, Social, and Political Thought in a Technical Age.* Ed. Ronald H. Stone. New York: George Braziller, 1968. 3–13.

Noble, Marianne. "Dickinson on Perception and Consciousness: A Dialogue with Maurice Merleau-Ponty." Deppman, Noble, and Stonum 188–206.

Noll, Mark A. "The Princeton Theology." *Reformed Theology in America: A History of Its Modern Developments.* Ed. David F. Wells. Grand Rapids: Wm. B. Eerdmans, 1985. 15–35.

———. *Between Faith and Criticism: Evangelicals, Scholarship, and the Bible in America.* San Francisco: Harper and Row, 1987.

———. *America's God: From Jonathan Edwards to Abraham Lincoln.* Oxford: Oxford UP, 2002.

———. "Edwards' Theology after Edwards." *The Princeton Companion to Jonathan Edwards.* Ed. Sang Hyun Lee. Princeton: Princeton UP, 2005. 292–308.

———. "Jonathan Edwards' Use of the Bible: A Case Study (Genesis 32:22–32) with Comparisons." *Jonathan Edwards Studies* 2.1 (2012): 30–46. Web.

Norcross, George. *A New Year's Sermon Delivered in the Second Presbyterian Church.* Carlisle, Pa.: Valley Sentinel Steam Printing Office, 1876.

———, ed. *The Centennial Memorial of the Presbytery of Carlisle; A Series of Papers, Historical and Biographical, Relating to the Origin and Growth of Presbyterianism in the Central and Eastern Part of Southern Pennsylvania.* 2 vols. Harrisburg, Pa.: Meyers Printing and Publishing House, 1889.

———. *Forty Years in the Wilderness: A Sermon Delivered to the Second Presbyterian Church, Carlisle, Pennsylvania, on His Fortieth Anniversary, January 3, 1909.* Carlisle, Pa.: Cornman Printing Co., 1909.

Oberhaus, Dorothy Huff. *Emily Dickinson's Fascicles: Method and Meaning.* University Park: Pennsylvania State UP, 1995.

Ostriker, Alicia. *Stealing the Language: The Emergence of Women's Poetry in America.* Boston: Beacon, 1986.

Park, Edwards A. *Memorial Collection of Sermons.* Boston: Pilgrim Press, 1908.

Parrington, Vernon Lewis. *Main Currents in American Thought.* 2 vols. New York: Harcourt, 1958.

Pauw, Amy Plantinga. *The Supreme Harmony of All: The Trinitarian Theology of Jonathan Edwards.* Grand Rapids: Wm. B. Eerdmans, 2002.

Peake, Arthur S. *Christianity: Its Nature and Its Truth.* New York: Thomas Y. Crowell & Co., 1903.

Porter, David T. *Dickinson: The Modern Idiom.* Cambridge: Harvard UP, 1981.

Porter, Ebenezer. *The Young Preacher's Manual, or a Collection of Treatises on Preaching.* 2nd ed. New York: Jonathan Leavitt, 1929.

Ramsey, Paul. Editor's Introduction. *WJE* 8:1–122.

"Rev. George Norcross, D.D." *Biographical Annals of Cumberland County, Pennsylvania.* Chicago: Genealogical Publishing Co., 1905. *USGenWeb Archives.* Web. 4 April 2014.

Richards, Eliza, ed. *Emily Dickinson in Context.* Cambridge: Cambridge UP, 2013.

Rogers, Jack B., and Donald K. McKim. *The Authority and Interpretation of the Bible: An Historical Approach.* San Francisco: Harper and Row, 1979.

Ross, Bruce. "Fables of the Golden Age: The Poetry of Marianne Moore." *Twentieth Century Literature* 30.2–3 (1984): 210–30.

St. Armand, Barton Levi. *Emily Dickinson and Her Culture: The Soul's Society.* Cambridge: Cambridge UP, 1984.

Schafer, Thomas A. Editor's Introduction. *WJE* 13:3–90.

Schreiner, Susan. *The Theater of His Glory: Nature and the Natural Order in the Thought of John Calvin.* Grand Rapids: Baker Academic, 1991.

Schulze, Robin. "Marianne Moore's 'Imperious Ox, Imperial Dish' and the Poetry of the Natural World." *Twentieth Century Literature* 44.1 (1998): 1–33.

———. "Textual Darwinism: Marianne Moore, the Text of Evolution, and the Evolving Text." *Text: Transactions of the Society for Textual Scholarship* 11 (1998): 270–305.

———. *The Degenerate Muse: American Nature, Modernist Poetry, and the Problem of Cultural Hygiene.* Oxford: Oxford UP, 2013.

Seelbinder, Emily. "The Bible." Richards 69–77.

Sewall, Richard B. *The Life of Emily Dickinson.* Cambridge: Harvard UP, 1980.

Shuger, Debra K. *The Renaissance Bible: Scholarship, Sacrifice, and Subjectivity.* Berkeley: U of California P, 1994.

Siegfried, Regina. "Bibliographic Essay: Selected Criticism for Emily Dickinson's Religious Background." *Dickinson Studies* 52.2 (1984): 32–53.

Sielke, Sabine. *Fashioning the Female Subject: The Intertextual Networking of Dickinson, Moore, and Rich.* Ann Arbor: U of Michigan P, 1997.

"Signify, v." *OED Online.* Oxford UP, March 2014. Web. 11 April 2014.

"Sir George Adam Smith Has Lived Till Now." *Christian Century* 59.12 (1942): 373–74.

Slatin, John M. *The Savage's Romance: The Poetry of Marianne Moore.* University Park: Pennsylvania State UP, 1986.

Smith, Claude A. "Jonathan Edwards and 'The Way of Ideas.'" *Harvard Theological Review* 59 (1966): 153–73.

Smith, Gary Scott. *The Seeds of Secularization: Calvinism, Culture, and Pluralism in America, 1870–1915.* Grand Rapids: Christian UP (Eerdmans), 1985.

Smith, George Adam. *The Book of the Twelve Prophets, Commonly Called the Minor.* 3rd ed. Vol. 1. New York: A. C. Armstrong and Son, 1898.

———. *Modern Criticism and the Preaching of the Old Testament.* New York: A. C. Armstrong and Son, 1901.

Smith, Henry Boynton. *Faith and Philosophy: Discourses and Essays.* New York: Scribner, 1877.

Smith, John E. Editor's Introduction. *WJE* 2:1–90.

Smolinski, Reiner, and Jan Stievermann, eds. *Cotton Mather and Biblia Americana, America's First Bible Commentary: Essays in Reappraisal.* Grand Rapids: Baker Academic, 2010.

———. Editor's Introduction. Smolinski and Stievermann 1–58.

Stalker, James. *The Life of Jesus Christ.* New York: Fleming H. Revell, 1891.

Stein, Stephen J. "The Spirit and the Word: Jonathan Edwards and Scriptural Exegesis." Hatch and Stout 118–30.

———. Editor's Introduction. *Notes on Scripture. WJE* 15:1–46.

———. Editor's Introduction. *The Blank Bible. WJE* 24:1–118.

———. "Edwards as Biblical Exegete." *The Cambridge Companion to Jonathan Edwards.* Ed. Stephen J. Stein. Cambridge: Cambridge UP, 2007. 181–95.

———. "Cotton Mather and Jonathan Edwards on the Epistle of James: A Comparative Study." Smolinski and Stievermann 363–82.

Steinman, Lisa M. *Made in America: Science, Technology, and American Modernist Poets.* New Haven: Yale UP, 1987.

Stewart, Carole Lynn. *Strange Jeremiahs: Civil Religion and the Literary Imaginations of Jonathan Edwards, Herman Melville, and W. E. B. Du Bois.* Albuquerque: U of New Mexico P, 2011.

Stonum, Gary Lee. *The Dickinson Sublime.* Madison: U of Wisconsin P, 1990.

Svetlikova, Anna. "Alternative Viewpoint: The Literary Life of Jonathan Edwards." *Understanding Jonathan Edwards: An Introduction to America's Theologian.* Ed. Gerald R. McDermott. Oxford: Oxford UP, 2009. 145–50.

Sweeney, Douglas A. "The Biblical World of Jonathan Edwards." *Jonathan Edwards Studies* 3.2 (2013): 221–68. Web.

Thuesen, Peter J. Editor's Introduction. *WJE* 26:1–113.

———. "Jonathan Edwards and the Transatlantic World of Books." *Jonathan Edwards Studies* 3.1 (2013): 44–54. Web.

Tomlinson, Charles, ed. *Marianne Moore: A Collection of Critical Essays.* Englewood Cliffs: Prentice-Hall, 1969.

Turner, James. *Without God, without Creed: The Origins of Unbelief in America.* Baltimore: Johns Hopkins UP, 1985.

———. *Language, Religion, Knowledge: Past and Present.* Notre Dame: U of Notre Dame P, 2003.

Upham, Thomas. *Elements of Moral Philosophy, Embracing the Two Departments of the Intellect and the Sensibilities.* Vol. 1. Portland: William Hyde, 1839.

Wadsworth, Charles. *God's Culture. A Thanksgiving Sermon, Preached in the Arch*

Street Church, on Thursday, November 29, 1860. Philadelphia: J. W. Bradley, 1860.

———. *Sermons.* New York: A. Roman and Company, 1869. *Internet Archive.* Web. 12 October 2012.

———. *Sermons.* Philadelphia: Eagle Book and Job Printing Department, 1905. *Internet Archive.* Web. 12 October 2012.

Warner, John Riddle. *Sermons by the Rev. John R. Warner, D.D., with a Sketch of His Life by His Daughter, Mary Warner Moore.* Philadelphia: J. B. Lippincott, 1895.

Weber, Donald. Editor's Introduction. *Jonathan Edwards,* by Perry Miller. Amherst: U of Massachusetts P, 1981.

———. "The Figure of Jonathan Edwards." *American Quarterly* 16 (1983): 157–60.

Weinstein, Josh A. "Marianne Moore's Ecopoetic Architectonics." *Interdisciplinary Studies in Literature and the Environment* 17.2 (Spring 2010). *Oxford Journals.org.* Web. 29 June 2014.

Weisbuch, Robert. *Emily Dickinson's Poetry.* Chicago: U of Chicago P, 1975.

Williams, David R. "The Wilderness Rapture of Mary Moody Emerson: One Calvinist Link to Transcendentalism." Ed. Joel Myerson. *Studies in the American Renaissance.* Charlottesville: UP of Virginia, 1986. 1–16.

Willis, Patricia C. "Monkey Puzzler, True Curio." *Marianne Moore Newsletter* 3.1 (1979): 12.

———. "MM in Brooklyn." *Marianne Moore Newsletter* 4.2 (1980): 24.

Wilson, John F. Editor's Introduction. *WJE* 9:1–110.

Wolosky, Shira. *Emily Dickinson: A Voice of War.* New Haven: Yale UP, 1984.

———. *Poetry and Public Discourse in Nineteenth-Century America.* London: Palgrave Macmillan, 2010.

Zakai, Avihu. *Jonathan Edwards's Philosophy of Nature: The Re-enchantment of the World in the Age of Scientific Reasoning.* London: T & T Clark International, 2010.

Zapedowska, Magdalena. "Critical History II: 1995 to the Present." Richards 321–31.

Index

This page constitutes a continuation of the copyright page.

Portions of chapters 2 and 3 appeared in earlier in "'In Love with the Image': Transitive Being and Typological Desire in Jonathan Edwards," *Early American Literature* 41:2 (2006).

Emily Dickinson's poems are reprinted by permission of the publishers and the Trustees of Amherst College from THE POEMS OF EMILY DICKINSON: VARIORUM EDITION, edited by Ralph W. Franklin, Cambridge, Mass.: The Belknap Press of Harvard University Press, © 1998 by the President and Fellows of Harvard College. Copyright © 1951, 1955 by the President and Fellows of Harvard College. Copyright © renewed 1979, 1983 by the President and Fellows of Harvard College. Copyright © 1914, 1918, 1919, 1924, 1929, 1930, 1932, 1935, 1937, 1942 by Martha Dickinson Bianchi. Copyright © 1952, 1957, 1958, 1963, 1965 by Mary L. Hampson.

Quotations from Emily Dickinson's letters are reprinted by permission of the publishers and the Trustees of Amherst College from THE LETTERS OF EMILY DICKINSON, edited by Thomas H. Johnson, Associate Editor, Theodora Ward, Cambridge, Mass.: The Belknap Press of Harvard University Press, Copyright © 1958 by the President and Fellows of Harvard College. Copyright © renewed 1986 by the President and Fellows of Harvard College. Copyright © 1914, 1924, 1932, 1942 by Martha Dickinson Bianchi. Copyright © 1952 by Alfred Leete Hampson. Copyright © 1960 by Mary L. Hampson.

Permission for the use of the following letters and notes of Marianne Moore, as may be found at the Rosenbach Free Library of Philadelphia, and cited as particular volumes, uncollected poem "Inheritance" [Vol. I:02:03], uncollected poem "Kay Nielson's Little Green Patch" [Vol. I:02:46], Letter to Reinhold Niebuhr from Moore 5/20/52 [V:45:15], Niebuhr Letter to Moore 5/26/54 [V:45:15], notes from the Reading Notebook of Marianne Moore [VII:01:01, VII:01:03 and VII:07:12 respectively], written by Marianne Moore, note from Religion Notebook [VII: 08:03] written by Marianne Moore, and a note from the Religion File [VII:09:11], written by Marianne Moore is granted by the Literary Estate of Marianne C. Moore, David M. Moore, Administrator, Literary Estate of Marianne Moore. All rights reserved.

Lines from "The Jerboa," "The Plumet Basilisk," The Labors of Hercules," and "The Monkey Puzzle" are reprinted with the permission of Scribner, a Division of Simon & Schuster, Inc., from THE COLLECTED POEMS OF MARIANNE MOORE by Marianne Moore. Copyright © 1935 by Marianne Moore, renewed 1963 by Marianne Moore. All rights reserved. Lines from "By Disposition of Angels" and "The Icosasphere" are reprinted with the permission of Scribner, a Division of Simon & Schuster, Inc., from THE COLLECTED POEMS OF MARIANNE MOORE by Marianne Moore. Copyright © 1951 by Marianne Moore, renewed 1979 by Lawrence E. Brimm and Louise Crane. All rights reserved.

Lines from "The Jerboa," "The Plumet Basilisk," The Labors of Hercules," "The Monkey Puzzle," "By Disposition of Angels," and "Tell Me, Tell Me," "To a Snail," "To a Giraffe," "Injudicious Gardening," and "The Icosasphere" from THE COMPLETE POEMS OF MARIANNE MOORE by Marianne Moore. Used by permission of Faber and Faber, Ltd. Lines from "To Browning," "In the Days of Prismatic Color," and "Roses Only" from BECOMING MARIANNE MOORE: THE EARLY POEMS, 1907–1924, by Marianne Moore, edited by Robin G. Schultze. Used by permission of Faber and Faber, Ltd.